CW01084033

The Sounds of the Cities

'Nearly Famous'

THE ROCK MUSIC SCENE IN HULL
AND THE EAST RIDING,
SCARBOROUGH, YORK, SCUNTHORPE
AND GRIMSBY
DURING THE SWINGING SIXTIES

Ray Moody BA(Hons), PGDip (Econ Dev), Cert Ed

Rockumentary Press
FILEY

i

First published in 2001

by

ROCKUMENTARY PRESS
Seabreeze Cottage
11 Cliff Top
FILEY
North Yorkshire
YO14 9HG

Typeset in 11 point Palatino

Design and Typesetting by The Central Print Unit
Cover printed by The Central Print Unit
Printed and Bound in Britain by
Central Print Services, Hull University, Inglemire Lane, Hull

ISBN 0-9541793-0-7

The Great Old Days have gone and all the

Grandeur of the earth

There are not Caesars now or kings

Or Patrons such as once there used to be

Amongst whom were performed most glorious deeds

Who lived in Lordliest renown

Gone now is all that host

The splendours have departed

Acknowledgements

I never intended to write this book, but felt for such a long time that somebody should, before the history disappears. While taking the task on myself I would like to thank the following people and organisations for their help and kindness and hope that in some ways at least, whilst recording history, I have also revived fond memories of another generation's youth. Many thanks to:

Richard James Percy (Scarborough)
Pete Green
Brian Sleight
Rod Ellis
Kevin Hutchinson
Dave Carmichael
Allen Melling
Norman Moore
Alf Simpson
John Science
Neville J M Moore
Barry Nettleton
Terry Wincott
The Hull Daily Mail
Rhona Liley
Dave Bradfield
Janet Bradfield
Mike Ward
Paul Sutton
P Whitewood
Goole Times
Vic Harbord
Alan Knight
Bill Gillanders LMPA

Mike Trickett
Mick Whitfield
Tony Trickett
Johnny Hawk
Mavis Winkler
David Wells
Rich Hodgson
John Hutchinson
Pat Cornell
Pete Hudson
Craig Austin
Mike Boone
Bob Mason
Gary Burroughs
Dave Brown
Keith Stutt
Robin Taylor
Malcolm Ladd
Dave Bell
Ken Platten
Pete Cuthbert
Roger Kendall
Robert Finch
Maurice P O'Neill

P Whitewood
Tony Beasty
Jill Morris
Tony Gosling
Phil Calvert
David Johnson
Colin Carr
Dave Park (Canada)
Jerry O'Connell
Ron Mitchell
Julie Heggarty
Leslie Skillings
Eddie Baird
Justin Purington (USA)
Ron Newlove
Rob Thomas
Dave Spenceley
Stephen Whitmore
Kevin Corbett
Pete McLeod
Underman
Marc Higgins

George Cundill
Charles White (Dr Rock)
Scunthorpe Entertainer
Melvin Barrowby
Steve Ellis
David Wiseman (Sixties'
Souvenir)
John Burgess
John Larder
Michael Chapman
Allan Black
Colin Havercroft
Jim Shann (Australia)
Jon Bentley
Cliff Wade
Scunthorpe Entertainer
Pamela Johnston
Tom Ward
John David Parker
Scunthorpe Telegraph
Isle of Wight
Maurice Martinson

Dedicated to the Greatest Sixties Radio programme
of them all:

David Wiseman's 'Sixties Souvenir'

'The Flame Still Burns'

Would that I,
could take that train,
Just once again,
To stare at that,
From which I came,
Oh, would that I

Photographs kindly provided courtesy of the following people and organisations:

Dave Park (The Strollers)
Pete Green (The Mods, The Rats, Mick Ronson, Dean Curtis and The Phantoms)
The Hull Daily Mail
Grimsby Telegraph and Argos (Calmen Waters)
George Cundill (The Agents)
Dave Bell (The Semi-Tones)
Jill Morris (The Aces)
Rich Hodgson (The Urge)
Jerry O'Connell (The Penjants)
Craig Austin (The Dimples, The Imps, Gospel Garden, Methusulah)
Michael Chapman (Michael Chapman)
Allen Melling (The Winsors)
Dave Johnson (The Dominoes)
Colin Carr (The Clubmen)
Allan Black (The Mandrakes, The Mutiny)
Colin Havercroft (The Phantoms)
Jim Shann (The Cotton Pickers)
Justin Purington (The Crestas)
Pete McLeod (The Hammer)
Cliff Wade (The Roll Movement, The Misfits)
John Hutchinson (The Tennesseans)
Dave Spenceley (The Alpha-Beats, Sweet Sugar Soul Set, Sweet Sugars)
John Gladwin (The Amazing Blondel)
Jean Crossley Studios (ABC, Roger Blooms Hammer)
Dave Brown (Brave New World)
Brian Cooke (Mandrakes, Tennesseans)
Kevin Corbett (Plague '66, That Feeling, The Variations)
Mike Ward (The Avengers)
Leslie Skillings (Mandy and the Girlfriends)

Special thanks to **Richard James Percy** for permission to reproduce photographs of the Incas, the Moonshots, the Blue Stars and the Mandrakes from his book

'Scarborough In the 1950s and 1960s'
published by Alan Sutton Ltd 1994

While the publishers have made every reasonable effort to trace the copyright owners for any or all of the photographs there may be some omissions of credits for which we apologise.

INTRODUCTION

Rock music was a long time in its American cooking pot, gradually coming together via a mixture of the black blues and white Hillbilly music, through R & B and country, to rock 'n' roll. It arrived in this country from the USA in the mid-Fifties, led at full charge by Elvis Presley and Bill Haley. But by 1960, Bill Haley had been discovered to be a plump 'old man' with a 'kiss curl' and Elvis had been tamed by the United States Army. Various other influential rock stars including Buddy Holly and Eddie Cochran were dead, Little Richard had got religion and leading rock 'n' roll DJ, Alan Freed, had been persecuted, prosecuted and taken off the airwaves. The Establishment took control of popular music in America. It cleaned it up and toned it down, so that by the arrival of the 1960s, all that was coming over the water from that country were 'wholesome' boy and girl pop singers singing 'wholesome' pop songs.

For a moment, while a cohort of British rock groups, like the Alamo, took up residency in Hamburg, rock music endured an enforced lull. And it has been suggested, that had the 'Beat Boom' not exploded in Britain in 1963 as a direct result of these same groups serving their Hamburg apprenticeships, then it might well have died. As it was, it didn't and that year in Britain, led by the Beatles, rock music was reborn.

Almost overnight, teenage lives were changed forever as they gained a totally separate identity from their parents. A Teen market quickly developed and like the outbreak of World War III, there was a 'Call-to-Arms'. This time, however, instead of reaching for guns, those not content to simply 'bop' or tap their feet and listen to the new sounds, reached for the electric guitar. Life for them took on another dimension, for now there were guitars to learn to play, groups to be formed, group names to be thought of, records to listened to over and over again until copied 'note perfect'. Musical instrument shops began to be wistfully stared into, rehearsal rooms had to be found, endless practices needed to be attended, gigs were sought, sheet music and guitar strings were bought.

New words entered the vocabulary, like 'plectrum', 'jack-plug', 'Vox' and 'Fender'. (A fender previous to this, had been something which had stopped hot coals from burning the carpet!) And surrounding it all there were girls and admiration, pop shows to watch, styles to copy. From that point on, society changed, mostly for the better, but sadly, ultimately, some of it for the worse. The only thing that was for certain was that life would never be the same again.

Many of the newly formed groups didn't get very far, some often never got beyond the initial rehearsals or even the imagination. Some did, a few even going on to fame and occasionally fortune. But as fast as it had arrived in those revolutionary times, by the start of the 1970s somehow it had changed and while there was certainly still a 'group scene', that naiveté, drive and freshness had gone, the revolution was over and it just wasn't the same.

'In the early 1960s, when a young, hungry, unknown beat group were playing rock 'n' roll music in the sweaty, steamy clubs of Hamburg and Liverpool, what spurred them on was the unshakeable belief that one-day they would get to the 'Toppermost of the Poppermost' ... and they did. This book provides a record of those rock groups locally, who in that same decade also tried to reach that ultimate rock pinnacle and perhaps didn't always quite get there!

VIVE LA SHADS

I spent my childhood in Hull and was introduced to its live contemporary music scene at the age of 12, but my interest in popular music had been stirred much earlier, as a young child growing up in the late 1950s. My earliest recollection is that of my mum getting me out of bed late one evening when my dad had left for his ten-till-six shift on the railways. The two of us would often stay up together to watch late night television. One evening, half asleep, I remember seeing Little Richard live in concert, a small black man, dressed in an overlarge suit, exhaustively jerking himself about as he stood to play the piano. Sweating profusely, he mopped his face with a large handkerchief as he rattled off such great numbers as 'Keep A Knockin', 'Tutti-Frutti', 'Good Golly Miss Molly' and 'Lucille'.

It was a world away from the clean cut, antiseptic and boring British singers around at that time. Light years away from the music my father made us listen to on such depressing radio programmes as 'Sing Something Sinful'! It was exciting and it was different.

Not long after this, during tea-time on a Sunday evening, we began switching our Redifusion radio set to Channel 'B', to listen to Alan Freeman's 'Pick of the Pops'. At first, I didn't really take much notice of the programme, as there were still so many dreary records being played. But then I heard a record, which I just had to own, it was called 'Pasadena' by the Temperance Seven. Thankfully, my mum bought me the record, but being too poor to own a luxury like a record player, in order to be able to play it, we had to borrow an old fashioned black-cased gramophone from my granny. This had a heavy metal play-head, which stuck an inch long nail-like needle into the record. It also wasn't electric and had a clockwork motor that needed to be constantly wound-up. Nevertheless, I spent hours winding up the gramophone and soon wore the record out by over-playing it. But the Temperance Seven, just like Little Richard, were in their own way, interesting and different.

A short time later, amidst Hull City Council's early 1960s 'Slum Clearance' programme, while exploring with my younger brother in one of the many derelict houses stood awaiting demolition, we found a more modern 'electric' record player. It lay like a 'jewel' amongst all the junk and rubbish which had been discarded by the late occupiers. After excitedly running home with it and plugging it in, we soon discovered that it had been left behind because it wasn't working. Fortunately, my parents managed to 'scrape-up' enough money to pay to have it repaired and I eagerly looked around for some records to play on it. Being unable to afford to buy brand-new singles costing six shillings and sixpence a time, I searched around for some second-hand ones and found a 'junk' shop on Hessle Road, Hull where ex-jukebox singles could be bought for only one shilling and sixpence each. After initially toying with a copy of Rolf Harris's 'Sun Arise' followed quickly by Joe Brown's 'Picture of You', I then struck gold when I discovered the 'Shadows' classic 1960 hit, 'Apache'.

The record was atmospheric and brilliant and I played it over and over again. That unique combined sound of electric guitars and drums, with the drums evocatively creating the effect of Indians on the warpath and the guitars conjuring up feelings of both fear and bravery, I'd never before heard anything sound quite like it. When soon afterwards, the Shadows latest recording, 'Wonderful Land', was played on the radio, the guitar playing sounded so pure and created such emotions that it sent shivers down my spine. The notes being played seemed to sound like words. The guitar was actually 'talking'! My older brother, had also been enjoying the records and both of us were, thereafter, determined to become 'Kings of the Guitar', like 'Shadow' Hank B. Marvin, with his sceptre, a red solid-bodied electric guitar, a Fender 'Stratocaster'.

As good as he was, however, and while he certainly played his part, Hank couldn't provide the catalyst necessary to 'completely' re-launch rock music. And it wasn't until late 1962, after a fairly sterile period musically, that the Beatles arrived on the scene (direct from serving their apprenticeships in Hamburg) and the whole Sixties' pop revolution really began.

Around this time, in a rare moment of generosity, perhaps in the realisation that neither my brother nor myself were going to ride horses and become famous jockeys and possibly in the hope that one of us might be the next Hank B. Marvin, my father bought us an old acoustic guitar. It hung on a nail in the window of 'Pools Corner', a 'Second-hand' shop situated at the corner of Plane Street, in Hull. Because we were quite poor and the guitar cost £4, it had to be paid for in two instalments. But once the final payment had been made, the guitar was brought home and both my brother and myself, worshipping the instrument like a God, eagerly set about trying to play it.

At first, mum taught us how to pick out simple melodies to the latest pop songs. But we soon realised that we would have to graduate beyond this if we wanted to get anywhere. So we turned to the only help that seemed to be available, which was a two and sixpenny 'Teach Yourself Guitar' book bought from the 'Paragon Music Stores' in Hull. Not only did it show diagrams of how to play 'chords' but also contained the music to such latter-day 'hits' as 'Little Brown Jug', 'Song of The 'Vulgar' Boatmen' and 'Massa's in the Cold, Cold Ground'!

The book must have been written about 30 years previously but was the modernist (and cheapest!) thing the shop had if you

7

wanted to learn to play the guitar in 1963. Although, I did hear later, that some 'progressive types' had managed to get their hands on a copy of Bert Weedon's 'slightly' easier to understand guitar tutor 'Play In a Day'. But this did cost five shillings and our financial resources were severely limited. Also, for me, almost a teenager, starting out on the 'Road to Rock', Bert Weedon looked old and had connections with the music of the past, therefore, as a role model, was a non-starter!

Even so, our own book was so dated that the guitar player featured on the front was wearing full evening dress and it must have been written for someone wishing to play guitar in a pre-war dance band. Purchasing it also did very little to improve our guitar playing as no matter how we stretched and placed our fingers on the fretboard to match the chord symbols in the book, the sound created still seemed to make little sense. The problem was that since leaving the shop, the guitar had never been properly tuned. Not possessing a piano, we hadn't been able to afford the six shillings and sixpence required for a set of 'pitch pipes' to tune it by. Not that we understood how pitch pipes worked and what you actually did with them. And while they remained at six shillings and sixpence we were unlikely to find out! They were just some seemingly unique device we'd read about in our 'Teach Yourself Guitar' book. But they were desperately needed as we couldn't distinguish the sound of an 'E' from a 'D'. It was much more a case of the guitar strings being tuned too low or more usually too high, as our bare arms bore testimony, often bearing the red 'whiplash' marks caused by over-tightening our steel 'Cathedral' guitar strings.

Around this time, the ABC Regal Cinema in Hull announced that it was to hold an audition to spot young talent to perform during its weekly Saturday morning children's matinee. By now, both my brother and myself, by restricting ourselves to the top strings of the guitar were able to pick out the tune to the Spotnicks 1963 hit, 'Hava Nagila', note perfect. Excited, we decided to audition and become stars like Hank and were convinced that once the management of the cinema heard us playing 'Hava Nagila' they'd marvel at our obvious talent and we'd be signed-up and on our way to the big time! Unfortunately, we then realised that to avoid competing with each other only one of us would be able to play that particular tune at the audition and so I was cajoled into quickly learning another.

When the great day arrived and we were about to set-off with our one guitar, there was immediately an argument as to which of us should carry it, as there was a certain kudos in being seen in the company of a guitar in those halcyon days. Because neither of us would back down (being on the verge of stardom!) we had to compromise and decided that we'd both carry it. Unfortunately, my taller brother managed to grab the more prestigious end at the front and I had to settle for a much less prominent position at the rear. Nevertheless, we set-off like this for the short walk to the cinema, a two-headed, four-legged guitar, neither of us willing to relinquish our grip on our sections of the instrument until we arrived at the audition. On the way, we ignored the bemused looks we got from passers-by, looks that we proudly put down to being discerned as future pop stars!

Unfortunately, the audition turned out to be a disaster. My brother bravely did his bit first and received a smattering of applause from the Manager and his bored staff who were sitting at the front of the empty cinema. Then I made my way on to the stage, standing in front of the huge hanging silver stage curtains, the same ones that would form the backdrop to the Beatles and Rolling Stones concerts only weeks later. The spotlight in the darkened cinema fell on me and I realised for the first time that there was such a thing as stage fright. Instead of simply picking out the tune to 'Don't Bring Me Down' by the Pretty Things, I panicked, and having completely forgotten what I had learnt, began to wildly strum the guitar strings. At the same time I gave out an impromptu 'wailing' of the lyrics. Despite the fact that I was making a din, it still seemed like an eternity before a voice from out of the darkness at the front of the stage put me out of my misery and shouted, 'Next!' Apparently, our obvious talent had not yet been appreciated.

Fortunately, not long after this, in those fevered musical times, my brother saw a teenager on a bike with a guitar strapped to his back. Running alongside, he asked him if he knew where we could get 'guitar lessons'. Not stopping, the boy shouted the name and address of his music teacher and we entered the next stage on our musical journey.

Unfortunately, there wasn't really any one around in those early days to show you how to play 'rock' guitar and this kind lady actually taught piano and earned a little bit of extra money by being able to 'decipher' the two shilling and sixpenny 'Teach Yourself' Guitar books! But she was able to tune the guitar for us and did teach us to read our EGBDF and FACE, also our C's, D's and G's, and the occasional minor and seventh chords. Beyond that, however, we were on our own. Quite literally, as after about three months of weekly lessons we seemed to have exhausted her and she took to sitting in the next room while we ran through our repertoire. To spur us on to greater performances, or when she occasionally noticed that we had stopped playing, she would 'shout' encouraging remarks to us - her favourite being, 'I can hear you boys!', which she would repeat during breaks in Television programmes or in lulls in conversations with the neighbours.

Our graduation came quite unexpectedly one evening, when my brother unwittingly tramped dog dirt through her house, leaving it 'clarting' the plush carpets and relieving himself of the bulk of it on the piano pedals, where he had been resting his feet!

THE BEAT GOES ON

The early rock music scene in Hull mirrored the national scene perfectly. There was the mid-Fifties' arrival of rock 'n' roll and Teddy Boys with greased-back hair, drape jackets, drainpipe trousers and side-burns. Then the Lonnie Donegan led 'Skiffle' craze of the late 1950s with a rush for acoustic guitars, tea chest basses and washboards. The Vipers Skiffle group appeared at the Palace Theatre during 1957 followed by the 'King of Skiffle', Lonnie himself turning up at Hull's ABC Regal Cinema. Locally, Hull's teenage skiffle outfits at this time included the Cotton Pickers, the Blackjacks, the Aces and the Kingston Five. They played such venues as the Halfway House, the Kingston Hotel and various local youth clubs and church halls.

In 1958, all the way from the USA, the legendary Buddy Holly and the Crickets also appeared at the ABC Regal and later, Britain's top rock group Cliff Richard and the Shadows would turn up there as well.

As the Sixties' dawned, nationally we began to see the arrival on the scene of instrumental groups such as the Shadows, the Tornadoes, the Spotnicks, the Ventures, the Safaris and Duane Eddy. Their influences encouraged teenagers to move on to solid-bodied electric guitars.

However even though local venues such as the ABC Regal, the 'Kevin' Club in the Market Place, and the Majestic Ballroom in Witham had been bringing rock 'n' roll outfits to Hull since the late 1950s, a glance at the Entertainment's page of the Hull Daily Mail, even by late 1962, would 'appear to' show, like nationally, that rock music had far from taken root. The majority of local venues were still booking dance bands and quartets with names like Bert Kinsley and his Swingers, the Stanley Bempton

11

Orchestra, Harry Smith and his Madcap Seven. Venues were also still very much catering for an adult rather than a teen audience. There were one or two Jazz venues, notably the Windsor Hall, Argyle Street, Hull and occasional evenings at the Gondola Club down Little Queen Street. But, even though Uri Gagarin had taken a space flight and there had been 'Ban the Bomb' marches, nuclear threat and 'Beatniks', most families were still tuning into radio programmes such as 'Two-Way Family Favourites' where you were more likely to hear songs about runaway trains going over the hill and 'blowing', than you were to hear a rock 'n' roll record.

But a starting pistol was about to go off and the country was about to erupt. The arrival on the scene of the Beatles and the 'Mersey Beat' late in 1962, created an avalanche, which like a snowball rolling down hill, both locally and nationally caused an awakening. In the towns, cities and villages of the UK, Beat Groups 'seemingly' sprang up from nowhere. In Hull, a Beat Contest held at the Skyline Ballroom as early as January 1963, attracted more than 10 local groups. The phenomenal success of the Beatles and their contemporaries throughout that year encouraged more and more groups to appear on the scene and by 1964 it was estimated that the total number of beat groups in Britain far exceeded 10,000.

As with all popular trends, Hull showed great enthusiasm and in the wake of this 'beat boom' Hull City Council during the summer of 1964 began to hold 'Beat Nights' in the open air theatres of the City's East and West parks. Twice a week, in answer to Liverpool's 'Mersey Beat', two local groups representing Hull's rival 'Humber Beat' began to each play a forty-five minute to one hour set. The first of these shows was advertised on a billboard outside of the gates of Hull's West Park and my brother and I eagerly looked forward to seeing it.

12

On the evening of the show we took our seats in the park's open-air theatre early, keen not to miss anything. When the groups van's arrived and the various members clambered out, we closely watched their every movement as they carefully unloaded their equipment and transferred it onto the theatre's stage. First their guitars, then their amps and finally their fantastic sparkly-coloured drum kits with the names of their outfits boldly emblazoned on the bass drums. We sat transfixed as the drummers slowly began to put their kits together and the guitarists strategically positioned their small 15 and 30-watt Vox and Selmer valve amplifiers. The excitement began to mount as the amplifiers were switched on and two or three minutes of silence was followed by the sound of crackling, hissing and humming, plus the occasional snatch of some distant radio programme. Knowledgeable opinion in the audience had it that this apparently indicated that the 'amps' had 'warmed-up'! The guitarists then plugged their guitars in and ten minutes of incessant tuning followed. Meanwhile, the vocalists had begun testing their microphones and were constantly repeating the words 'One, two, one, two!' (We carefully memorised this apparently key phrase and later practised it at every opportunity!) The audience grew expectant as Twelve-bar chords were struck by the guitarists and final crucial decisions were taken as to whether to have treble controls up or down!

The whole ritual looked intensely exciting and extremely technical. But as we sat watching, the hard wooden slatted park seats began to bruise our backsides and we had to keep making vain attempts to swot midges, which as the sun slowly began to set over the park, started to mercilessly bite our heads. But then the pain and itching were forgotten, for at long last, the technicalities over, the first group were ready to take the stage. The Parks Department's compere approached the microphone and after blowing into it several times (a technique we also carefully noted!) introduced them, 'Ladies and gentlemen, sit back and listen to the pulsating sounds of ... Len Bone and the Vertebrae!'

The echoing sound of drum beat and the metallic clang of guitar strings played through primitive valve amplifiers resounded out over the park as Len and his outfit broke into their first number, 'Some Other Guy Now ... '. Were these the same ordinary mortals we had seen leaving their van only half-a-hour since? In their dark 'Undertaker' suits they certainly looked different, as though taking on another life form, like slipping into 'group mode'. The beat was hypnotic and Len's voice came over dark and mysterious. A few of the teenage girls in the audience jumped-up and started dancing on the loose pebbles covering the ground, others began rhythmically tapping their feet.

The Vertebrae played their way through the standard R & B set for that period which consisted of tracks that the Beatles would have been playing in Liverpool's Cavern Club only a year or so earlier. Wearing a waistcoat that resembled skeleton ribs and looking fresh from the graveyard, Len leered like a ghoul as he growled into the microphone and the group had a good solid sound. By the end of their set, we were ecstatic and our feet continued tapping long after they had left the stage.

Yes, this only confirmed what we already knew, more than ever now we wanted to be members of a beat group. The guitar was a magical device, which like the 'Eye of Zoltec' (the guy in the Victor comic wore) emitted strange powers to its wearer, it turned erstwhile spotty teenagers into Gods. As the midges bit harder and bumps began to appear on our heads, we eagerly waited for the next group to take the stage.

The second beat group on the bill that evening turned out to be much more 'flashier'. They were introduced as, 'Ricky Knight and his fabulous Crusaders'. Ricky wore a red Lurex jacket and made his entrance on stage by 'leaping' over the drum kit. The group were very much more 'alive' and exciting to watch and evidently it paid off because after changing their name to the

'Hullaballoos' they went on to release several records. They also followed the Beatles in touring America as four blond 'Mop-Tops', appearing on several package tours along with a string of other popular Sixties' groups.

We went to literally dozens of these Beat Nights and saw most of the local groups around at this time. Their names all began with the prefix 'The' including the Aces, the Blueberries, the Zodiacs, the Texans, the Sunsets, the Zircons, the Tennesseans, the Tycoons, the Cossacks, the Phantoms, the Crestas, the Gemini's, the Mustangs, the King Bees, the Riverbeats, the Rats, the Fabians, the Magpies, the Rascals, the Martians and the one exception to the rule, Ye Barons.

As an imaginative 12-year-old the names were exciting and I would be disappointed if a group didn't somehow live-up to their image. If I went to see the Cossacks then I expected to see 'Cossacks', if I went to see the Tennesseans then I expected to see 'Tennesseans'. I did, however, attend some 'Beat Nights' with trepidation, wondering what on earth a 'Zircon' or a 'Blueberry' might look like!

The various groups 15 cwt Bedford, Thames and Commer vans, with names such as 'Barry Graham and the Mustangs', or the 'King Bees' boldly emblazoned on their sides could be seen all over the City. The Rats van not only had the group's name on it, but also a picture of a large rodent painted on its side. Some outfits, such as the Riverbeats and the Crestas, were a little bit more conservative and had their name neatly printed on a flyer in the back window of their van. A few groups vans, such as those owned by the Rats, the Scorpions and later, the Strollers and Plague '66 were also often covered in their fans lipstick scrawled graffiti. Some of the groups further promoted themselves by plastering their flyers all over the city. One in particular displayed the name 'Ye Barons' while another proclaimed 'Gonx for R & B'.

Many of the local groups, like their Liverpool contemporaries, sought a gimmick, something they would be remembered for other than just their music. Whilst Liverpool outfits such as the Undertakers, dressed all in black and reputedly carried their guitars in coffins and Manchester's Freddie and the Dreamers made fools of themselves by performing 'bandy-legged', not to be outdone the Hull groups had their own ideas. For example, the Hullaballoos grew their hair really long and dyed it blond, which was extremely daring for the time, especially in Hull! Meanwhile Barry Graham and the Mustangs attempted to cultivate an air of 'respectability' about themselves. Keeping their hair short and neat they wore smart suits and tried to impress people by letting it generally be known that they spent their leisure time 'horse riding'. The Rats went even further, talking in their own 'Hip' language and calling it 'Rat Chat'. Meanwhile, the climax of a Zircons concert would see them 'high-stepping' as they played the Can-Can. But, arguably, it was the Winsors who had the totally unique gimmick of being the only local beat group in these days of growing hair-length, to feature a bald-headed singer!

As well as having a gimmick, most groups would also try to dress differently. Some still wore bright red or blue sparkly suits as made fashionable by early rock stars such as the Shadows. Many others wore matching Italian suits and slim ties like the Beatles. The Zircons, for instance, managed to do the Can-Can dressed in tailored maroon suits. Some groups such as the Flyaways and the Martians attempted to live up to their space-age image by dressing in 'space suits' made out of a satin material. The Rats and the C-Beats went for the full 'Beat' look and wore very 'Cavern' looking V-necked leather jerkins. Driffield's Syndicate 5 wore blue and white hooped, long-sleeved Tee-shirts and the Tennesseans wore red shirts and black ties. Other groups, with less money to spend, simply wore similar gear on stage such as four black bri-nylon polo-necked shirts bought from Boyes, of Hessle Road, Hull. All of the groups wore 2 to 3 inch high Cuban heeled boots as made fashionable by the 'Fab Four'.

Many groups also had matching guitars and Burns guitars, being reasonably priced (but sounding pretty naff!) were particularly popular. A few local guitarists, such as Martin Bridges of the Martians would also occasionally show off their talent to the audience by playing their guitars behind the back of their heads. Drum solos were also very popular and one or two drummers fixed-up light bulbs in their bass drums so that when they hit the bass-drum pedal the group's name lit up.

A few local outfits would also move in unison together on stage, following a pre-arranged dance sequence copied from the Shadow's 'Walk'. In attempting to get the edge on their rivals, some groups often went 'over the top' with this and their 'walks' took on quite sophisticated sequences. Two steps to the left, three to the right, one backward and then two forward. Some routines were carried out so quickly and so stiffly that as the various group members shot backwards, forwards and sideways with their guitars, they made such exaggerated movements and smiled so fixedly, that they often looked quite afflicted, even demented, like mad men stepping on burning coals!

Other local groups, such as for example, the Strollers, the Crusaders, the Sunsets and the Winsors, simply relied on the 'good looks' or 'personality' of their singers to win their audiences over. A few local outfits, including the Rats, the Moonshots, the Aces, the Scorpions, the Mustangs, and the Swinging Dukes did also have the advantage of having their own fan clubs to clap along.

But much more important than the gimmicks was the music. In 1964, R & B was King. Nine groups out of ten at the Hull Parks

17

Beat Nights would play tracks such as Wilbert Harrison's 'Kansas City', Tommy Tucker's 'High Heel Sneakers', Carl Perkins 'Everybody's Trying To Be My Baby', the Coasters 'I'm A Hog For You Baby' and 'Ain't That Just Like Me'. Most groups also knew the Chuck Berry Songbook inside out with songs such as 'Roll Over Beethoven', 'Sweet Little Sixteen', and 'Memphis Tennessee'. Buddy Holly songs were also still very popular. But as the Beatles and the Rolling Stones progressed throughout the 1960s then most groups would follow them.

The same thing was happening in every other town and village of Humberside, the East Riding and beyond. Usually, but not always, only the group names were different. In Scunthorpe it was the Dimples, the Chechakos, the Imps, the Cadillacs, the Nightriders, the Decoys, the Four Cents and the Kraakans. In York it was the Misfits, the Hornets, the Escorts, the Cheavours, the Viceroys, the Impacts, the Vampires, the Corvettes, the Easybeats, the Clubmen and the Boneshakers. In Scarborough it was the Moonshots, the Blue Stars, the Strangers, the Iguanas, the Tennesseans and the Flintones.

Despite the obvious talent of many of these local groups, in 1964 there was still a certain newness, freshness and even amateurishness about it all.

This certainly was the beginning.

CLUB A-GO-GO

Many venues opened their doors to the arrival of the 'beat groups'. These included school halls, dance halls, city halls, village halls, church halls, youth clubs, cinemas, small clubs and coffee bars, basically anywhere that could hold a group and an audience.

For the churches and village halls, beat groups provided another fund raising activity to go alongside Jumble Sales and Beetle Drives. Performing on dusty, splinter ridden stages to a back-drop of last year's pantomime, the R & B sounds of the beat groups often baffled local vicars and the various village hall committees. To some 'Hip' vicars it offered an opportunity to show a token acceptance of a quickly changing world. Nevertheless, the walls of the church halls would reverberate to the backbeat of the beat groups as teenage girls danced awkwardly around their handbags on often bare wooden floorboards. But for three hours on a Friday or Saturday evening the wooden huts became 'Beat Scenes' where the music would only be interrupted by the heady half-time glass of 'well watered' orange squash.

The Coffee Bars had sprung up in the late Fifties' and early Sixties'. One of the most famous was the '2 i's' Coffee Bar in London where many stars including the Shadows, were spotted. These were basically small clubs, which served snacks and soft drinks and often had a small dance floor area and a jukebox. Many coffee bars and small clubs had opened up by this time, often in disreputable looking basements and cellars. While Liverpool had its 'Cavern', 'Casbah', 'Jacaranda' and 'Blue Angel', Hull had its 'Kevin', 'Gondola', and 'Kon Tiki', later its 'Sombrero' and Barracuda. Out in the East Riding and along the coast, Driffield had its Club Bohemia, Skipsea had its 'Linzi

Coffee Bar featuring its 'Drogo's Den', Bridlington had its 'Dolphin' and 'La Caverne', Scarborough had its Condor, Gemini and Candlelight and York had its Enterprise Club. Just like in Liverpool, live groups played at all these venues.

York's Enterprise Club was established as a 'Beat Cellar' as early as 1961 and was the first club in town to hold regular dances for teenagers. Club proprietor, Neil Guppy was a former St John's College student. Between 1961 and 1965 the Enterprise Club's membership grew from 400 to 1000 teenagers. All of York's beat groups played the Enterprise.

In 1964 the Zarf Club down Stonegate became another York club venue. It boasted a coffee bar, a very groovy juke box with the latest Mod and Soul records, a cellar where local bands played and an upstairs stage were top underground groups such as the Graham Bond Organisation performed. At the far end of that floor, in an unlit area, were placed lots of old settees and armchairs where you might care to make your own fun!

Skipsea's Linzi Coffee Bar with its 'Drogo's Den' was another early Beat Cellar. In 1963 singer/guitarist Dev Douglas was resident there and soon afterwards he gained a recording contract. In 1964, Ricky Knight and the Crusaders took over the residency and they too would also sign a recording contract.

In Hull the 'Kevin' Club (1958-1964) in the Market Place (managed by Roy Tilly) had been featuring live chart topping groups on its circular stage since the late 1950s. These included Billy Fury (1960), Vince Eager (1960), Acker Bilk (1961), Screaming Lord Sutch (1961) and Johnny Kidd and the Pirates. Among the many local groups who played there were the Aces, the Rascals, Scott Madison and the Rangers, Tony Martin and the Sunsets, and the Winsors.

Another Hull venue to open around this time was the 'Kon Tiki' Club, which was hidden away down an alley off Whitefriargate. Inside, both Star and local groups played away to a backdrop of a South Sea Island setting, complete with fake palm trees. In its dark and steamy atmosphere 'mod' girls danced the night away.

But by 1964, major 'Mod hangout', the Gondola Club in Little Queen Street, had become Hull's main small club venue. While top local beat group, Tony Martin and the Sunsets (later the Mods) were resident there, many star groups and musicians played the Gondola. These included the Pretty Things, Johnny Kidd and the Pirates, Jimmy Powell and the Five Dimensions, the Undertakers, Wayne Fontana and the Mindbenders, Dave Berry and the Cruisers, Freddie and the Dreamers, Little Walter, Rocking Henry and the Hayseeds, Frankenstein and the Monsters, the Graham Bond Organisation and the Alex Harvey Band.

While being pop stars in their own right, several of these groups featured members who would go on to even greater fame and fortune. For instance, when Jimmy Powell and the Five Dimensions played the 'Gondola' they featured a young 'Rooster-haired' Rod Stewart on harmonica, while the Graham Bond Organisation contained two future members of the legendary rock band 'Cream', namely Jack Bruce and Ginger Baker.

When Gondola Club proprietor, John Science, was short of an act he would contact Vance Arnold and the Avengers, who would come down from Sheffield. Vance Arnold's real name was Joe Cocker but it was considered inappropriate at this time to use it!

In the autumn of 1962, John was contacted by an agent who informed him that he had a Sunday night date available for a

Liverpool group recently returned from Hamburg. Could he use them? Unfortunately, the Gondola Club was fully booked, but to help the agent out, John contacted Hull's Majestic Ballroom who agreed to put the group on. Little did John realise that he had just turned down, soon-to-be world superstars, the Beatles!

Apart from the Coffee Bars, the small clubs and the church halls the other main live music venues were the dance halls. Hull's Majestic Ballroom in Witham, was one of the leading local dance halls during the first half of the Sixties', to feature rock groups. A Top Rank Ballroom managed by Cyril Hatwell, after starting life as a cinema, the 'Majestic', in 1959 became a traditional dance hall featuring a big band fronted by vocalist Leon Riley. But by the early 1960s it had begun to run Sunday evening 'Beat' dances and these soon turned out to be much more profitable, they ran until 1965. Some of the top acts to perform there during this time included Gene Vincent (1964), the Hollies (1963) who had recently had their first record 'Just Like Me' released, Billy Davies (who at the time was ex-Shadow Jet Harris's Girlfriend), Sounds Incorporated (1963), Gerry and the Pacemakers (1963), Billy J. Kramer and the Dakotas, Freddie and the Dreamers (1963/64), Herman's Hermits, Manfred Mann, and Screaming Lord Sutch on two occasions.

Unquestionably, the most famous of all the groups to play at the Majestic were the Beatles. They appeared there twice within the space of six months. The first time, Ringo Starr had only just weeks earlier replaced Pete Best on the drums. It was on an evening in October 1962 before the release of their first single. Because it was Hull Fair week, only about 40 people turned up for the gig, at which they were supported by Hull groups the Aces and Scott Madison and the Rangers. But when the Beatles made their second appearance there, in February 1963, their first single, 'Love Me Do' had just charted and while the venue had the capacity to hold 950, the Management felt that it couldn't turn the rest away and so allowed a total of 1500 in! The Beatles were only paid £50 for the gig and were also booked for a further appearance at the Majestic later that year, but because of their tremendous success they could afford to break their contract. Local groups playing the Majestic at this time included the Aces, Tony Martin and the Sunsets, Barry Graham and the Mustangs, Scott Madison and the Rangers, and the Winsors.

The Skyline Ballroom in Hull was another of the main dance halls to book local beat groups. It had begun gradually by featuring outfits such as Scott Madison and the Rangers at its quite formal Dinner dances. Then in 1963 'Beat Contests' began to held there with local groups such as the Rebels, the Gazelles, the Panthers, the Rascals, Ye Barons, Barry Graham and the Mustangs, Tony Martin and the Sunsets, the C-Beats, the Martians, the Crusaders and the Rangers, competing against each other. Many of the winners and competitors at these beat contests then began to be featured at special 'rock 'n' roll' evenings. Beat Contests were by this time becoming very popular and were also held at Hull's Locarno Ballroom and out of town at such venues as the Gaiety Cinema Scarborough, Scunthorpe's Baths Hall, the Rialto Cinema York and Hornsea's Floral Hall. Two of the biggest local ones were the Yorkshire and the Tyne Tees Beat Contests. There were also national Beat Contests with regional heats organised by such pop papers as the Melody Maker and the 'People' newspaper.

Several Hull cinemas had also since the early Sixties' begun to feature local groups, often in-between films. The Dorchester in the city centre, the Astoria on Holderness Road, the Langham on Hessle Road and the Mayfair on Beverley Road used beat groups such as the Burn's Beat Combo, the Night People, the Batmen and the Rascals to attract teenagers in, especially on a Sunday Evening.

Hull's ABC Regal Cinema, as part of the national touring circuit, brought many pop package tours to the City during the 1960s. These featured such stars as Roy Orbison, Chuck Berry, the Moody Blues, the Kinks, Marianne Faithful, Gerry and the Pacemakers, Gene Pitney, Long John Baldry, the Rolling Stones and the Beatles.

The Beatles returned to Hull in October 1964, this time to play the Regal. After arriving at the cinema early the 'Fab Four' were given a tour of the building, during which Paul McCartney spotted an old upright piano. He immediately sat down at it and gave an impromptu performance, rattling off a medley of old fashioned pub songs with John Lennon, George Harrison and Ringo Starr, stood around him joining in on the choruses. Where is the piano now? It might be worth a fortune!

Having already appeared in Hull at the City Hall in 1963, supported by Johnny Kidd and the Pirates and Hull's Aces, the Rolling Stones also played the ABC Regal in 1964. It was the first time in their history that one of their concerts was filmed in colour and like the Beatles before them, the Stones went down a storm.

Another Hull Cinema, the Cecil, also opened its doors to occasional pop package tours. One in 1965 was headlined by Herman's Hermits who were that week in the charts with their hit single, 'I'm Into Something Good'. The concert also featured the Honeycombs and Hull's recent conquerors of the USA, the Hullaballoos.

Another less likely venue, which brought some legendary groups to the City during the early Sixties', was the Beverley Road Baths. In 1963, 'Five Live' Yardbirds played there featuring one Eric 'Slowhand' Clapton and later, in 1965, Eric Burdon and the Animals appeared there as well.

On the local scene, several Hull pubs had begun to feature the City's groups, most notably the Halfway House and Ferryboat Inn. But from 1965 the Hull City Hall and Hessle Town Hall began to hold beat dances, which featured two or even three local groups a night.

Out at Beverley, the Regal Cinema, Hodgson's Ballroom and the Memorial Hall were also big promoters of local beat groups with the Regal featuring three groups a night and the Memorial Hall up to six!

On the River Humber too, the Hull to New Holland ferries ran 'Riverboat Rock' cruises, featuring the beat groups of the area. Groups also often used the New Holland ferry to shorten their trip for gigs in Grimsby. Venues here included the South Bank Jazz Club and the Hacienda Coffee Bar, also Grimsby's 'Gaiety' Dance Hall (Mecca) and the yearly Jazz festival which featured most of the top Sixties' groups including the Animals, the Small Faces, Screaming Lord Sutch (with Paul Nicholas) and Jimmy Witherspoon. Close by in Cleethorpes the Witch Doctor Club and 'The Village' were also being played by the region's groups.

In Scunthorpe the Drill Hall, the Baths Hall and the Jazz Workshop, together with a few local pubs (The Sherpa Hotel and Queen Bess) provided regular venues for both star and local groups.

Down the East Coast, the Withernsea Pavilion and Hornsea Floral Hall also became regular venues for both star and local groups, with the Bridlington Spa Royal Hall providing a regular supply of top hit groups throughout the Sixties'. These included Otis Redding, Sam and Dave, P. J. Proby, Ike and Tina Turner, the Rolling Stones, the Kinks, the Four Pennies, the Move, Jimi Hendrix, the Nashville Teens, Tom Jones, and the Troggs, to name but a few.

The Brid Spa, like the Beverley Regal, also became a place where East and North Riding groups met and played support. Hull groups would also often play some of the thriving Scarborough venues such as the Cricketers Arms, the Candlelight Club, the Condor Club, the YMCA and the Olympia. Regular gigs were also to be had in Filey at the Belle Vue Club, Filey Pavilion and the Brigg Cinema.

For those Hull groups who made it out to York, apart from the Enterprise and the Zarf Club, there were many other venues available, including the Mandrake Club, the Tramways Club, the Burns Hotel, the Rialto Cinema, the Big Coach, the Empire, the Assembly Rooms, the Wildman Pub on the Tadcaster Road and the Boulevard Night-Club. All over Hull and the East Riding, from Grimsby to Scunthorpe and York to Scarborough the 'Big Beat' was reverberating throughout the area.

HEART FULL OF SOUL

In 1964 my 15-year-old brother left school and after finding a job, was able to save up enough money to buy a second-hand 'Hofner' electric guitar. Soon afterwards I used the money from my paper-round and traded in our 'acoustic' to buy an even cheaper second-hand electric guitar, a 'customised' (three large oval shaped rubies had been stuck on it!) light blue and check-maple Guyatone LG50 bought from Sellitt and Soon, of Holderness Road in Hull. This shop was an Aladdin's Cave of 'cheap' second-hand group gear and we took a Sunday afternoon walk there most weekends to stare in the windows at the frequently changing range of guitars, amplifiers and drums for sale. Rosetti 'Lucky 7' guitars and Shaftsbury amplifiers were prevalent. After a group had 'packed-it-in', this was often the place where their gear ended up, appearing at times like a 'beat graveyard' with dejected second-hand bass drums bearing the names of recently departed groups. Many of the guitars, drums, and amplifiers for sale often dated back as far as the Second World War. Our first cheap microphone bought from there looked suspiciously as though it had last seen service inside a WWII tank! But it was the place to pick-up bargains if you were entering the group scene on a budget.

However, having now done a 'Bob Dylan' and 'gone electric' we had no amplifier. Fortunately, my brother knew a member of local group, the Night People, who sold him a second-hand Vox AC15 amplifier, which we both plugged into. Most of the local groups by this time were using Vox AC30 twin speaker valve amps (the twin-speaker models having been especially produced on a request by the Shadows). Others were using the 'Selmer' equivalent and both were now covered in a black material.   Not only did we have half the wattage shared between us but our own amp was a pre-1958, one speaker model, covered in an old fashioned looking beige coloured material, over-flatteringly termed 'blond'. (Today worth a fortune!)

Many of the early groups had started out like us with cheap guitars and equipment. Small green suitcase style Elpico amps and even valve radio sets had often initially been used as amplification for guitars. Linear Concorde amps were used for PA's and cheap, often nameless, strangely shaped blocks of wood with pick-ups and strings attached to them were used as guitars! Now, 'fully equipped' the two of us were also ready to form a band and 'hit the road'. And like so many hopeful young musicians before and after us we placed an advertisement in the Hull Daily Mail seeking 'band members'. The response was seemingly fruitful as we managed to get a reply from a drummer who was due to appear on Television's weekly talent show 'Opportunity Knocks'. Not only could he drum, but he also did impromptu Chinaman impressions, squinting his eyes, folding his arms and balancing a cymbal on his head. We rehearsed together two or three times and the drums brought the music to life, it was like adding a missing link, making us sound like embryo 'Shadows'. But the drummer had no transport and we had no transport (as both our fathers only owned bikes) and so we were having to catch buses or pay for a taxi to each others house's to rehearse. After a Conductor refused to allow his drum kit on to a Beverley Road bus he pinned his hopes on his 'Opportunity Knocks' audition and we never saw him again.

We re-advertised and this time (despite it being the heat of summer) got a 'singer' wearing 'shades' and dressed in a tightly buttoned-up black plastic Mac. (Apparently Bob Dylan had recently been seen wearing one!) At our first rehearsal (sweating profusely in the Mac!) he kept mumbling something about a PA and where was the Echo Box? Not possessing a PA he plugged his microphone into the Vox AC15 amplifier along with the two guitars and kept complaining as we ran through our repertoire that we were playing every song in a different key to the one he was singing in. We decided not to see him again!

By this time, we had begun rehearsing in an old church hall. The place was far from inspiring. There was no heating and so on an evening it was freezing. It also had a creepy caretaker who would lurk about, jangling his keys, in the darkened recesses beyond the main hall. The sound of the key jangling would grow remarkably louder as it neared the time to leave. Just like Igor in the Frankenstein movies he would obediently obey his Master's orders and ensure that you never got a second longer than the two hours you had paid for. But places to rehearse were hard to find and throughout years of practising, they so often seemed to be like that, cold, dirty, soul-destroying places where any artistic fervour, like any heat, would soon disappear. But after being banned from practising in their 'front rooms' most groups were thankful for being able to use church halls, village halls, scout huts, barns and even 'chicken-huts' to rehearse in. Not that you were always safe there, as groups would still often be prone to eviction as surrounding neighbours and irate local vicars complained that decibel levels were getting too high!

Learning songs at rehearsals could also often prove difficult. Picking the song up off a record meant first getting your hands on a copy of the record. Buying records was expensive and we didn't know anyone that we could borrow them from. When we did buy them, like other group members we'd sit with our ears tuned to the record player, listening to a song over and over again. Each time we played it, the record would pick up more and more scratches from the needle and inevitably, it would begin to 'jump'!

We sometimes found it difficult to pick up certain chords or lyrics from the records and would play a song so many times that we felt quite 'wappy'. Sometimes we'd buy the sheet music but this was often in a different key to the record and contained no real bass lines. The sheet music also occasionally missed out chords or included unnecessary, obscure, or even wrong ones! A compromise used by us and many other groups, would be to first try to pick the song up off the record and then to stand furtively by the sheet music rack in Gough and Davy or the Paragon Music Stores checking and memorising the chords or lyrics. Groups would also often query songs with each other backstage at gigs or stand out front checking what chords other groups were playing up on stage. Some groups did have the advantage of having members who were particularly good at 'picking up' off the record, such as Dave Cuthbert of the Strollers, Pete Green of the Mods and Mick Ronson of the Crestas.

In our quest to team up with fellow musicians we had other enquiries to our 'box adverts' but usually found that the applicants weren't too keen on forming a new group with two young inexperienced teenagers. They were either just checking out what was happening on the local scene, or even simply trying to find out where we rehearsed so that their rival group could steal the hall!

However, undaunted by the lack of drums we continued to rehearse and felt ready for our first gig. The problem was how did you get one as there seemed to be few agents about? So once again we used the local paper, 'Bookings Required!' Unfortunately, the few replies we had were from pubs, who once they saw two small, thin 13 and 15 year old boys armed with guitars, soon realised that we looked far too young to play on licensed premises. But keen to play and desperate for our first gig we decided to enter a talent contest that was being held during the summer evenings in the local parks. Many of the more established local groups, including the Crusaders, the Martians, the Phantoms, the Strollers, the Cock-a-Hoops, the Zircons and the Semi-Tones, would still regularly enter such competitions. A gig was a gig, especially for new groups, who full of enthusiasm would be willing to play anywhere in their eagerness to gain experience.

Our Round One heat was held at the open-air theatre in Hull's West Park. We travelled there on a No. 63 bus along with our one Vox AC15 amplifier, the two guitars, plus an extension lead and plug-box my father had proudly made for us. For the first round heats, each of the acts were put into categories. We were placed in the guitar/vocal category and were competing against a guy in his late teens who would later go on to form recording group 'Red Dirt'. He sat on a stool and playing an acoustic guitar, 'growled' his way through Bob Dylan's 'You Ain't Goin' Nowhere' and 'Mr Tambourine Man'. We followed him on and treated the audience to 'FBI' and 'The Frightened City' by the Shadows, followed by the Yardbirds, 'Heart Full of Soul'. Despite being in the charts, as I bent the notes, the last song seemed a little bit contemporary for some of the older members of the audience and as my brother and I were sharing the Vox amplifier, each time one of us added gusto to our guitar playing the others guitar would sound proportionally quieter. Never-the-less we were given a good round of applause and the compere later adjudicated that we should go through to the next part of the competition.

So the 'Raydens', as we had now decided to call ourselves, had made it through to the Second Round. This time the show was being held at the open-air theatre in Hull's East Park. Because there were now fewer acts, the contest no longer had any categories and so everyone was competing against everyone else. When the cue came over the PA system for the Raydens to appear on stage, we were waiting backstage in a shed which served as a dressing room. (We had been advised that as 'potential stars' we mustn't mingle with the audience!) Unfortunately, somebody wishing to cut down on the competition or believing that the show would benefit from our absence had locked us in and we were only able to make our escape by climbing through the extremely narrow shed window. Dishevelled, but on stage, we plugged our guitars into the Vox AC15 and began our set. This time we left out 'Heart Full of Soul' and instead played 'Paint it Black' by the Rolling Stones. At the end of the show the audience were asked to sound their applause for each of the acts on the bill and this was measured on a 'clapometer'. Those receiving the loudest applause would go through to the quarter-finals of the competition. The fact that most of the acts on the show were troupes of 10 to 12 dancing girls who had each brought at least two relatives along to clap on their behalf, didn't seem to matter. When the time came to vote on our act, despite our mum and granny trying desperately to make up for our lack of extended family, it was to no avail and we were out of the competition and our gigs came to a temporary halt.

With the lack of success in trying to attract a drummer we decided to keep it in the family and brought our 11 year-old brother in on the act. Thanks to local Music Shop owner, J. P. Cornell, somehow, we managed to buy him a cheap second-hand kit of 'Beverley' drums and he began to have drumming lessons with a local bandleader based at the Skyline Ballroom in Hull. Despite the fact that the lessons had never got beyond the snare drum, we decided to look for more gigs and now a fully pledged 'beat group', changed our name to the 'Raydenmics'.

We were in luck, in that another talent contest was advertised, this time it was being held at the Broadgates Psychiatric Hospital near Beverley. Fortunately, we had by now acquired our own transport. Unfortunately, it wasn't a 15 cwt van with our group name boldly emblazoned on both of its sides, but a 1940s motorcycle and sidecar, group name on a sheet of paper in the sidecar window! It did however make out of town gigs possible and saved us money on taxis.

The talent show was being held during the dark winter evenings of 1965. When the night of the first round of the competition arrived, we lifted the lid of the sidecar and in climbed my younger brother and our mum who was acting as our manager. Around them and on top of them, we loaded the Vox AC15 amplifier, two guitars, a microphone and stand, and a set of drums. I was lucky in having what I thought was a privileged position on the back of the bike with my by now, 16 year old brother 'steering'. Loaded up and barely able to get the lid of the sidecar down, we set off.

Carrying so much weight the motorcycle found it difficult to pick-up speed and the sound of cymbal crashes accompanied the roar of the engine each time we went over a bump. By the time we had crawled our way to the outskirts of Hull the evening air had become extremely cold and on the back of the bike we were freezing, with only occasional heat from the bike's straining engine offering us any relief. As we rode on through the dark and misty East Yorkshire countryside and past an eerie looking Beverley West Woods, it had become so cold that I had to cling on to the roof of the sidecar to stop my frozen body from falling off. But, eventually, almost blocks of ice, we arrived at the hospital.

The cold night air had badly affected us and before unpacking the equipment, with our legs frozen into a 'U' shape, we slowly 'dismounted' and 'staggered' inside to find the toilets. We discovered that they were individual cubicles which had doors that opened directly on to the main corridor. Perhaps because of the nature of the hospital, each cubicle only had 'half a door', which for some strange reason was hung mid-way up the doorframe! Therefore, because of our shortness in stature, if we had used them, our lower regions would have been on full view to anyone passing by who had turned up for the show. Being shy and bashful teenagers, we daren't risk it and had to spend the rest of the evening cross-legged!

To take our minds off our throbbing bladders we set our gear up on the stage and seeing another drum kit, realised that top Beverley group the Strollers were on the bill. Having seen them on several occasions, we knew just how good they were and despite the fact that they were a member short mentally began to settle for second place. But as usual we were up against various troupes of dancing girls, one of who's pants flew off during the Can-Can! Despite the handicap of full bladders we actually went down quite well and gained a few young fans in the audience, but we still didn't get through to the next round of the competition.

It is only years later, when you hear that even someone as great as 'Elvis' could still only manage to come second in a local talent competition and that the early Beatles stopped entering talent competitions because they kept losing to a metaphorical 'woman playing the spoons,' that you begin to realise just how subjective they are and they can be a really negative experience.

Also, call me cynical if you wish, but it only really dawned on me a few years later, when my hormones were playing up, why so many contorting female dance troupes always seemed to win their way through to the finals!

GOT MY MOJO WORKING

Not only had a multitude of venues sprung up for the local beat groups, by 1965 the first Hull recording studio had also opened its doors. Called the Malconi Studios it was situated on Hessle Road close to the 'Flyover'. The four-track studio was able to produce demo discs of its recording sessions and many local groups began to beat a path to its door. These included the Fabians, the C-Beats, the Mods, the Phantoms, the King Bees, the Winsors and the Avengers. The following year another Hull recording studio opened its doors and it would still be open more than 30 years later. This was Keith Herd's 'Fairview' studio in Willerby. The recording studio was initially based in the front room of Keith's house where egg boxes were stuck on the walls to dampen the sound and recording operations were conducted through the kitchen serving-hatch window! The studio soon moved out into a converted stable at the rear of the house, where even so, some early recording artists claim that initially horses had to be removed from the stables before recording could commence. Knowledge of the recording skills of Keith Herd, a budding Joe Meek cum George Martin, soon began to spread and he too began playing host to a string of local groups. These included the Small Four, Mandy and the Girlfriends, the Mods, the Strollers, ABC, the Rats, and later the Mandrakes, Michael Chapman, Roger Bloom's Hammer and Treacle.

Feeling that it was time they had something down on vinyl, the Raydenmics also decided to produce their first demo recording. Not for us the Malconi or Fairview studios, but a smaller establishment, much smaller indeed. In fact the Recording Booth standing in Paragon Railway Station, Hull, where 'demo discs' could be made for a mere two shillings and sixpence a time. Normally used by rail travellers recording messages for their loved ones, the booth was really only built to accommodate one person. After first furtively checking for Railway policemen we took an acoustic guitar, a pair of bongo drums and an harmonica into the booth. The only way we could play the instruments was by contorting ourselves into various positions. My younger brother sat on the floor with the bongos, my older brother stood astride him, forced to hold his guitar in an upright position due to the lack of space. Meanwhile I also had my own legs 'akimbo', trying to blow on a harmonica with my face pressed to the machine's operating mechanism. Despite the cramped conditions, one of us managed to free an arm and insert a coin into the payment slot. (I'm fairly certain that it wasn't my older brother!) We then waited for the red light, and the off, then burst into our own self-penned number 'Summer Trees'. The resulting demo disc (released on the 'Calibre' label) is still in existence for those brave enough to want to hear it! But had any of us become a Jimi Hendrix or a Paul McCartney then it might today be worth a fortune.

Whilst local groups now had venues and recording studios, the publicity machines had also been working. Local, weekly newspaper, the Hull and East Yorkshire Times from late 1964 until the early 1970s began a weekly 'Teen Scene' feature. This put local groups in the spotlight and provided information generally on what was happening on the local scene. Many of the groups featured tended to be quite positive about the progress they were making and fame always seemed to be 'just around the corner'. Similar articles were to be found in the Scarborough 'Mercury' with its 'Youth' column, the 'Scunthorpe Star' with its On The 'Steelbeat' column the 'Yorkshire Evening News' with its 'Trend' column and in Grimsby's 'Telegraph and Argus' with its 'Showcase' feature.

There were also several attempts at publishing a local pop magazine featuring the groups of the area. The first, produced in Driffield in 1964, had the title of 'Beatcomber'. A good quality, well-written magazine, unfortunately only one edition was ever produced. Nevertheless, this contained articles on Hull's 'Aces', Bridlington's 'Mark Antony and the Avengers', Selby's 'McCoys', Driffield's 'Roadrunners' and Scarborough's 'Moonshots'.

York went several steps further, publishing numerous editions of the Ousebeat magazine. This featured articles on most of the York groups including the Viceroys, the Counterpoints, the Rockafellas, the Ousebeats, Steve Cassidy and the Escorts, Dal Dyman and the Tycoons and the Cheavours.

Local music shops had also been benefiting from the 'beat boom'. In Hull these included J. P. Cornell, the Paragon Music Stores, and Gough and Davy. Out at Scarborough it was Deans Music. York also had a branch of Gough and Davy but generally, most local musicians would buy their guitars and amps in Leeds at stores such as 'Kitchens' where they had more choice. We always bought our 'Cathedral' guitar strings and two and sixpenny copies of the latest hits on sheet music from the Paragon Music Stores. Our guitars and amplifiers were usually purchased from J. P. Cornell of Spring Bank, Hull.

Cornell's was the 'Groups' shop. Pat Cornell, the owner, had been a drummer in various local dance bands including those of Norris Walker, Ceres and the Edwin Harper band. He first set his music shop up on Spring Bank, Hull, in the late 1940s and moved to his popular Spring Street corner site during the early Fifties'. He remembered the 'Skiffle' craze as starting a boom in the demand for guitars. Fender guitars and Vox amplifiers quickly became market leaders and the shop was an agent for both. Hull's Mick Ronson and Johnny Paterson both bought their first guitars from Cornell's. On a Saturday in the 1960s, local musicians would be in and out of the shop all day. Such people as Mick Ronson could often be seen 'holding court' in there, with local musicians trying out new guitars, assistant Johnny Paterson selling them and upstairs, Keith Herd, soldering iron in hand, repairing some group's amp or equipment.

Whilst most groups would generally 'hustle' for their gigs there was clearly locally an opening for someone to bring the new groups and venues together. In 1965, the Scorpions drummer, Pete McLeod, saw this gap in the market and set up an Entertainments Agency. Initially operating from a shed in the back garden of his parents Kirkella home, by 1967 he had become so successful that he needed to set up more permanent offices. Another young budding entrepreneur, Hull College student Tony Hodges, began to run the 'Beatscene', a club based at changing venues. One weekend it would be held at the Kirkella Memorial Hall and for example, featuring the Fabians while the next weekend it would be at the Hessle Town Hall and featuring the King Bees.

Many parents also found a new lease of life managing their son or daughter's pop group, especially mums. These included a Mrs Bridges, a Mrs Chapman, a Mrs Carey and a Mrs Moody. Several other local names began to be linked with managing groups. These included Pete Bocking, Jack Wigley, Barry Paterson, John Walmsley, Jackie Bender, Michael Moore, Joe Wilkinson, R C Kitching, John Ranby and Barry Hastings.

In Scarborough, beat group managers included Dave Cook, Brian Cooke, Ron Gillet and Peter Pitts. The Peter Pitts Agency was brimming with talented local groups including the Tennesseans, the Methods, the Trolls, the Kerbsiders, Chow's Men and the Iguanas. Ron Gillet managed the very popular Moonshots and was also an early manager of the Mandrakes.

Out at York, Syd Hartness managed several   top groups including the Roll Movement, Gideon's Few and Scunthorpe's 'Gospel Garden'. Enterprise Club owner Neil Guppy also acted as an agent for most of the town's local groups, putting them on every weekend at his club. These included the Counterpoints, the Vampires, the Viceroys, Del Dyman and the Tycoons, and the Ousebeats.

But arguably, the most successful agent locally at this time was Cleethorpe's Martin Yale. Yale had links with Record Producer Bunny Lewis, hit songwriter Chris Andrews and Manchester's prestigious promoters, Kennedy Street Enterprises. He was responsible for getting the Rats and many others their recording contracts and also got several local groups, such as the 'Mods', some top support gigs. In 1965 Yale managed stars like Dave Berry and Joe Cocker and organised various regional Beat Contests. He had his finger on the pulse of the rock music scene and offered many local groups much useful advice, from selecting their names, down to what to wear on stage. He was for instance responsible for getting Peter King and the Majestics to change their name to the rawer and more happening 'Rats' and for Tony Martin and the Sunsets changing their name to the Mods. Martin Yale was also extremely good at promoting his groups. Perhaps his cheekiest stunt was to send the Rats along with a piece of cheese as a present for the producer of a top Television pop show they were appearing on!

A certain camaraderie was beginning to develop backstage amongst the local groups. At venues such as the Hull City Hall, the Beverley Regal, Burton Constable Hall and the Scarborough's Olympia, in the small dressing rooms at the back and sides of the stage (when they weren't 'chasing' girls!) groups would meet and talk. The talk would more often than not be about music and the songs that the different groups had learned to play. Guitarists would be querying each other about the chords in certain songs, checking who was playing the right ones! Tricks would also occasionally be exchanged on the guitar. Group members would be 'talking' equipment and trying out one another's amps and guitars. Talk was also about what was good and what was bad on the scene. There would be the occasional criticism of other groups and the venues played. But a group's worst critics were usually themselves, they knew when they had played well and when they hadn't.

Out front at the various venues, girls would often hang about the stage ('groupies!') and they would be able to name the members of several of their favourite local outfits. Visiting groups would often be asked if they knew the members of rival groups as the girls eagerly awaited their return to that venue. Some girls would also follow their favourite local group from gig to gig. This could prove risky for some group members who having perhaps sworn their undying love the night before, were often to be found in the arms of another at the next gig!

A few Hull groups had by this time actually managed to sign 'recording contracts' and release records. These included the Aces, the Hullaballoos, the Rats and the Mustangs (who had changed their name to the Majority) but non of them had managed to make the UK charts. The Hullaballoos had come the closest with their single 'I Gonna Love You Too' reaching No. 56 in the US charts. But all four groups, or their records, had been featured on national Television programmes such as 'Thank Your Lucky Stars', 'Discs A Go Go', 'Juke Box Jury' and the legendary 'Ready Steady Go'.

Further down the coast, a couple of Scarborough groups had also produced records. These included the Incas with 'I'll Keep Holding On' which had sold 15,000 copies. And some of the former 'Moonshots, who had teamed up with some of York's

'Viceroys' and become the Shots. Their release, 'Keep A Hold Of What You Got Now Baby', had also sold well, despite this, both records had failed to Chart, but things in the area certainly looked promising.

TURN, TURN, TURN

By the summer of 1965, beat group activity had reached a new zenith. There were now even more groups on the scene and even more venues. But by the end of the year, the terms 'beat' and 'beat group' were beginning to become dated and were giving way to 'pop' and 'pop group'. There was a definite feeling of change in the air and in the music. That year, an extremely influential young American guy called Bob Dylan left the mainstream folk scene and on his milestone album 'Highway 61 Revisited', went 'electric'. With songs such as 'Positively 4th Street' and 'Like A Rolling Stone', he showed groups (including the Beatles) that rock lyrics could be serious and have meaning. They didn't just have to be about 'Boy meets girl', 'Boy falls in love with girl', 'Boy gets packed-in by girl', 'Girl wants boy back', etc, etc.

The Beatles had also been progressing, first with their classic 1965 album 'Rubber Soul' and then the following year when they produced the very influential 'Revolver'.

Many of the first wave of beat groups had originally developed out of 1950s rock 'n' roll and 'skiffle' like the Beatles. For the first half of the Sixties' they held sway on the local scene and newer groups often found it difficult to break into regular venues such as for example the Beverley Regal where the older more established groups were still very popular. But the 'Big Beat' was beginning to attract younger crowds and a lot of the older customers at venues like the Regal were beginning to move on. As we reached the mid-Sixties' many first wave group members were also getting married or settling into relationships and careers. Some didn't want to follow the Beatles and move on to the new sounds. Locally, like nationally, many of these groups began to either disband or move slowly away from the mainstream pop scene and into the Working Men's Clubs and cabaret. Some moved onto the club circuit in the belief that the 'pop phenomena' was a temporary thing and a young person's game. There was also a generally held belief that you were finished if you hadn't 'made it' by the time you had reached the ripe old age of 2I! Therefore, In order to survive as a musician, some thought that you needed to get accepted by a more mature audience.

But there was no shortage of young musicians to replace them and a new wave of local groups began to appear on the scene. Groups influenced by the music of the Rolling Stones, the Beatles, the Yardbirds, the Kinks, the Small Faces, the Who, the Byrds, the Beach Boys, Black Soul artists, the Mod culture and Bob Dylan. There was a move away from R & B and revolution in the air as the Swingin' Sixties' really began to swing.

New boutiques opened up in Hull city centre and record stores such as Hammonds 'Pic-a-Disc' did brisk business. Parka clad Mods roared around the city on their Union Jack and chrome panelled Lambretta scooters, spending their evenings hanging out at the Gondola Club.

Early in 1966, the local College Students Union began to hire Hull's Skyline Ballroom and started to bring a new wave of top rock groups to the City. These included, Cream, John Mayall, Jimi Hendrix, the Small Faces, Traffic, Geno Washington and the Move. All of whom were supported by our top local groups.

One of the best places to see local groups playing live on a Saturday evening in 1966 was at the Hull City Hall. On a Friday and Saturday in Beverley it was at the 'Regal'. Unfortunately, both venues (for members of the audience) had the disadvantage of being 'trouble spots'. At the City Hall, the chances of being head-butted by a drunken Trawlerman, while stood watching the group performing live on stage was extremely high! But the music was 'usually' worth the risk despite ringing ears (caused by the loudness of the groups, not the Trawlermen!) for several hours afterwards. Every Saturday night, three local outfits, introduced by compere Ron Downing, could be seen playing live. Their names had now also begun to change and there was much less use of the prefix 'The'. Now the names were 'Plague 66', ABC, Sons of Witch, Roger Bloom's Hammer, Disturbance, Birds Groove, Locomotion, New Religion, the Strollers, the Sweet Sugar Soul Set, the Urge and the Mandrakes.

One of the most exciting of this new wave of local groups were 'Plague '66', their performance was 'electric'. Not only did they sound good, but looked good as well, often to be seen dressed in knee length fur coats and turquoise-blue psychedelic flares. Influenced by the black soul artists of American labels Stax, Atlanta and Motown, Plague 66's set consisted of soul classics, featuring Otis Redding, Wilson Pickett, Marvin Gaye, and James Brown numbers. Wherever they played, fans would crowd around the stage and girls would often try to join them on it! The group created a brilliant atmosphere and there was always a feeling that when they took to the stage 'one' was witnessing a 'happening' which was strange, because on the stroke of midnight New Years Eve 1966 the group changed their name to 'That Feeling'. Featuring two singers up front (one wearing wellington boots!) they set trends and it was noticeable that other local groups appeared on the scene and attempted to emulate them. But most failed to capture the unique excitement that this group could create.

Another very polished and popular outfit by this time were Beverley group the Strollers. The Strollers were one of the first of the younger, new wave groups. They featured a great front man, a chirpy, tambourine-slapping singer known affectionately as 'Garth'. On stage, looking like Davy Jones of the Monkees he often sported a caftan and a very 'mod' looking cap (thrown into the audience at Burton Constable Hall one evening and lost). The group had excellent harmonies and led by a Farfisa organ, were especially good at Beach Boy, Who and Beatle numbers. So professional was the Strollers sound and so closely did they copy the original records that one evening while playing at a club in Scarborough, a member of the audience actually demanded his entrance money back, as he told the proprietor, 'He'd come to see a 'live' group, not one miming to records!'

Out at York, the Roll Movement claimed to be the town's first Mod group of the Swingin' Sixties'. Looking and sounding like a soulful 'Small Faces', singer Cliff Wade possessed a voice, which came across like a mixture of Wilson Pickett and Paul McCartney. The group soon developed a big fan following, especially amongst girls! So much so that coach loads of loyal fans made the trip to Brighton to support them when they won their way through to the finals of the 1966 Melody Maker Beat Contest Final.

In Scunthorpe, suave rock group the 'Dimples' had released the single 'Love Of A Lifetime' and had promoted the record on Television's 'Scene At Six Thirty', but despite being a very popular 'live' act their single failed to reach the charts.

Scarborough had also seen the birth of several new groups, one in particular were fast making an impression on the local scene. Fronted by a very young looking vocalist called Allen Palmer, the Mandrakes, were quickly gaining a reputation for being able to play Top Ten songs better than the original.

Most of the newer local groups (following the lead set by the Rolling Stones) were now moving away from the 'suited' image of their predecessors and were becoming much more casually dressed on stage. Many groups had also been influenced by US Soul shows and the antics of groups on Television's 'Ready Steady Go' and were attempting to do more on stage. Several started using Go Go dancers in their act. One local band, 'Disturbance' emulated top recording group the Move and began 'sledge-hammering' television sets to pieces on stage. Another, Market Weighton's 'Sons of Witch', began smashing their amps and guitars up at the end of their set in an attempt to copy the Who. This was much to the satisfaction of J P Cornell, Gough and Davy, Dean's Music, Kitchen's and other local musical equipment suppliers.

Around Hull and the East Riding we were also witnessing some of the last performances by some of the area's great first wave groups, including the Tycoons, the Tennesseans, the Magpies, Jonty and the Strangers, the Moonshots, the Blue Stars, Mark Antony and the Avengers, Del Dyman and the Tycoons, Wally and the Falcons, Tony Martin and the Mods, the Imps and the 'original' Rats.

A WHITER SHADE OF PALE

In the summer of 1966, every local teenager lucky enough to own a transistor radio set had it tuned to Radio 270, a pirate radio station transmitting from a ship anchored off the East Coast near Scarborough. That July, having just turned 15 and with the Kinks Number One smash hit 'Sunny Afternoon' blaring out over the airwaves, I left school. Within weeks I had got an office job and now earning the substantial sum of £4 a week, was over a period of a year, able to purchase a string of 'every-so-slightly' improving electric guitars. First, a Burns 'Nu Sonic', followed quickly by a 'Futurama', then a Watkins 'Rapier' and finally, a Hagstrom. This was thanks to local Music shop owner J. P. Cornell having a range of second-hand guitars available, which could be purchased on payment of £5 deposit and £1 per week. No credit references were required, providing he or assistant Johnny Paterson knew your face. Instead of paying the £5 deposit you could also trade in your old guitar, which I did. Around this time we also managed to purchase another Vox AC15 amplifier, two Reslo-ribbon microphones, a Linear Concorde amp for use as PA and to go with it built two 4 x 12 speaker columns. My brother had now turned 17 and having quickly passed his driving test was also able at last to buy a cheap second-hand 15 cwt van, first a Bedford and later a Thames.

Still experiencing difficulty in contacting an agent to get us gigs on the local circuit, but now having access to a typewriter, I began to write to Youth Clubs, dance halls and church halls, in an effort to get our own gigs. I was quite successful and we were soon playing reasonably regularly. We also changed our name to the 'Shapes' as we were now a 'psychedelic' outfit who featured a light show! The light show was actually four large empty paint tins, in the bottom of which holes had been pieced, electric light bulb holders fitted and coloured bulbs inserted. But 1967 was the age of Psychedelia and we were witnessing the advent of the 'Fuzz Box' and the 'Wah, Wah' pedal. There was a surrealistic feel to it all. Records like Procol Harum's 'A Whiter Shade of Pale', Pink Floyd's 'See Emily Play' and Cream's 'Tales of Brave Ulysses' together with the arrival of Jimi Hendrix on the scene had taken pop music into another dimension. Even the gawkiest of teenagers walked around with a copy of the Beatles 'Sgt Pepper' album under their arm.

Group names changed to match the new music. Locally we had the arrival of the 'Gospel Garden', 'That Feeling', the 'Scarlet Farmyard' and the 'Purple Haze'. Further down the coast Scarborough had their more subtle 'Purple Mist', 'New Religion' and the remarkably named 'Strawboa Fantasy'. No longer was the music just to be danced to, but to be listened to as well. Flowered shirts hit the new boutiques along with hipsters and everyone wore 'granny' specs.

Two more Hull based groups had signed recording contracts and released records. Roger Bloom's Hammer released the single 'Polly Pan' and the Small Four released the track 'One Up On Me'. Despite the 'Hammer' receiving airplay on both the BBC and several Pirate Radio stations, including reaching the Top Thirty on local station, Radio 270, elsewhere their record failed to chart. The same fate befell the Small Four's single.

London based 'Hull' group, the Majority, had released several more singles including the great track 'One Third' and songs written by both Ray Davies of the Kinks and various members of the Ivy League. But all of their releases had so far failed to chart.

In York the Roll Movement had signed to the Go label and released the single 'I'm Out On My Own', but this too failed to chart. The combination of York's Viceroys and Scarborough's Moonshots who had originally come together to form the Shots had now evolved into the 'Smoke'. With the release of their great single 'My Friend Jack Eats Sugar Lumps' they looked to be well on their way to becoming the first group from the area to reach the Top Thirty. Unfortunately, their rise up the charts stalled at Number 45 when the BBC banned the record from receiving further airplay because of the sudden realisation that the song was about taking LSD! Nevertheless, the record reached No.2 in the German Top Thirty and was a hit throughout Europe.

Former Scarborough 'Tennessean', John Hutchinson, returned to England from the pop scene in Sweden where he had enjoyed a hit record. While in London he quite by chance met a guy named David Bowie. Impressed by 'Hutch' and his Swedish style clothes Bowie invited him to join his group the 'Buzz' who were resident at London's Marquee Club. Hutch later recommended that former fellow Tennessean, Derek Boyes should also join Bowie and the group.

For several months Hull produced its own pop magazine featuring the groups of the area. Psychedelia was at its height and the magazine was given the title 'Groovy'. It was marketed as Yorkshire's 'In' magazine and had the advantage of using colour photographs. The various editions featured local groups in various psychedelic poses, wearing the latest gear which had often been 'borrowed' from the local boutiques. The first edition included articles on the Rats, Roger Blooms Hammer, Ways 'n' Means and ABC. The December 1967 edition (probably the last) featured a colour photo of the Mandrakes on its cover and saw them dressed in some pretty 'way-out' clothes. This edition also featured articles on Grimsby's Rumble Band and York's Roll Movement.

We entered the age of Psychedelia with enthusiasm, going to Jumble Sales to find suitably loud multi-coloured materials to make up into 'way out' flared trousers and waistcoats. Not earning sufficient to afford to buy a 'Wah Wah' pedal outright, the plans for building one were featured in 'Practical Wireless' magazine. Despite not knowing the slightest thing about electronics and the local electrical shops not possessing half the parts, we made various substitutions for the detailed resistors, transistors and capacitors and eventually soldered something together. Whether it would have worked or not is extremely doubtful. But we never got to find out, for in our eagerness to try it, as the first foot-pressed down on it in the hope of an expectant 'Wah', the unencased prototype was irreparably crushed into the carpet!

We also at this time sought 'inspiration', just like we had read Bob Dylan and Donovan had done before they had become successful songwriters, 'Hitting the road' with nothing but a guitar, a bedroll and a copy of Jack Kerouac's beat poems in their back pockets. Our slightly more diluted version was to take an acoustic guitar, a tent (with no groundsheet), a couple of blankets and a copy of the NME to the cliff tops at Fraisethorpe, just below Bridlington. In the depths of winter we intended to camp for two or three days in a foot or so of snow in the hope of enlightenment! Luckily, the plans never quite came to 'full' fruition!

Our gigs, too, had their moments. The one and only time I wore my bright red Zulu War British army military tunic at a gig we attracted most of the girls in the audience on to the stage. This was apparently much to the annoyance of the local youths. The result was that during the lead break of 'Hi Ho Silver Lining' I felt a sudden sharp agonising pain in my right hand and almost dropped the plectrum. Looking down I saw blood flowing freely from an open wound on my throbbing thumb as a large sharp lump of coal fell away from it. We had apparently made some of the local youths jealous. Gritting my teeth I played on, but having seen the huge pile of coal for the boiler-house on the way in, spent the rest of the evening singing and playing guitar in a crouching fashion, very much in the mode of Gerry 'Pacemaker' Marsden. Holding my guitar under my chin as a shield and wondering from which direction the next consignment of coal was likely to arrive!

At a gig at the Beverley Youth Centre, we supported local group 'Limited Company' who were particularly good at Beatle songs and had great harmonies. After the gig our van broke down and we had most members of the Youth Club pushing it through the streets of Beverley in the early hours of the morning shouting, 'Give It Bacon!' Later we discovered that our rear lights had disappeared, but I doubt if bacon would have worked anyway, as it was petrol that was required!

At yet another gig, on the Longhill Estate in Hull, we seemed to make one of the local youths unhappy and he too threatened to do us physical damage outside. By early 1968, impatient for fame, we decided that we weren't getting anywhere fast enough as the Shapes and further encouraged by these occasional threats of violence, decided that it might be better if we all tried to 'make it' in different bands who might have 'bigger members'! At the same time, to try and enjoy some of our youth, which had until then been totally given over to rehearsing, paying for equipment and trying to get the next gig.

THIS WHEEL'S ON FIRE

After the psychedlia of 1967 and the influx nationally of many new and exciting sounds, 1968 was perhaps an indecisive year musically as most of the more influential chart groups consolidated their positions and other newer outfits waited in the wings. There were one or two notable hits this year including Arthur Brown's 'Fire' and Simon Dupree's 'Kites' but generally, while the rock machine drove steadily onwards there were yet no further 'new sounds' in the air.

But things were changing, all of the Pirate Radio Stations including our own local station Radio 270, which had kept us up-to-date with all of the latest hit records had now been outlawed and had gone off the air. This was despite the best efforts of York group, the Roll Movement, who had taken part in a sit-down protest in Scarborough in an attempt to try to prevent the closure. The Police had broken this up and despite their best efforts pop music would now be provided by new national station Radio 1.

On Television, the legendary 'Ready, Steady, Go' had also gone from our screens and groups now queued up to perform on the newer 'Top Of The Pops'. Groups also began to appear on weekly TV shows such as Dee Time, the Lulu Show and the classic 'Twice A Fortnight'.

Locally, several groups underwent a metamorphosis. The Rats for a short while became 'Treacle' and had their management taken over by ex-Majority drummer Don Lill. Out at Beverley, two former members of the Penjants had joined the Strollers, including Mick Ronson contemporary Laurie Burnett and their repertoire had taken on some of the West Coast sounds of America. Meanwhile the remaining members of the Penjants had become the Scarlet Farmyard.

Out at Scarborough, the Strawboa Fantasy were evolving into 'Brave New World'. Meanwhile the Mandrakes had poached 12 string guitarist, Allan Black from Bridington group the Mutiny. They had then folded with vocals 'Snips' going off to form the Hull based 'Chest Fever'.

There had also been secret meetings held with some of the members of Hull's Rats and Scarborough's Mandrakes with talk of a Palmer/Ronson supergroup. Secret rehearsals had been held but the idea did not come to fruition.

Meanwhile, John Hutchinson had been invited to return to London to rejoin David Bowie in a outfit called Feathers which included Bowie's current girlfriend, Hermione Farthingale. When she left, Bowie and Hutch gigged as a duo and went into the recording studios to produce some demo tapes. During these sessions they recorded a track called 'Space Oddity' on which Hutch played the part of 'Ground Control' to David Bowie's 'Major Tom'.

In Grimsby, local blues band the Aztecs, had changed their name to Calmen Waters and were soon vying with the Rumble Band for billing as top group in town.

In York the Roll Movement had disbanded shortly after overturning their van in the winter snow and ice. This had led to vocals, Cliff Wade, going solo and releasing the single, 'You've Never Been To My House' on the Morgan Blue Town label. Cliff had also recorded sufficient material for an album, which unfortunately, would not be released until 30 years later. Meanwhile, original Roll Movement bass player, Pete Shaw, had joined local 'supergroup' Matchbox and later Roll Movement member, Steve Howden, had formed future recording band Red Dirt. Another York group, the Angel Pavement were also soon to release two very good singles, 'Baby You've Got To Stay' and 'Green Mellow Hill'.

Back in Hull, after releasing a further single, which had also failed to reach the Top Thirty, Roger Bloom's Hammer had evolved into the simpler 'Hammer' with Roger Bloom leaving the band and being replaced by former 'Peighton Checks' vocalist, John Parker.

Hull based folk/rock guitarist Michael Chapman, was spotted by the Who while supporting them at Hull University. So impressed were they by his performance that they tried to arrange for him to be signed to their label, Track Records. Although this didn't quite work out, shortly afterwards Michael joined EMI's Harvest label and began recording his first album, which he would give the title 'Rainmaker'.

Out at Scunthorpe, the Gospel Garden, after playing the top London club circuit, touring the country and releasing a single, had now evolved into the rock band Methuselah and having gained yet another recording contract, released an album.

Down in the Smoke Hull group the Majority, having spent three years releasing a string of eight singles, all of which had failed to chart and during which time they had rubbed shoulders with the likes of the Beatles, the Beach Boys and Jimi Hendrix, now featured as the backing group on the near chart topping classic Barry Ryan single 'Eloise'. Two of the original Hull members had now left the group and been replaced by Londoner's.

Locally, several groups went into Keith Herd's Willerby studios to record demo tapes. Most notably the Mandrakes who had came down from Scarborough complete with vocalist Allen (Robert) Palmer to record several of their own songs. These included the Palmer tracks, 'It's The Hardest Thing In The World' and 'Babysitting'!

The Rats alias 'Treacle' had also been in the recording studios. The session included the original track 'Bernie Gripplestone' with Keith Herd, like Beatles producer George Martin, playing tapes backward to add some psychedelic sounds. The end result was a song sounding very similar to Pink Floyd's recent hit single 'Arnold Layne'. The Rats had also recorded some more typical rock and blues material on which Mick Ronson applied his guitar playing prowess.

The rise of Jimi Hendrix, Jeff Beck and Eric Clapton had brought lead guitarists to the fore. At local gigs both audiences and rival group members eagerly watched the guitar styles of the likes of 'Ronno', Les Nichol, Mick Dytche, Steve Howden, Paul Sutton (The Prof), Ron Hales, Cliff Wade, Rich Hodgson and Laurie Burnett.

All night rock concerts held at Burton Constable Hall, East of Hull had begun to bring some of the top up and coming groups to the area. The concerts featured such 'progressive' groups as the Move, Family, Fairport Convention and Spooky Tooth to name but a few. Top local groups including the Mandrakes and the Strollers, also featured.

The Skyline Ballroom and the Brid Spa had continued bringing the latest hit groups to the area, including Simon Dupree and the Big Sound and Amen Corner. Several other Hull venues were also featuring top groups, including Cottingham Civic Hall who had attracted both the Soft Machine and Jethro Tull.

In Scarborough new club venue 'Scene One, Scene Two' was also booking chart groups, including the Small Faces, Manfred Mann and the Bonzo Dog Do Dah Band. The Candlelight Club had also seen a visit by Fleetwood Mac.

Out at York, the 'Beathive' on Dalton Terrace, the Cliffe Ballroom, the Folk Hall in New Earswick and the 'Mulberry Bush' in Malton together with the Assembly Rooms, the Enterprise Club and the La Bamba Club were now providing regular gigs not only for York groups, but for Hull, Scunthorpe, Grimsby and Scarborough groups as well.

SOMETHING IN THE AIR

By 1969, several of the top groups, including 'Cream', had split and many so called 'Supergroups' such as 'Blind Faith' were being formed. Once again there was another noticeable change in the music and a sense that 'something was in the air'. From America the Doors, the Band and 'Creedence Clearwater Revival' had imported some very influential sounds. In Britain the Beatles had returned to their rock roots with the release of their classic double 'White' album. The 'blues' were also enjoying an electric revival in the capable hands of groups like Fleetwood Mac. And a guy named David Bowie, who would shortly have strong connections with the City of Hull, released his eerie 'Space Oddity'.

We made our first ever visit to London that year, sleeping in the back of our old Thames van. It was a week after the Rolling Stones had held their free concert in Hyde Park in memory of recently departed guitarist, Brian Jones. We spent our sunny afternoons, lazing like sleepy bull toads on the grass in Hyde Park. We swam in the Serpentine and drank ice-cold coke in the park's glass-plated Bee Hive Restaurant. We hung out in the Piccadilly of the Swingin' Sixties', visited Carnaby Street and the Marquee Club in Wardour Street and travelled up and down every escalator on every Tube station in London. We visited all of the music shops we had previously only read about in adverts in the New Musical Express, including 'Orange' on Old Crompton Street and 'Sound City' on Shaftsbury Avenue. Somehow the visit captured the last vestiges of a post-war London and yet at the same time the height of the Swingin' Sixties'. But already the first dying rays of Sixties' sunlight were beginning to form into a sunset over Waterloo Station.

Back in Hull the local scene had been changing yet again and some of the stalwart top local groups of the Swingin' Sixties', including the Strollers, had finally called it a day. New sounds were in the air and a new culture too. Groups now had access to better equipment including improved Shure and Beyer microphones, Marshall amps and higher wattage PA systems. Many more local guitarists were now also using quality Fender and Gibson guitars.

Some of the most popular local groups now playing around the City of Hull were the Rats, Calmen Waters, the Mandrakes, Coastal Erosion, Variations, Red Dirt, Sweet Sugars and Chest Fever. While all of these bands were great, one of the best of them was Calmen Waters.

A blues band from Grimsby, Calmen Waters played their own original blues material and 'electric' interpretation of blues numbers by artists such as B B King, Albert King, Freddie King, Muddy Waters and Elmore James. Looking like four wild Hillbillies they had the longest hair of any band in the area and were brilliant to watch. While playing regularly in Hull, their 1969 performances included several trips down to London to appear at the legendary 'Marquee' Club.

Still retaining their blues roots, the Rats in 1969, had taken to including several 'Cream' numbers in their set, including 'Crossroads', 'Sunshine of Your Love' and 'White Room'. They also played John Mayall's 'Telephone Blues' and 'Mick's Boogie'. Songs with long lead breaks in the middle so that Mick Ronson, wearing a tie and dye Granddad shirt and knee length boots, his long blond hair parted down the middle, could 'show his stuff'. This was often punctuated by the superb harmonica playing of vocals, 'Benny' Marshall. Rats drummer, John Cambridge had now left the group and gone down to London to join recording outfit, 'Juniors Eyes'. Former Driffield Road Runner, Mick 'Woody' Woodmansey had replaced him.

Out at Scarborough, new club the 'Penthouse' had opened and it soon became another venue attracting top groups to the town. The cream of Scarborough's local groups also played there. These now included Brave New World, Dizzy Wheela, Lazy Poker and the Mandrakes. Scarborough's highly rated Mandrakes, had made almost weekly visits to Hull throughout the late Sixties'. I saw them play twice in 1969, once when they had taken on a female singer to replace Allen (Robert) Palmer and earlier, at a Free Festival held in Hull's East Park. That concert must have been one of the last occasions Palmer appeared with the band and they performed like stars. Wearing green leather high-heel boots, reputedly bought during their recent successful tour of Denmark, the Mandrakes played their way through their own versions of such songs as the Beatles 'Dear Prudence' and Traffic's 'Heaven Is In Your Mind'. But arguably the highlight of their set was when lead vocal, Palmer, gave a brilliant solo performance of Leonard Cohen's 'Suzanne'.

Chest Fever were also a band with presence. Fronted by enigmatic Bridlington vocalist 'Snips', their set included the Rolling Stones, 'Lets Spend The Night Together' which would have every member of the audience rocking. But the climax of their performance was an absolutely brilliant version of Bob Dylan's classic 'Like a Rolling Stone'.

The late Sixties' had seen the steady rise of Michael Chapman, whom I had met in 1967 when he lived down Arnold Street off Anlaby Road in Hull. Whilst originally coming from Leeds, he spent many years in the City and after signing his recording contract, produced such classic albums as 'Fully Qualified Survivor' and 'Window' which must have been strongly influenced by his Hull and East/North Riding surroundings.

Another popular performer returned to the local scene was folk/rock guitarist 'Hutch'. John Hutchinson's membership of various outfits fronted by David Bowie, including a residency with him at London's Marquee Club at the height of the Swingin' Sixties' and a more recent membership of a duo with him, had given Hutch a really professional sound. Playing acoustic guitar and often with bass support, he performed such tracks as the haunting Joni Mitchell song 'Michael from Mountains', the Beatles, 'Blackbird' and a brilliant track by American group 'Diijo' entitled 'Life Is A Circus'.

Scunthorpe duo, the Amazing Blondel, who had come out of rock group 'Methuselah', also frequented the City and had a large following. Looking like renegade members of 'Jethro Tull', they had great audience rapport and would go on to record several albums. Their first, 'The Amazing Blondel' sold particularly well in the area and included such great tracks as 'Bethel Town Mission', 'Shepherds Song' and 'Love Sonnet'.

One of the best local gigs I attended that year in Hull was at the Leo Schultz High School. It was organised by the Sixth Form and featured the 'Michael Chapman Band', Spreadeagle and the 'Amazing Blondel'. All three bands played brilliantly that night. I particularly remember John Parker, the vocalist of 'Spreadeagle' as he stood on the top of Michael Jackson's future co-writer, Rod Temperton's keyboard, looking like a Greek God as dressed in an 'off-white' bed sheet he belted out a rock version of a song from the musical 'Oliver'.

The Sixties' seemed to move towards its climax with one of the occasional all-night concerts, which had been held at Burton Constable Hall, East of Hull, throughout the late Sixties'. It featured such stars as 'Chicken Shack (including Christine Perfect later to join Fleetwood Mac), the Pretty Things and the Third Ear Band, as well as several top local groups. Thunderclap Newman were supposed to top the bill but failed to appear and were replaced by the 'Nice' who turned out to be brilliant. Playing tracks from their 'Ars Longa Vita Brevis' album, Keith Emerson didn't just use his hands to play his keyboards but stuck knives into them as well and spent half the set playing them backwards! Creating some fantastic sounds, yet, apparently coming off stage, like so many bands before and since, suffering from the delusion that they hadn't played well! Local groups featured that evening included the Rats, the Mandrakes, Calmen Waters and Hutch. There was no trouble as we sat from dusk till dawn listening to band after band. I remember that It was a strange feeling, lying on a hard stable floor half-asleep and hearing the blues played live at 5 o'clock in the morning. David Bowie later summed it up in his song title, 'Unwashed and Somewhat Slightly Dazed'!

But unquestionably the musical highlight locally of the late Sixties' were the free Rock concerts held in Hull's East and West parks. Behind the concerts were Barry Nettleton and Rick Welton who combined their names and together formed the Hull 'Brick' Company, the aim of which was to promote the live music scene in Hull. Rick Welton at this time managed the Hull Arts Centre while Barry Nettleton worked at Hull University as a photographer. Barry, in particular, enjoyed putting on promotions. One of his early ventures was to run the 'Freedom Folk', later 'Phase Two', both folk clubs being based at the Blue Bell Inn in Hull's Market Place. Featuring such people as Ralph McTell, Mike Cooper, Al Stewart and Michael Chapman the club attracted good audiences. Alongside the folk club Barry also ran various other promotions, hiring local venues and putting top local groups on.

The idea for the free concerts had come out of the Rolling Stone's 1969 free concert in London's Hyde Park. In attempting to stage these events the Hull Brick Company faced strong local resistance but when the concerts were eventually sanctioned the Hull City Council provided much help. While bringing bands such as Junior's Eyes, Edgar Broughton, Wishbone Ash, and Ian Dury's Kilburn and the Highroads to Hull, the concerts also enabled many local bands to get an airing.

While all of the free concerts were great, one of the very best of them featured 'Mighty Baby' who had just released their album 'House With No Windows'. London group 'Juniors Eyes' also played that gig and performed their single 'White Light'. During their set, drummer John Cambridge, apologised for the non-appearance of David Bowie at the concert. Bowie had been billed to appear, but that week had entered the charts with his first hit single, 'Space Oddity'.

Perhaps the most memorable free concert was that headlined by Wishbone Ash. That Sunday afternoon the group heralded the advent of twin-lead guitars as they played their way through many great tracks from their eponymous first album, including 'Blind Eye', Jailbait' and 'Lady Whiskey'. Several local bands appeared alongside them including Snake Eye, Chest Fever, the Amazing Blondel, Michael Chapman, the Rats, the Mandrakes and Brave New World.

KNOCKIN' ON HEAVEN'S DOOR

In 1970, the Brick Company further expanded the live music scene in Hull by opening the 'Brickhouse'. This was a converted Methodist Church situated down Baker Street and for a year it provided the City's only live music club. While featuring a new wave of rising stars such as Hawkwind, Sharks, Arthur Brown's Kingdom Come, Groundhogs, Captain Beefhart and Rory Gallagher, the emphasis was also very much on home-grown music. Local bands supported all of these visiting outfits and there was a local night as well at which they could show their stuff.

Alongside the 'Brickhouse', the Hull Brick Company also ran a national touring network, working notably with Wishbone Ash and Mott The Hoople. The Company would book major venues around the UK, such as City Halls, and offer a three-band bill. These would for example feature 'Wishbone Ash, ''Stackridge' and one of the Brick Company's own two managed bands 'Red Dirt' and 'Nothineverappens'. This gave both Red Dirt (later Snake Eye) and Nothineverappens a national profile with many London Agents seeing both bands and a lot of interest being created.

Among the Hull Brick Company's many other promotions that year included putting David Bowie's newly formed 'Hype' on at Hull University. The band featured Hull's John Cambridge on Drums and Mick Ronson on guitar. Former fellow Rat, Benny Marshall, also joined Bowie and the group up on stage, playing harmonica on the track 'Unwashed and Somewhat Slightly Dazed'. Apart from Hype's inaugural 'live' gig at London's Chalkfarm Roundhouse, it is believed to be one of the earliest occasions Mick Ronson had played live with Bowie and it was rumoured that he caught a bus to the concert from his home on the Greatfield Estate. Another person Mick Ronson had recorded with, Michael Chapman, played support.

Barry Nettleton and the Hull Brick Company, did nearly get their fingers burnt bringing top groups to the City. Their 1970 promotion of the Who live at the Hull City Hall nearly ended in disaster. A few weeks before the band were due to appear, their drummer, the late Keith Moon, accidentally ran over and killed his chauffeur and the Who immediately cancelled all of their scheduled gigs. Two thirds of the tickets for the Hull show had already been sold with much of the proceeds being spent on further advertising. Desperate, because of the money, which had been laid-out, and the money that would have to be paid back, Barry Nettleton wrote to Pete Townsend whose address he had been fortunate to be able to obtain off Michael Chapman. Townsend was made aware of the 'Brick Company's plight and obligingly wrote back saying that, "He would see what he could do!"

Several weeks later, Barry Nettleton received a further letter from Townsend advising him that the Who were going to give a concert in Leeds on a forthcoming Saturday. This was going to be recorded and the Who could probably come up to Hull the following day, on the Sunday, as it would be nice to have a 'back-up' tape.

The Who were paid £1000 to play the Hull City Hall. The concert was a sell-out and just like the Leeds gig was recorded. Because of better audience reaction it has been suggested that much of the Hull recording was used in preference to the Leeds concert, on the Who's 1970 album, 'Live at Leeds'.

While in 1970 there was an end of the decade 'bash' at the Hull City Hall, featuring Michael Chapman and friends, arguably, musically the Sixties' climaxed on the 28th, 29th and 30th August 1970. Not in Hull, but on the Isle of Wight, where together with over half-a-million other young people of our generation we sat through three days of music featuring the rock giants of the Sixties'. Never again would so many, or could so many huge rock stars be assembled together in the same place. These included Jimi Hendrix (who died three weeks later), the Doors (featuring Jim Morrison who died less than a year later), the Who, the Moody Blues, Jethro Tull, Joe Cocker, Leonard Cohen, Donovan, Ten Years After, Procol Harum, Taste, Emerson, Lake and Palmer, Country Joe and the Fish, Free, Family, Joni Mitchell, Tiny Tim, Joan Baez, John B Sebastian, and the Bonzo Dog Do Da Band.

It was a grand finale to the Sixties', a salute to a truly revolutionary decade in which rock music was reborn, developed and sophisticated. A decade in which the structure for an industry slowly began to be created. It was also a goodbye to the past and a final shaking-off of the post-war world.

Anyone who ever dreamt of being a rock star in the Sixties' would have been at that festival. We bought our tickets at the Paragon Music Stores in Hull, which as It happened proved to be a waste of money, because the day after we arrived, the event, like Woodstock before it, was turned into a free festival.

But it was worth every penny, three days of peace, love and music. Bob Dylan's 'haunting' song 'Lay, Lady, Lay' proved to be the anthem of the event with the record constantly being played in-between performances. Hippie flags flew on the wind and two-fingered fraternity greetings saluted us everywhere. Long hot summer days of music were followed by cool evenings as we warmed ourselves alongside huge rubbish burning campfires. As the flames flickered in the darkness, sat in the early hours of the morning listening to Jimi Hendrix or Leonard Cohen performing only a few hundred yards or so away was like being in some kind of rock 'n' roll heaven.

WHEN THE MUSIC'S OVER,
TURN ON THE LIGHT

When one walks the streets of Hull today it seems hard to believe that so many legendary bands once played here as it became customary for so long, to say that 'No one ever comes to Hull!' Yet, would anyone believe that the Pink Floyd played the Hull Art College Dance back in 1967 complete with a semi-sane Syd Barrett. Or that Eric Clapton and Cream played here in 1966 and that Jimi Hendrix's wailing guitar must have sounded out above the rooftops over Jameson Street one evening in 1967. Is it also credible that 'Travellin' Wilbury' Roy Orbison and a 'duck-walking' Chuck Berry played here in 1965, or such legendary bluesmen as John Lee Hooker, Muddy Waters, Champion Jack Dupree, Little Walter, Sonny Boy Williamson and Arthur 'Big Boy' Crudup. Not forgetting such lesser mortals as the Who, the Kinks, the Small Faces, Traffic, the Yardbirds, the Animals, or even the Beatles and the Stones.

Wherever one looks in the City and the towns and villages of Humberside and the North and East Ridings today, ghosts and echoes hang about those now often closed and silent buildings, like Hull's Skyline Ballroom, where rock groups once blasted out their sound. Sadly, some buildings, like the Beverley Regal, have been demolished and have now gone forever. No longer on that stage, will the ghosts of the groups of the past, stare out at the large glass panel in the centre of the dance floor with its underground lighting, or be dazzled by the great mirrored ball which once hung overhead. Some venues, however, such as for example the Hornsea Floral Hall, the Scarborough Spa and the Hull City Hall are still there, almost unchanged and inside amidst the shadows, it is easy to imagine that one can still hear the 'backbeat' of the beat groups of the past.

Pop music in the Sixties' appeared to offer so much, a possible way out, a potential lottery win with fame and girls thrown in. It provided the chance to be somebody when you had left school at 15 without ever dreaming of staying on for O' levels. For the first time ever there was the possibility of not having to work, like our parents had done, for so very little reward, from the cradle to the grave.

The problem was that everybody wanted to 'make it' in the Sixties' but nobody really knew how. Many of the local groups had a great sound and had become popular on the local scene, but were often stumped as to what to do next. After the success of the Beatles, the Record Companies had rushed to Liverpool to sign up 'Mersey Beat' groups, but it is doubtful if any ever came to Hull to listen to those influenced by the sound of the 'Humber'. So that with the lack of visiting A and R men, when impresario 'Hughie Green' came to the City and held auditions for his televised weekly talent show, then many local groups (but certainly not all!) rushed for an audition, because this at least looked like a way to the top. The fact that Hughie Green was an old guy from another generation who probably hated pop groups and pop music didn't seem to matter, his show 'appeared' to offer a route, albeit a traditional one, to the big time.

There was also an insular nature to many of the local groups. While certainly, there were exceptions, such as John Cambridge, John Hutchinson, Martin Bridges, the Rats, the Dimples, Gospel Garden, Barry Graham and the Mustangs, Cliff Wade, Mick Ronson, the Shots, the Roll Movement and the Tycoons, the majority of local groups wouldn't have dreamt of moving away to London where the pop scene was really happening. Yet, as I suggested earlier, to get an A and R man to visit Hull in those days, like now, but with the added burden of no M1, M62 or Humber Bridge would have taken a minor miracle and been like getting a visit from the Queen.

Many of the local groups also didn't seem to last very long. While once again there were exceptions such as for example the Strollers, the Rats, the Semi-Tones, the Winsors and the Mandrakes, many local groups had a very short life span, most only surviving a matter of months rather than years. There was an urgency to 'make it'. I remember my brother suggesting to me in our rock 'n' roll daydreams of 1967 that we might not 'make it' until the 1970s! It was light-years away and a depressing thought. If a group weren't getting anywhere within a relatively short period of time then they either packed it in, or there was a reshuffle of musicians and a change of name in the hope that this time it would come up with that winning formula. Many musicians also tended to remain within the same small clique.

Yet some local groups did get to sign those elusive recording contracts. In Hull these included the Aces, the Rats, the Mustangs, the Hullaballoos, the Small Four and Roger Blooms Hammer. But arguably, none of them could be put down to being spotted by an A and R man while playing in Hull. A few local outfits, including the Amazing Blondel and Michael Chapman did get noticed by top groups they were supporting, who actively passed on details of their talent to their respective record companies. But there were many other local groups, such as for example the Strollers, who sounded just as great and as polished as many of the London groups, yet still didn't seem to get spotted. Also, the Mandrakes, who supported literally dozens of chart topping groups and often had rock musicians the calibre of Jim Capaldi and Steve Winwood standing in the audience watching and applauding them. Yet even though rated and often billed as 'Yorkshire's Top Semi-Professional group', no one apparently stirred-up enough interest for them to sign a recording contract.

What, therefore, made a group successful? Was it just being a great singer, drummer or guitarist? Clearly the evidence suggests that it wasn't, as there were so many talented musicians who never 'made it'. No, in the end you didn't just require talent you definitely needed to be in the 'right place', at the 'right time'. Locally, the Hullaballoos provide a good example of this. They were seemingly in the right place one evening in 1964 when they played a gig at Sproatley Village Hall. In the hall that evening were their future management who would go on to turn them into 'American' recording stars.

The evidence also suggests that it was better to go looking for your luck instead of waiting for it to come to you. That dream we all had, of playing a storming gig and hoping that somebody important would be there in the audience to see it, Nope, for the majority of us they never showed!'

So we might ask, locally, just how many potential John Lennons, Paul McCartneys and Jimi Hendrixes have been missed? How many great songs, have not been written that might have been? And what about pondering a few, 'What ifs?'

For instance, what if John Cambridge hadn't met and joined David Bowie in 1969, would Mick Ronson ever have gone back down to London? Or would he have spent the rest of his career like so many of his contemporaries, playing guitar on the local pubs and WMC circuit? What if Robert Palmer hadn't joined the Allan Bown, would the Mandrakes have ever have been signed? What if Calmen Waters had toured with Jimmy Witherspoon in 1969, would they have gained the exposure necessary to gain that elusive recording contract? What if just one of the Majority's singles had made the Top Thirty, would they have then become regular visitors to the charts? And what if the Smoke's 'My friend Jack' hadn't been banned from receiving further airplay by the BBC, would it have gone even higher up the UK charts than its final position at No. 45?

The answers to all of these questions and more, we will never know.

Hindsight too is a wonderful thing. Now, over thirty years later, there are probably many things as a member of a rock group in the Swingin' Sixties' we wouldn't do again, or we'd do much quicker. 'If only we'd, 'Hmmm, ...?'

Unfortunately, a problem with the rock 'n' roll roundabout is just when do you get off? Many got off when they got married, their girlfriends told them to 'pack-it-in' or their parents insisted that they get a 'proper job'. For some, being a member of a band simply provided a brief teenage flirtation before settling down to something more 'serious'. But what about the rest, for whom rock music had permeated their soul. When should they pack-it-in? Was it if you hadn't made it by 20, or 25, or 30? Or when it all became too frustrating as you saw those of your age group buying houses and cars, because they'd been able to keep a steady job while you were still penniless, trying to pick yourself up after yet another band had split or after facing yet another false dawn. Or does rock 'n' roll turn into going around and around the club circuit?

And when you do pack-it-in, what do you do with your weekends when there's no more gigs to go to and no more mid-week rehearsals to attend? When Saturday comes and you miss the van turning up and the camaraderie and often craziness of band membership. Miss the endless out of town journeys, sitting on the equipment in the back of uncomfortable vans, with amps and drum cases shifting about this way and that and the possibility of decapitation by the PA columns each time the brake pedals were pressed. Miss relieving the boredom of the long out-of-town journeys by hurling insults out of the van window, especially at young couples when you had occasionally suggested (from the safety of your speeding van) that you had, had intimate relations with someone's girlfriend! Miss the seemingly endless flatulence of group members (often of a competitive nature!) and the constant clamour to wind-down van windows. Miss 'mooning' out of the van door at the passing of a rival group's vehicle and the camaraderie of meeting up at the old 'greasy spoon' transport cafes and petrol stations. Miss the Roadies who came in all shapes and sizes and with all sorts of personalities. Miss the backstage trashing of dressing rooms and the occasional ripping of sinks off walls (when you weren't weeing into them)! Miss swinging on stage curtains like Tarzan and the occasional fights to try to get a group member out on stage wearing only their underpants! Miss the friendships formed with other groups when you shared the same bill and miss trying to outplay them on stage. Miss the thrill of appearing with and meeting and talking to 'rock stars'. Miss the girls and the adulation when the girls actually chatted you up! Miss the endless carrying in and setting up of equipment and the attempts not to carry out your share of the gear at the end of the gig. Miss the journey home with the flatulence often worse and the occasional dropping of one's fish and chips on the van floor amidst the debris of cigarette ends and worse. Miss the vans that broke down and the desperate telephoning home to relatives and friends pleading for them to come out and rescue you.

As a young musician developing through the Swingin' Sixties' I learnt a lot, not least that I was pretty limited as a lead guitarist and like so many failed lead guitarists turned to the bass. What I didn't realise was that all of my experiences, both the music and the bands I had listened to helped me to become a reasonable songwriter, going on in the 1970s to gain an independent recording contract and record in both Manfred Mann's and the Kinks studio.

But by 1970 I was still only just 18. We had been too young, too poor and too naive in the Sixties' to make it as a group. For us, the gigs had initially been difficult to get because of our ages. We lacked money because we were either too young to work or when we did work earned barely sufficient to live on never mind being able to buy any decent gear with it. We were also too young to sign hire purchase contracts and nobody was willing to stand as Guarantor for us.

Whilst friendships were formed amongst the group fraternity and chords were certainly swapped backstage, there were also definite rivalries at that time. Many groups saw others as potential competition and no one seemed to want anyone else to get on. There were no videos then to show you how to develop as a lead guitarist and no one else was willing to show you in case you got one step ahead of them. I did however, hear from a couple of sources, that Mick Ronson did actively encourage some young guitar players.

When I re-emerged into the local group scene in the early 1970s the whole scene had changed and it was to go straight into the WMCs. For while there were now plenty of established agents in the area there were very few other places to play. The growing popularity of discotheques had taken away all of the regular local dance gigs including the Hull City Hall and Beverley Regal and all of Hull's small clubs had closed. Unfortunately, even the Top Ten often proved too progressive on many of the 'local' WMCs and so you had to be very careful with your selection of material.

The WMCs were also really the antithesis of what rock music was about, they demanded uniformity and discipline, playing songs someone else might want to hear rather than what you really wanted to play. You were also often performing in front of audiences whose average age was about 50 when you really wanted to play to the young. The songs you were playing therefore often became 'musak'. Personally, after performing once legendary 1950s rock numbers in some rock 'n' roll medley night after night, for years afterwards I couldn't listen to them on the radio without wincing!

I therefore consider that the WMCs, especially in that immediate post-Sixties' period, were responsible for wasting much potential youth talent. Because if you wanted to play 'live' locally in the early 1970s you had to either play the WMCs or play your guitar in your bedroom. Not that it was really the WMCs fault, after all you were entering their territory. It was simply that the rock venues of the Sixties' had disappeared and locally, apart from WMCs and 'Chicken-in-a-Basket' type venues, there were now very few other places to play.

Today the contemporary group scene in Hull seems to be so much better as there are various venues where you can play your own original material and there are now pubs whose audiences appreciate 'rock'. (This is of course in some part due to the fact that the 'Children of the Revolution' have now all grown up!) There is also a great recording studio where several generations of budding rock stars have beaten a path to its door and many others have now sprung up. Rehearsal rooms too, complete with PA systems are also available. A lot has been learnt since those early days.

There were certainly brief flirtations with the 'big time' by various local groups in the 1960s and hearts were sent beating faster every couple of years or so as some group from the area looked as though it had at long last 'made it'. First, the Aces, followed by the Hullaballoos, the Rats, the Majority, the Incas, the Shots, the Small Four, the Dimples, Roger Blooms Hammer, the Roll Movement, Gospel Garden, Methuselah, Angel Pavement and the Rumble, they all had their brief moments of glory. Then came the turn of Hull's own 'guitar hero', Mick Ronson. As a member of the 'Spiders From Mars' he played the role of Sancho Pansa to David Bowie's, Don Quixote. In doing so he arguably provided the catalyst which launched Bowie as a rock superstar.

In a three year period, Mick Ronson played classic 'rock' guitar on and arranged some of Bowie's finest albums including the immortal 'Ziggy Stardust'. When in 1972 while performing live on Tops of the Pops, David Bowie put his arm around Mick Ronson's shoulder and invited him, to join in on the chorus of 'Starman' it really did look as though at long, long last a group from this City had 'made it' and Hull would finally become established on the 'rock map'.

But somehow it never happened and following the death of 'Ziggy', while Mick Ronson certainly became a 'minor' rock legend with his name and career details to be found in any encyclopaedia of rock, arguably, nationally, we had to wait for well over another decade for the arrival of the 'Housemartins' to prove, at long, long last, and beyond any shadow of a doubt that you can come out of Hull and as well as playing great music can write brilliant, thoughtful lyrics.

In those early days, to learn to play guitar, you had Hank B. Marvin as your role model, or worse, Bert Weedon. It wasn't really until a band such as the Yardbirds came along that you began to realise that there was much more to playing guitar than what Hank or Bert were dishing out. But bands like the Yardbirds had been influenced by bluesmen such as John Lee Hooker, Elmore James, BB King, Muddy Waters and Robert Johnson. They therefore had a head start. We didn't get the blues down Hessle Road ... well at least not the blackman's version!

THE SOUND OF THE CITY

They came in all shapes and sizes. Some could have 'made it' while other others only lasted a matter of weeks. Some still resembled their fathers. They played the game in smart suits, shirts and ties, turned their amps down and attempted to appease another generation's audience. Others were progressive, they grew their hair long and told them that 'The Times They Were A-Changin'.

Some might have become legends while others made hardly a ripple. Now, over 30 years later, as the echoes finally die away it's too late to matter. But the one thing they all had in common was that for a period of their young lives they either sang, strummed a guitar, or banged a set of drums in the hope of becoming rock or pop stars.

Some are still playing today. In the pubs and clubs of the City and beyond, ageing, often balding, faceless musicians who might perhaps have once been only a step away from fame and fortune are still banging those same drums and twanging those same guitars. The only difference is that now for 98 per cent of them the fever to 'make it', like their hair has gone.

But for all of them, when on moonlit nights, they hear tracks like Procol Harum's 'A Whiter Shade of Pale' or the Animals 'House of The Rising Sun' being played on their car radio, the hair rises on the back of their necks and shivers run up and down their spines. As though hearing a clarion call, they are momentarily whisked back in time to their youth and remember longingly that they were part of that revolutionary decade. A decade in which anything seemed possible and the 'Summer of Love' might just have lasted forever.

I went to see one of them recently, a white haired guy wearing a hat. Was this really the same person whose albums I had played endlessly 30 years ago, believed every lyric and still do. But when he sang and played the guitar I knew that it was him. The voice hadn't changed and both the guitar playing and the songs were as great as ever. No, there was no doubt about his identity. Had we all grown old, I wondered, or was it just him?

In the end I suppose the question needs to be asked, 'Just how many local groups did really make it back then?' Ok, well if not the groups then individual band members? Well I guess it all depends on what you mean by 'making it' and as some cynic once said, 'Did anyone really 'make it' anyway?' No, in the end it might simply be a case of, 'How far did you get?'

Only you can answer that, and while for some there were certainly, heartaches, false dawns and disappointments along the way. There was also fun and laughter and excitement and we were all ... oh, so 'nearly famous'.

'LEST WE FORGET'

THE GROUPS OF HULL
AND THE EAST RIDING,
SCARBOROUGH, YORK, SCUNTHORPE
AND GRIMSBY

1960 - 1970

ABC	1966 - 1967	HULL

Drums	John Cambridge (Attack) replaced by Keith Stutt (Birds Groove)
Bass	Steve Powell (Attack)
Lead	John Rowe (Gonx)
Lead	Les Nichol
Vocals	John Hebblewaite

Potted History: 'ABC'

ABC were formed out of the Attack. Their name was suggested to them by Steve Marriott of the Small Faces backstage at Hull's Skyline Ballroom.   A very popular group, their influences included the Beatles, Cream, Jeff Beck and Jimi Hendrix. The group had a great image and two of its members sported Hendrix style hair-do's.   In 1967 ABC had the privilege of supporting the 'Pink Floyd' at the Hull Art College Dance. Other local gigs they played included the Hull City Hall, the Beverley Regal and the La Bamba Club in York. The group also recorded at Keith Herd's Fairview Studios in Willerby. The songs included Gladys Knight and the Pips 'Stop And Get A Hold Of Myself' and their own original track 'LSD'. But by the end of 1967 the band had split with John Cambridge joining the Rats and Les Nichol going off to form the William Cotton Blues Band, later joining Scunthorpe based recording group 'Gospel Garden'.

ACES	1959 – 1963	HULL

Drums   Brian Sleight

Bass   Johnny Paterson

Rhythm   Henry Temple

Lead   Tony Gosling replaced by Trevor
                                          Woodward, Steve Trice

Vocals   Johnny Hawk, Antonio Montana

Other Members: Rob Coggle (Washboard), Rick Kemp

Potted History: 'THE ACES'

The Aces were formed in 1959 when Tony Gosling got together with Johnny Paterson, Henry Temple, Brian Sleight and Rob Coggle after he had wandered into Hull's Hopewell Road Youth Club. The group originally played 'skiffle' and featured Rob on Washboard; but they gradually began playing rock 'n' roll music. By the time Tony Gosling left the group to go to College in 1961, they had developed into Johnny Hawk and the Aces. This version of the group also at one time featured future Steeleye Span bass player Rick Kemp. Johnny Hawk and the Aces were the first Hull group to use a Watkins 'Copy Cat' Echo and Johnny Paterson was also the first person in Hull to own a Fender 'Precision' bass guitar. The group eventually evolved into the Four Aces.

The Aces (Hull - 1959/1963)

Johnny Hawk and the Aces (Hull - 1961)

The Aces (Hull - 1963)

ACES	1963 -1964	HULL

Drums   Adrian Gatie replaced by
Doug Thurlow (Rangers)

Bass   Johnny Paterson replaced by
Michael Howard

Lead   Brian Gatie replaced by
Norman Crumpton

Vocals   Eric Lee

Potted History: 'THE ACES'

The Aces had developed out of 'Johnny Hawk and the Aces', changing their name to 'Eric Lee and the Four Aces' and then on gaining a recording contract to simply the 'Aces' to avoid confusion with American singing group the 'Four Aces'. The 1963 line-up of the Aces recorded three singles for Parlophone. Their first, 'Wait Till Tomorrow' I remember listening to on Hull's own phone-in Teledisc Service, by dialling Hull 211411. The B-sides of all the Aces releases were written for them by their guitarist, Brian Gatie.

The Aces were resident for a period between 1962/3 at Hull's Majestic Ballroom in Witham, which was part of the Top Rank circuit. Their contract involved them performing at other Top Rank venues and while with Top Rank they supported the Beatles. Very busy gigging both in and out of town the Aces had several entrepreneurial ideas. These included hiring Ellougton Village Hall and putting a dance on each week with their popularity ensuring that they performed to a full house. When they had other gigs, or as their support, they would book other local groups to play at the hall including the Mods, the

90

Mustangs, the Cossacks, the King Bees and the Mariners who around this time featured Mick Ronson. The Aces also organised 'Riverboat Rock' cruises, holding dances and playing live on the Hull to New Holland Ferry.

Between 1962/64 the Aces were Hull's top group and in 1963 when they supported the Rolling Stones at the Hull City Hall (who had just released their first record, 'Come On') the loyal audience kept chanting, 'We want the Aces!' But when the Stones appeared they soon won the crowd over and demonstrated that they were going to be big stars.

Unfortunately, non of the Aces singles reached the charts and they had the ignominious experience of their first single being voted a certain 'miss' on Television pop show 'Juke Box Jury'. However, this was no big deal as the type of people making up the panels of JBJ often seemed to know little about pop music and often voted many hit records, including Long John Baldry's No.1 million seller 'Let the Heartaches Begin', a certain miss!

Discography:

Singles:

'Wait Till Tomorrow' c/w 'The Last One'
    1963   Parlophone   R5094
'I Count The Tears' c/w 'But Say It Isn't So'
    1964   Parlophone   R5108
'I Apologise' c/w 'It Don't Matter No More'
    1964   (Unreleased)

AGENTS	1964 -1965	DRIFFIELD

Drums   George Cundill

Bass   Barry Sharpless replaced by
                     Peter Robinson

Rhythm/Vocals   Eddie Butler replaced byPaul Nolan

Lead   Alan Wilmott

Potted History: THE FABULOUS 006 AND THE AGENTS'

The full name of this group was the 'Fabulous 006 and the Agents' but promoters often shortened it because of the expense in advertising expenditure! The Agents played Top Ten hits and ballads especially numbers by the Drifters. Local gigs included Driffield's Buck Inn and Keys Hotel. Out of town they played at the Seabirds pub in Bridlington and the George Hotel in Scarborough. The Agents also often appeared at the Driffield Town Hall alongside other local groups and had gigs in most of the villages in the East Riding. George Cundill acted as the group's manager and remembers gig fees ranging between £8 and £10. He also recalls the time the Agents played the Kon Tiki Club down Whitefriargate in Hull. The group had just taken on a replacement bass player. Unfortunately, he was so much in love that he couldn't bear the thought of being parted from his girlfriend in the audience. To overcome this problem he made himself an extra-long guitar lead. That evening while the rest of the Agents and his amplifier performed up on stage, he sat playing his bass guitar in the audience with his girlfriend right beside him! When Eddie Butler left the area the Agents soon afterwards disbanded. George Cundill and bass player Barry Sharpless, helped to form the 'Exodus', while lead guitarist Alan Wilmott joined local group the 'Young Ones'.

ALPHA-BEATS 1964 - 1966 **HULL**

Drums John Spenceley

Bass Colin Bell

Rhythm John (Zak) Mackay, Steve Moore

Lead Paul Shallcross, Alan Wright

Vocals Dave Topham

Potted History: 'THE ALPHA-BEATS'

The Alpha-Beats drove around in an old Bedford van that they bought for Seven Pounds, Ten Shillings. John used a cheap set of Beverley drums which he bought from Cornell's. The Alpha-Beats played local youth clubs, Swanland Village Hall and the tiny Toc H Club in Anlaby. John Spenceley and Dave Topham went on to form the Sweet Sugar Soul Set while Zak went on to form Disturbance.

007 and the Agents (Driffield - 1965)

The Alphabeats (Hull - 1965)

94

The Amazing Blondel (Scunthorpe - 1970)

ALPHABETICAL ALARM CLOCK	circa 1969	SCUNTHORPE
Drums	Roger Parot	
Bass	Mick Brown	
Rhythm	Paul Duffin	
Lead	Richard Pryztupa	
Vocals	Jock McKay	
Potted History:	'THE ALPHABETICAL ALARM CLOCK'	

The Alphabetical Alarm Clock were perhaps the most unusually named group to come out of Scunthorpe during the Swingin' Sixties'. Local gigs included playing the Alpine Room which was based at the Open Heath Hotel. Scunthorpe had a thriving group scene at this time, which included the Peighton Checks, the Pitiful Souls, the Classics, the Worrying Kind and 'Methusulah'.

AMAZING BLONDEL 1969 - 1976   SCUNTHORPE

John Gladwin   Lead Vocals, Second Lute, theorboe, cittern, double bass, second guitar, tabor, tubular bells

Terry Wincott   Crumhorn, recorders, pipe-organ, vocals, tabor pipe, tabor flute, piano, harmonium, lute, harpsichord, mellotron, bongos, percussion

Eddie Baird (1970)   First Lute, cittern, vocals, glockenspiel, dulcimer, first guitar, 12 string guitar, percussion

Potted History: 'THE AMAZING BLONDEL'

The Amazing Blondel were formed by two former members of the 'Dimples', 'Gospel Garden' and 'Methuselah', all of which had been recording bands. The Amazing Blondel were original, two (later three) talented multi-instrumentalists who featured numerous woodwind instruments, a harmonium, crum horn, lutes and various other medieval instruments in their act. They appeared like wandering minstrels at the time of King Richard The Lionheart. John Gladwin quotes his formative influence for the future outfit as Elton Hayes who played a very 'lute' like sounding acoustic guitar in the background of the 1950s Television series 'Robin Hood' which starred Richard Greene. While the Amazing Blondel were inspired by Elizabethan composers such as William Byrd and John Dowland they wrote their own material, and there was a 20th Century folksy feel to everything they played. Their music was therefore more of a romantic notion of how mediaeval music might have sounded. Nevertheless, to help them to achieve their 'authentic' sound, AB had some of their instruments especially made for them by Master Craftsman, David Rubio.

97

John Gladwin (The Amazing Blondel)

The idea for forming a duo came about when as members of heavy rock band Methuselah John and Terry noticed their audiences getting a bit wild during their set. To cool things down a little they began to perform a duet. With John on guitar and Terry on Bongos they would play a piece called 'The Lincoln Tales'. They soon began to find that this went down better than the rest of the set. So John began writing some new songs and Terry taught himself to play a variety of woodwind instruments, they then left 'Methuselah' and began playing folk type gigs. One evening, at a gig in Middlesborough, Eugene McCoy, a presenter on the Television programme 'Masterchef', was heard to exclaim, "Very Blondel!", after Richard the Lionheart's wandering minstrel - and the 'Amazing Blondel' were born. Using their previous recording company connections the duo released an album, 'The Amazing Blondel'. This sold particularly well in the area and mint copies are now worth several hundred pounds! The original idea had always been to turn the duo into a group and by 1970 they had added a third member, Edward Baird.

As a teenager Eddie had been a member of Scunthorpe outfits such as the 'Black Hawks', 'Johnny and the Boys' and the 'Kingpins' - all of these groups had virtually the same members - unless they occasionally found anybody else who could play, or who had better equipment! Latterly, Eddie had been in a guitar duo with partner, John Darbyshire and they had been writing and occasionally performing songs together. It was largely through this partnership that Eddie had come to the attention of John Gladwin and Terry Wincott.

The Amazing Blondel fitted well into the 'Hippie' summers of 1969/70, looking like renegade members of Jethro Tull as they performed at the various free concerts of that period, such as those held in Hull's East Park.

It was after a gig in Hull in 1970 supporting the rock band 'Free', that Blondel were recommended by them to Island Records. Free had been so impressed by their performance that on their return to London they raved about Blondel to the Head of Island Records, Chris Blackwell. Blackwell eventually contacted the group and invited them down to his office in London, where they performed for him with gusto. Liking what he heard, Blackwell signed Blondel and bought them a new PA system and van. They then began recording and many top musicians played on their albums including Paul Rodgers and Paul Kossoff of Free, Steve Winwood and Jim Capaldi of Traffic. Their albums were also produced by some well-known producers including two of them by ex Yardbird bass player, Paul Samwell-Smith.

The Amazing Blondel toured with many top bands including Free, Fairport Convention, Traffic, Procol Harum, Genesis and Cat Stevens. They also headlined various tours themselves. However, in 1973, after extensively touring Europe, including Sweden, Denmark, Norway and Finland, plus a three-week tour of the USA, John Gladwin left the group to pursue a solo career. He recorded an album, which sadly, due to an oil crisis, was never released. The remaining members of the group produced a further three LPs and spent several more years on the road.

The Amazing Blondel were indeed amazing and John Gladwin was an exceptional songwriter. He wrote so many beautiful, soft, lilting ballads and folk songs. Just a few of my favourites include 'Bethel Town Mission', 'Canaan', 'Willow Wood', Celestial Light' and 'Love Sonnet'. Unlike most of their contemporaries, who had followed the lead of contemporary American folk music, Blondel had gone much further back in time, producing unique, traditional English sounding folk music and presenting it in a fun and interesting way. One writer gave the Amazing Blondel's sound the brilliant label 'Psychedelic Folk'. But Blondel were not only just known for

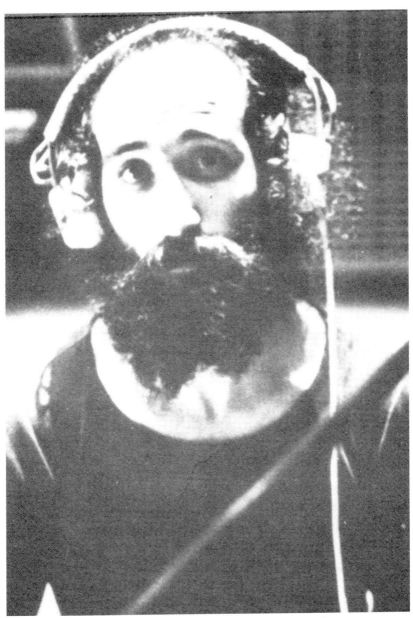

Terry Wincott (The Amazing Blondel)

their great songs, harmonies and musicianship but also for their on-stage banter and risquè 'musician' jokes, a humour probably developed during their many years on-the-road as members of top rock bands.

After an absence of almost 20 years, in 1995 the Amazing Blondel reformed and currently have 8 CD's available. Five of these are their original albums plus a compilation album 'Englishe Musicke' and a live album made up of recordings from their various tours of Europe during 1972/73. This album 'A Foreign Field That Is Forever England' goes a long way towards capturing the spirit of an AB concert. The group has also released a new album, 'Restoration' and are gigging again both home and abroad, including concerts in London, Norway and Italy.

I do not exaggerate when I say that to be able to once again sit through an Amazing Blondel concert and listen to the brilliant vocal harmonies and superb instrument playing on songs such as 'Celestial Light' is to be able to capture a piece of heaven on planet earth. I would also add, that very few bands can split and come back together over 20 years later and produce an album at least as good as, if not better, than some they produced in their youth. The Amazing Blondel certainly managed this with their album 'Restoration' and super tracks such as 'Benedictus Es Domine', 'Sir John Is In Love Again' and 'Highwayman'.

The Amazing Blondel have never been short of fans and in the early 1970s one budding superstar liked the Amazing Blondel so much, that he ran away with them (after hiding amongst their equipment after a concert). The guy's name was Dave Stewart, later to become a partner in the classic supergroup the 'Eurythmics'. Stewart did try auditioning for Blondel by playing then an unsolicited version of 'Streets of London' on a battered acoustic guitar, but after this failed to impress, he had to settle for being a Roadie, and quite rightly so!

Discography:

Albums:

'Amazing Blondel	1970	Bell Records	SBLL131
'Evensong'	1970	Island Records	ILPS9136
'Fantasia Lindum'	1971	Island Records	ILPS9156
'England'	1972	Island Records	ILPS9205
'Blondel'	1973	Island Records	ILPS9257
'Mulgrave Street'	1974	DJM	JLPS443
'Inspiration'	1975	DJM	DJLPS446
'Bad Dreams'	1976	DJM	DJLPS472
'Live in Tokyo'	1977	DJM	DJF20203
'Englishe Musicke'	1993	Edsel	EDCD 365
'The Amazing Blondel'	1995	Edsel	EDCD 421
'Evensong'	1996	Pinnacle	EDCD 458
'A Foreign Field That is Forever England'	1996	HTD Records	HTDCD56
'Fantasia Lindum'	1996	Edsel	EDCD459
'Blondel' (The Purple Album)	1996	Edsel	EDCD460
'England'	1997	Edsel	EDCD501
'Restoration'	1997	HTD Records	HTDCD70

Singles:

'Bethel Town Mission'	c/w	'You Don't Want My Love' 1970 Bell	
'Alleluia'	c/w	'Safety In God Alone' 1972 Island	
'Mulgrave Street'	c/w	'Sad To See You Go' 1974 DJM	
'Be So Happy'	c/w	'Queen' 1975 DJM	
'I'll Go The Way I Came'	c/w	'Liberty Belle' 1976 DJM	

Eddie Baird (The Amazing Blondel)

ANGEL PAVEMENT 1969 - 1971   YORK

Drums   Mike Candler (Roll Movement)

Bass   Graham Harris

Rhythm   Dave Smith

Lead   Alfie Shepherd

Vocals   Paul Smith (R G Simpson Band)

Potted History: 'ANGEL PAVEMENT'

A professional group, who while popular in this area, performed nationally. Local gigs included the Skyline Ballroom. Angel Pavement became so popular that they signed a recording contract and released two great singles, 'Baby You've Gotta Stay' and 'Tell Me What I've Got To Do'. Despite being very catchy numbers and similar to records that became hits at the time, they failed to chart. However, in 1970 the Angel Pavement were spotted while playing a London Club by a rich Mexican hotel owner. So impressed was he by the group that he arranged for them to play in Mexico and fixed up recording sessions for them over there. Before leaving Britain, Angel Pavement appeared live on the Yorkshire Television programme 'Calendar'. The group's first single was re-released during the 1990s on the compilation album 'The Best of and the Rest of Psychedelic.'

Discography:
'Baby You've Gotta Stay' c/w 'Green Mellow Hill' 1969 Fontana TF1059
'Tell Me What I've Got To Do' c/w 'When Will I See June ' 1970 Fontana TF1072
The Best of and the Rest of British Psychedelia 1991 Action Replay,MCAR1024

ANSERMET SWING	circa 1966	YORK

Drums	Steve Jackson
Bass	Glyn davis
Lead	Philip Reed
Vocals	Pete Humphreys
Potted History:	'ANSERMET SWING'

One of the strangest named of the York groups, local gigs included the Boulevard Nightclub. Steve Jackson would go on to join recording group 'Red Dirt'.

APPLE SPICE BAND	1969 - 1970	HULL

Drums	Graham Keenan
Bass	John Parker
Lead	Geoff Purschion
Vocals	Phil Wingfield replaced by Leslie Skinner
Potted History:	'APPLE SPICE BAND'

Originally known as 'Spice', to save mix-ups with a similarly named Hull group they later changed their name to the 'Apple Spice Band'. The ASB could often be seen performing at the free open air rock concerts held during the late Sixties' in Hull's parks. The ASB supported several top groups including 'Black Sabbath', 'Free' and 'Blodwyn Pig'. Most of the band members would go on to form 'Revelations' and 'Shiva'.

ASTRONAUTS   circa 1963   **HULL**

Drums

Guitar/Vocals   Ron Mitchell

Guitar   Robert

Potted History: 'THE ASTRONAUTS'

The Astronauts were one of many local groups to be named
after man's first tentative steps into space. Ron Mitchell had
first got into rock 'n' roll music after borrowing an early
'Crickets' album, called 'The Chirping Crickets'. He was
knocked out by it as he was a big fan of Buddy Holly. Ron also
knew that he wanted to be in a rock 'n' roll band when he saw
the adulation local singer/guitarist Dave Tenny got when he
made regular appearances at Hull's Sidmouth Street Youth
Club. The Astronauts played mainly local church halls and
youth clubs. When their guitarist, Rob, auditioned for local
group Ricky Knight and the Crusaders Ron was there as well
and he was also signed up. Ron went on to become the new
'Ricky Knight' and the group would eventually evolve into EMI
recording artists, the 'Hullaballoos'.

ATMOSPHERE   **1969 - 1970**   **HULL**

Drums   Phil Oaten

Bass   Pete Allen

Rhythm   Tony Stevenson

Lead   Pete Allison

Organ   Steven Petty

Vocals   Dave Wright replaced by   Ed Barley

Potted History: 'ATMOSPHERE'

Playing Top Ten music, this group were a 6th Form band who were originally known as 'Social Atmosphere'. I saw one of their first gigs, which was at the Haworth Arms in Hull. Some of the band members had brothers as their mentors who had been on the local group scene for quite a while.

ATTACK	**1965 - 1966**	**HULL**

Drums   John Cambridge

Bass   Steve Powell

Lead   Mike Tyson

Vocals   John Hebblewaite

Potted History: 'THE ATTACK'

Formed out of the Gonx,   the 'Attack' was a very 'Mod' sounding name. Unfortunately, there was already a recording group called the 'Attack' by this time. Nevertheless, local gigs included the Beverley Regal. The group didn't last long as the 'Attack' before evolving into the 'ABC'.

AVENGERS	circa 1963	PICKERING/ HELMSLEY
Drums	Dave Cook	
Bass	Jim Boyes	
Guitar	Tony Haystead	
Guitar	Ken Cook	
Vocals	Dave Mann	
Potted History:	'THE AVENGERS'	

The Avengers were one of the earliest East Coast beat groups. For their early gigs they had to borrow their equipment. The Avengers was a popular name for a beat group at this time due to the Television series which featured an immaculate 'leather clad' Emma Peel!

AVENGERS	1962 - 1967	BRIDLINGTON
Drums	Nigel Ward replaced by Dave Colman	
Bass	Mike Wood replaced by Dave Hammerton (Unit IV)	
Rhythm	Roy Dodgson	
Lead	Dave Cook replaced by Mike Wood Pete Romyn	
Keyboards	Nigel Ward	
Vocals	Mike Ward	
Potted History:	'MARK ANTONY AND THE AVENGERS'	

Mark Antony and the Avengers were a group with a big East Riding following. They had a bearded singer who looked like the archetype beatnik. The Avengers began life in the early Sixties' when Mike Ward, inspired by the Shadows and the Ventures got together with Mike Wood, Roy Dodgson and Dave Cook to form a similar instrumental group. Mike Ward was originally a drummer but with the arrival of the Beatles and the 'Big Beat' the Avengers decided to feature vocals. After each member of the band had, had a go at singing, Mike Ward was 'volunteered' as their vocalist and brother Nigel replaced him on the drums.

The first gig featuring the new line-up was at the 'Emmanuel Youth Club' in Bridlington. Mike Ward was so nervous that he decided to go on stage wearing a hood over his head and was hoping to remain anonymous. Unfortunately, unbeknown to Mark, in the true group spirit, the rest of the band had already told everybody in the audience just who this mystery 'hooded singer' was. So much for anonymity! But the Avengers had a good night and Mark soon got over his stage fright. The group then did lots of work in youth clubs, young farmers clubs, dances and barbecues and by 1964 were pretty well established as the top local outfit.

The Avengers supported many star groups, particularly at the Brid Spa. These included the Rolling Stones (twice), the Swinging Blue Jeans, the Kinks, the Hollies, Peter and Gordon, plus many others. Mike recalls that playing to three to four thousand young people at the Spa was a fantastic experience.

Because of their popularity the Avengers also headlined at the Brid Spa themselves. Every couple of months or so, complete with support act they would play to about 1,500 young people! 'It was really quite amazing, but the group scene then was new and exciting.'

Probably the group's all time low was just after this period when guitarist Roy Dodgson was killed in a car crash - Mike remembers that they played a gig a few days after this and it was very difficult for them to carry on. The Avengers decided not to replace Roy as such and Nigel Ward taught himself keyboards (in about three months!) he then played a Hammond organ to replace the rhythm and Dave Colman joined on the drums. About the same time Dave Cook left the group due to work pressures and Mike Wood took over on lead guitar, being replaced on the bass by Dave Hammerton. Before too long Mike Wood also left due to work pressures and he was replaced on the lead by Pete Romyn. Around this time the Avengers began to change their musical direction, due both to Nigel's influence and the great sound of the Hammond organ. The group began featuring several 'Animal' numbers in their set. They also got more into soul music especially numbers by Lee Dorsey, Wilson Pickett, Otis Redding and Sam and Dave.

Gigs continued to pour in, including every month playing at the American Army base at Menwith Hill. They also had regular gigs at Leeds University where their new sound went down particularly well.

Mike feels that for a little while they got a little bit ahead of the local music scene as the type of new music they were now playing had yet to hit Bridlington!

One of the high spots of the Avengers career was playing at the Cavern Club in Liverpool. Cavern Club DJ and promoter 'Bob Wooler' had spotted them while they were playing at Liverpool's 'Peppermint lounge'. Wooler telephoned Mark Ward to arrange the Cavern Club gig, for which they were paid £10. This hardly seemed worth the trip but they had a friend at college in Liverpool on whose floor they were able to spend the night. Playing the Cavern was a really exciting experience, the group were actually performing on the same stage where the Beatles had first been seen by Brian Epstein. Mark remembers that the place was 'heaving' and that they had a great night.

The Avengers also recorded a four track demo tape at the Malconi Studios on Hessle Road in Hull and produced a demo disc down in London's Denmark Street. But the group eventually disbanded in 1967 when Mark got involved in his restaurant career and didn't have time for the band anymore. Today Mark, 'minus the hood' is back singing again.

Mark Antony and The Avengers (Live at The Cavern)

Mark Antony and The Avengers (Bridlington - 1964)

AXE   **1969 - 1970**   **EAST RIDING**

Drums   Ken Markham

Bass   Bruce Kirton

Organ   Mike Freeman

Lead   Dave Smith

Vocals   Roger Bloom (Hammer)

Potted History: 'ROGER BLOOM'S AXE'

This was Roger Bloom's re-emergence on the scene after his lay-off after leaving he 'Hammer'. He had taken over from his brother Harvey Brookes on vocals and changed the name of the 'Harvey Brookes Skuttle' to Roger Bloom's 'Axe'. After being busy professionally, including gigs at the Top Ten Club in Hamburg (where the Beatles had perfected their art) and a tour of Denmark, the band folded in January 1970. Ken Markham went on to drum for recording star Dave Berry.

AZTECS	1967 - 1968	GRIMSBY

Drums   Barry Milner

Bass   Tony Houseman

Rhythm   Brian 'Bip' Clifford

Lead   Noel Skelton

Vocals   Andy Johnson

Potted History: 'THE AZTECS'

The Aztecs were a very busy Grimsby band who tended towards the blues. They played Youth Clubs and Dance Halls in Grimsby, Lincoln and Scunthorpe. They also had regular gigs in York at such venues as the Assembly Rooms. Most of the members would go on to turn pro and develop into one of the finest bands in the area, 'Calmen Waters'.

BARE SOLE	1969 - 1970	HULL

Drums   Ron Newlove

Bass   Brian Harrison

Rhythm   Dave George

Lead   Richard Foster

Potted History: 'BARE SOLE'

A local businessman invested in Bare Sole in the belief that they had the potential to 'make it'. Busy in Hull their out of town gigs included the Enterprise Club, York. Bare Sole supported several top groups at the Brid Spa including the Small Faces (who by this time were fronted by Rod Stewart') and Roger Chapman's 'Family'. They also recorded a demo tape at Keith Herd's Willerby Studio, which their Manager took to Decca Records but unfortunately it was unsuccessful.

BATMEN	1960 - 1964	HULL
Drums	Dave Bradfield	
Bass	Brian Hairsine	
Rhythm	Ray Marshall	
Lead	Ray Elleringham	
Potted History:	'THE BATMEN'	

Originally called Vince Ford's Batmen, the Batmen dressed completely in black like the superhero, including bat masks and bat capes. To match their style of dress the band produced their own on stage special effects, creating a 'Bat out of Hell' backdrop, long before 'Meat Loaf'. Prior to every out-of-town gig the group would buy 'dry-ice' from BP Chemicals in Hull and use it on stage to create a mist. They would also sprinkle the stage with blue 'Omo' washing powder and shine an infrared light on it to create an eerie effect. A very popular group, busy both in and out of town, local gigs included the Mayfair Cinema on Beverley Road and La Caverne Club in Bridlington.

After taking on new drummer Dave Bradfield, the Batmen turned professional and were booked for a tour of the American Army bases in France. Unfortunately, after crossing the channel the group crashed their van. Having to stop to make repairs they eventually arrived at the first army base in the early hours of the morning. Too late to play the gig, they made enquiries of a US army officer who sat playing cards with his buddies, as to what they should do. He advised them in just two words! Distraught and weary after all the travelling the Batmen made a frantic phone call to their Manager Pete Bocking, in Hull. He

The Batmen (Hull -1964)

Ray Charles and The Beat Boys (York - 1961)

contacted Cleethorpes agent Martin Yale, who had set the tour up. Yale managed to sort things out and arranged for the Batmen to spend the rest of their French trip at another US army base in Verdum. However, their troubles weren't yet over as they had been promised £20 a week each, to be paid to them by a local continental agent. Unfortunately, the agent displayed all the characteristics of being a Nazi in hiding and being true to his image only ever paid the group their first week's wages. They therefore had to spend the rest of the month existing on this, which meant a very restricted diet. The only occasional decent meal they had was in the US Army base Mess. The rest of the time they were hungry. However, they were fortunate in that on mentioning their plight in passing to an American army sergeant, he arranged for them to be given several large boxes of dehydrated field rations. That evening, returning from the base to the hotel annexe in the village where they were staying, they eagerly unloaded the numerous boxes of rations from the van. Too tired to start cooking they went to bed to dream about the feast they were going to have in the morning. Unfortunately, no sooner had they fallen asleep than the door of their hotel room burst open and they were arrested by the local French Police and taken to the village Police Station. The Gendarmes had apparently had been tipped off by the locals (who were probably still suffering from the effects of Nazi occupation) that the group had been seen unloading several large suspicious looking boxes from their van! The Batmen explained that they had quite legitimately been given the food by the US Army base, but despite being released, they never saw their rations again and spent the rest of the month hungry!

On their return to the UK, the Batmen's professional career continued not to run smoothly. They were booked to undertake a winter tour of Scotland. Unfortunately, on the journey the group's van heater stopped working and they had to drive through thick snow to each of their tour dates in a freezing cold van. They played at Cooper-Angus and Ockingleck and because of the popularity of Mersey Beat, at every gig were on strict instructions from agent, Martin Yale, to pretend to be from Liverpool. They managed this by introducing each of their numbers with a nasal accent and included plenty of 'whacks' and 'yeah, yeah, bloody yeah's'.

The Aeriels (Hull - 1965)

BEAT BOYS	1959 –1963	YORK
Drums	Tony Broadhead	
Bass	Rodney	
Lead	Geoff Wilson	
Vocals	Ray Charles Broadhead	
Potted History:	'RAY CHARLES AND THE BEAT BOYS'	

Ray Charles and the Beat Boys were one of York's earliest groups. They played rock 'n' roll music around such then York pubs as the Burns Hotel, the White Horse (Coppergate), the 'Castle', the 'Big Coach' (Nessgate) and the Lonsboro Arms (Petergate). Singer, Ray Broadhead was a half cousin of the late comedy star Dustin Gee and he remembers an early gig where a young Dustin jumped up on stage and shared the vocals. Dustin was apparently so thrilled by the experience that he went on to form his own group, Gerry B and the Rockafellas, which would ultimately lead on to him becoming a top comedy star.

BEAT CULT circa 1965 SCARBOROUGH

Drums Dave Ayre (Kerbsiders)

Bass Dave Pinkney

Rhythm Tom Ward (Kerbsiders)

Lead Pete Liley (Moonshots)

Vocals Chris Wade (Sonics)

Potted History: 'BEAT CULT'

'Beat Cult' were formed out of the various comings and goings of Scarborough group, the 'Sonics', whose members included Brian Sharpe. The only original member of the Sonics in the above line-up is Chris Wade. The Sonics had originally changed their name to 'Downtown Cult' before eventually settling on 'Beat Cult'. Beat Cult played R & B and had a regular gig at Scarborough's YMCA.

BIG CHANGE   **1967 - 1968**   **SCARBOROUGH**

Drums   Dave Hann (Genghis Khan)

Bass   Bob Fox (Trolls)

Lead   Dave Brown   replaced by Paul Leggett

Keyboards   Stan Dolphin replaced by John Prendergast

Vocals   Mick Bowen (Trolls)

Potted History: 'BIG CHANGE'

By 1967 there were clear signs that the post-war world was being left behind and a New World was being entered into. Big Change were brought together via local agent Peter Pitts. They made their debut at the Brid Spa, playing Tamla Motown and Soul music. In their time Big Change supported such star groups as the Bee Gees (on their first tour of the UK) and Wayne Fontana. They had regular work in Redcar, Hull and York. Dave Brown had been playing guitar since he was about 12 and left the defunct Pickering group 'Genghis Khan' to help to form Big Change. The group eventually evolved into pro-band 'Brave New World'.

BIRDS GROOVE   **1966 - 1967**   **HULL**

Drums   Keith Stutt (Gemini's)

Bass   Brian Buttle (Gemini's)

Lead   Peter Green (Mods)

Keyboards/
Vocals   Steve Powell (ABC)

Potted History: 'BIRDS GROOVE'

'Birds Groove' were formed out of the break-up of the Gemini's. The group chose their 'way-out' name (which suited the times) from a general liking amongst the band for Charlie 'Yardbird' Parker (known as the 'Bird') and his music. Birds Groove played Jazz, Soul, R & B and particularly material by Jimmy Smith. Typical gigs included the Barracuda Club down Lowgate, Hull and the local FE College. Birds Groove supported several top groups including the Pretty Things and the Hull appearance of Eric Clapton, Jack Bruce and Ginger Baker, collectively known as 'Cream'.

BLIND LEMMON   circa 1969   **GRIMSBY**

Drums   Roger Wentworth

Bass   Simon Richard

Lead   John Chessman

Vocals   Mike Argumont

Harmonica   Ian Fee

Slide Guitar   Brian Ledgard

Potted History   'BLIND LEMMON'

A blues band formed by Grimsby College students who were influenced by legendary blues/rock band 'Cream'. Blind Lemmon wrote some of their own original material including a 15-minute long number with the brilliant title 'Blowing All Our Fuses'. Grimsby had several regular venues in the 1960s, which often featured Hull groups. These included the South Bank Jazz Club, which was played by the Cock-a-Hoops, Roger Blooms Hammer and the 'Mods', also, the 77 Club which was played by the Mods and the Honeys. Not far away, Cleethorpes also had its regular venue, 'The Village', which later became the Purple Onion Club, and was played by local groups the 'Rats', the 'Mandrakes' and Roger Blooms Hammer.

BLUEBERRIES **1963 - 1965** **HULL**

Drums   Robin Welton replaced by Dave Morris
                   (Buccaneers)

Bass   Michael Howard

Rhythm   Norman Crumpton

Lead   Tony Gosling

Potted History: 'THE BLUEBERRIES'

A very popular group on the local scene, I saw the Blueberries when they appeared at one of the Beat Nights held in Hull's West Park during the summer of 1964. The group got their name from the type of music they played, the 'blues' and 'Chuck Berry' songs, hence 'Blueberries'. Tony Gosling would occasionally feature on harmonica. The group got many of its gigs through 'showcases' and by 'word of mouth'. They often played out-of-town at such gigs as Filey's 'Brig Cinema' where they supported Ricky Vallence. Chuck Berry had, had a big influence on many of the early beat groups, most included his songs in their repertoire and some, including the Blueberries' incorporated his name in theirs e.g. Blueberries, Rockin' Berries and Dave Berry. When the group disbanded Tony Gosling and Dave Morris went on to form the 'Small Four'.

BLUE CIRCLE   circa 1967   **HORNSEA**

Drums   Stewart Wrangham

Bass   Tony Underwood

Lead   Terry Bateman

Potted History: 'BLUE CIRCLE'

Blue Circle played Top Ten hits including 'Hi Ho Silver Lining'. They rehearsed at the Victoria Hotel in Hornsea. Stewart Wrangham went on to drum for the Huddersfield based Jimmy Parker Soul Supply and Sheffield's 'Travellers Express'. I would hesitate a guess that rather than being named after a local cement company, this band were big fans of Scarborough group the 'Blue Stars' who in the mid 1960s played in Hornsea every month at the Floral Hall. 'Blue Circle' probably cribbed their name from theirs.

BLUE STARS　　　　**1962 - 1964**　　　　**SCARBOROUGH**

Drums　　　　　　　Ken Thomas

Bass　　　　　　　　Andrew Boyes replaced by
　　　　　　　　　　Graham Trowsdale

Rhythm　　　　　　　Bob Woodyatt

Lead　　　　　　　　Brian Thompson

Vocals　　　　　　　Rich Routledge replaced by Chris Bagnall

Potted History:　　　'THE BLUE STARS'

The Blue Stars were yet another popular Scarborough group. On forming they had brought the house down at an amateur beat contest held at Scarborough's Gaiety Cinema and had become an instant success in town. Managed by Ron Gillet, in November 1963 Rich Routledge took over their leadership and changed the group's name to 'Rikki and the Blue Stars'. The Blue Stars were one of the top Scarborough groups of 1963. Regular local gigs included the Olympia and St Saviours Church Hall. They also appeared at Hull's Kon Tiki Club. Despite being successful, Rich left the band in 1964 and Chris Bagnall replaced him as vocalist. The band later changed their name to the 'Incas'.

BONE   circa 1970   **GILBERDYKE**

Drums   Tony Carter

Bass   Fred Norton (Lucifer)

Rhythm   John Brien

Lead   Geoff Parsons

Vocals   Robert Eyson replaced by   Paul Mooney

Potted History: 'BONE'

Bone were a semi-pro progressive rock band who had plenty of gigs both in the area and out of town. They were perhaps not always the group you would want as your support band as they seemed prone to unfortunate incidents. For example, while supporting local outfit the Variations they used 'dry-ice' to create a smoke effect, unbeknown to them, the damp crept into the Variations organ and when they appeared on stage, and switched on, their organ blew-up! At a gig in London, Bone supported the Carol Grimes band and rather than carry in all of their own equipment gained permission to use the pro band's gear. Unfortunately, while playing the last number of their set, Tony Carter broke the Grimes band's, bass-drum pedal. Too embarrassed to own-up to it, as soon as they finished their set the group quickly made an exit! Some of Bone's members, including Tony Carter and Geoff Parsons, would go on to form mid-Seventies' new wave outfit 'Dead Fingers Talk'.   DFT recorded two singles and an album, 'Storm The Reality Studios' which was produced by Hull's Mick Ronson.

The Blue Stars (Scarborough 1964)

134

Brave New World (Scarborough - 1969)

BRAVE NEW WORLD	1968 - 1975	SCARBOROUGH

Drums/Vocals   Dave Hann replaced by Pete Jackson (1970)

Bass/Vocals   John More replaced by Paul Tindale (1969)
Phil Hegarty (1972)

Guitar/Violin   Dave Brown (Big Change)

Guitar   Pete Hudson (Strawboa Fantasy)

Vocals   Mick Bowen replaced by
John Labrum (1969)
Pete Rennison (1969)
Mick Bowen (1970)
Rob Winspear (1971)
Mick Bowen (1972)
Barry Palmer (1973)
Nige Gross (1973)

Potted History: 'BRAVE NEW WORLD'

Dave Brown formed this band during the summer of 1968. Most of the members were by now well-experienced musicians on the local scene. The group were given the name 'Brave New World' by their keyboard player Stan dolphin, who left the group before they played their first gig. This was at St. Mary's Parish House in Scarborough in September 1968. That night they were supported by the Minority Soul Sound from Loftus who featured Pete Jackson on the drums and he would also later join Brave New World. At one of their early gigs Brave New World accidentally set fire to Pickering Memorial Hall with one of their smoke bombs! The group initially played covers including Tamla and Soul music and such tracks as 'Rock Me Baby', 'Reconsider Baby' and a version of former Scarboro' 'Moon-Shots/Smoke' 'My Friend Jack Eats Sugar Lumps.' But the group were soon to become know for their own brand of self-penned rock material featuring twin-lead guitar and the electric violin of Dave Brown.

Brave New World were the winners of the Paris Beat Contest, with Philips Recording and Radio Francais airings - against the top groups of France. They were awarded the Diploma du Golf Drouot - Le Plus Celebre Club des Jeunes in Paris, before a jury composed of personalities of the Press, TV, Radio, Show business and Vedettes du disque. The band turned professional and undertook a nation-wide tour supporting rock band 'Warhorse' and they generally stole the show. During the early 1970s BNW went on to tour Europe and played many one off gigs supporting top bands and receiving excellent reviews in the music press. One particularly memorable occasion was playing support to 'Hawkwind' in front of 22,000 people in Harlow Central Park. Brave New World tried hard but never succeeded in signing that elusive recording contract. They eventually played their farewell gig at Scarborough's Penthouse on New Year's Eve 1974 playing their final note in the early hours of 1st January 1975. Sadly, vocals Mick Bowen died in 1996. An afternote is that BNW came back together for a Millennium gig held at the Scarborough Spa on the 1st January 2000. Their music sounded as fresh as ever, indeed, they showed that they could still earn a very good living on the rock circuit.

BUCCANEERS   1962 - 1963   **HULL**

Drums   Dave Morris

Bass   John Tomlinson

Lead

Potted History: 'DAVY JONES AND THE BUCCANEERS'

The Buccaneers were one of Hull's earliest beat groups and several of its members would perform throughout the Sixties. There was a children's Television programme on around this time with the title 'The Gay Buccaneers!' But I think this group's great name was probably a crib on 'Johnny Kidd and the Pirates', one of the few genuine British Rock bands to make an impression in the very early Sixties'.

Tony and The Cadillacs (Scunthorpe - 1964)

138

CADILLACS	1958 – 1970	SCUNTHORPE

Drums   Frank Coult replaced by Mick Cowling, Stuart Smith,

Bass/Vocals   Mal Evans replaced by Keith Harrison

Guitar/Vocals   Tony Borrill

Lead   Barry Garner replaced by Alan Harsley, Greg Tomlinson

Piano   Martin Danks

Other Members included: Jack Pearson (drums)

Potted History: 'TONY AND THE CADILLACS'

The Cadillacs were one of Scunthorpe's earliest beat groups and members Greg Tomlinson and Stuart Smith would go on to join Scunthorpe based recording group the 'Dimples'. Martin Danks became a member of Scunthorpe's 'Blues Syndicate' and Alan Harsley joined the 'Southlanders'.

Tony Borrill's original group was the 'Sun Spots' whose members also included John Hill, Dave Edwards and Keith Harrison. They were the first group to play at Scunthorpe's Sherpa Hotel and Queen Bess.

CALMEN WATERS 1968 - 1970   GRIMSBY

Drums   Barry (The Dog) Milner (The Aztecs)

Bass/vocals   Tony Houseman (The Aztecs)

Second Guitar   Brian Clifford (The Aztecs)

Lead   Noel Skelton   (The Aztecs) replaced by
                      Mick Dytche

Vocals   Andy Johnson (The Aztecs)

Potted History: 'CALMEN WATERS'

Calmen Waters were one of the finest bands ever to come out of this area. They played excellent 'electric' interpretations of blues numbers and wrote their own original blues material. Particularly impressive was their own 'Blues For Caroline' and 'Story of the Band', also Muddy Waters 'Going Down to Louisiana', Champion Jack Dupree's 'Hurry Down Sunshine,' Elmore James 'Dust My Broom' and 'Look-up On Yonder Wall'. If I'd had to put my money on just one local band to make it in the late Sixties', this would have been the one. Exciting to watch, brilliant guitar work, including bottleneck guitar, wild looking and sporting the longest hair in the district they were fantastic. Calmen Waters had evolved out of Grimsby group the 'Aztecs'. Soon after changing their name Noel Skelton left the group to turn pro with an outfit touring the American Army bases in Germany (on his return he would join the Rumble). Calmen Waters themselves then turned pro and Andy Johnson left the band. The four piece soon became one of the top groups in the area and had a huge fan following. In June 1969 they appeared at the legendary Marquee Club in London and went down extremely well, receiving several encores. They were then booked to play a 17 day tour of the UK supporting bluesman Jimmy Witherspoon. The tour was to open at the Marquee Club and that same evening the band were also to make an appearance at London's 'Bag-o-Nails' Club alongside the legendary Bo Diddley. Unfortunately, at the last moment the tour was postponed. But it was then arranged for them to appear at London's 100 Club. The gig was to be attended by the Head of Blue Horizon Records, Mike Vernon, who was apparently keen to sign them to his label. Despite this, big time success appears to have ultimately eluded them. However, in the early 1980s Mick Dytche did turn-up playing guitar on several albums by Steeleye Span's, Maddy Prior and Rick Kemp including 'Hooked On Winning' (1982) and 'Going For Glory' (1983).

I remember one of Calmen Waters' gigs in particular. It was at St. Judes Church Hall on Spring Bank in Hull. While waiting for the gig to start I was cajoled into buying six raffle tickets. Not normally a lucky person, I was surprised when the first number was called out later, that it was mine and was pleased when one of my heroes in the band came down from the stage and presented me with the first prize. But then I won the second prize, then the third and then the fourth. By which time as the guy out of the band kept coming backwards and forwards from the stage it was all becoming extremely embarrassing and the crowd was growing restless with one particular 'shirtless' individual beginning to glower at me quite menacingly. So when one of my remaining raffle ticket numbers was called out for winning the fifth prize, with the 'shirtless' individual's glowering eyes on me, I daren't own up to it. Thankfully, the sixth and final prize was won by him, a box of chocolates, which while holding the box in one huge hand and fending his friends off with the other (so he didn't have to share them!) he ripped the lid of the box with his teeth and after upending it, devoured the contents at one go, wrappers an' all! Well at least that's how I remember it!

Calmen Waters (Grimsby - 1969)

Calmen Waters (Grimsby - 1969)

CAROL'S KNIGHTS	circa 1965	HULL

Drums	Dave Johnson
Bass	Frank Murphy
Lead	Alan Morris
Vocals	Carol Peak
Potted History:	'CAROL'S KNIGHTS'

Carol's Knights played excellent cover versions of the latest pop hits. Their local gigs included the Beverley Regal. The guys went on to form the '5 Objeks'. The Knights were one of several local groups fronted by a girl singer, the others included Mandy and the Moonrakers (Hull), Sylvia and the Escorts (York), the Semi-Tones (Beverley), Twiggy's People (Hull), Purple Haze (Hull), the Ousebeats (York), the Variations (Hull) Maureen and the Freeways (Scunthorpe) and for a short while even Scarborough's 'Mandrakes'.

C-BEATS   1964 - 1966   **WITHERNSEA**

Drums   Rob Taylor (Relations)

Bass   Joe Speck replaced by Mike Wright
               (Scorpions)

Rhythm   Mally Todd

Lead/   Jay Dene
Vocals

Potted History: 'THE C-BEATS'

The C-Beats looked like real 'Beat merchants', they wore very 'Cavern' looking 'V'-necked black leather sleeveless jerkins. Local gigs included Hull's Barracuda Club down Lowgate. The group were very popular and won a Beat Contest held at Hull's Skyline Ballroom. They were then selected to take part in a National Beat Contest with the final being held in London. The C-Beats supported several top groups at the Brid Spa including the Moody Blues, the Kinks and Lulu. A later member of the band was Geoff Parrott. By 1967, the C-Beats had evolved into the 'Elite'.

The C-Beats (Withernsea - 1964)

CHALLENGERS   *circa 1963*   **YORK**

Drums   Steve 'Sticks' Bennett

Bass   Ian McClaren

Lead   Geoff Oakland

Vocals   Danny Adams

Potted History: 'DANNY ADAMS AND THE
                   CHALLENGERS'

The Challengers were one of the first York Beat groups to gain a recording contract. They released the single 'Bye, Bye, Baby' on the Philips label. The group had a management contract with the London based Noel Gay Agency. Local gigs included York's New Tramways Club in Mill Street. The group also appeared on television.

Michael Chapman

CHAPMAN MICHAEL

circa 1967

HULL

Potted History: 'MICHAEL CHAPMAN'

I first met folk/rock/blues/jazz guitarist, Michael Chapman in 1967 shortly after his arrival in Hull. At the time he was living in a dingy house divided up into bedsits, down Arnold Street off Anlaby Road. My brother and I had gone to the house to see someone else and didn't know that Michael lived there. The person we went to see lived on the first floor of the house in the room opposite his. What I remember most vividly is the sea of empty brown beer bottles that surrounded Michael's doorway, seemingly dozens of them crowding out on to the landing. While we stood waiting, his door opened a little and a hand stretched out, holding yet another empty bottle, which was quickly added to the pile. After this, when visiting the house, we met Michael (wearing his trademark denim shirt) on several occasions and he would sometimes bring his acoustic guitar down to the communal living room and sit and play us and the rest of the tenants some of his songs. He also once gave us some good 'genuine' advice.

Michael Chapman was born in Leeds on 21 January 1941. From an early age guitars fascinated him and he would often walk into the centre of Leeds just to stare at one in a shop window. He began playing the guitar in his early teens and was self-taught. In the early days he recalls that there wasn't really anyone to listen to but his later influences included Django Rheinhardt, Jimmy Giuffre, James Burton, Scotty Moore and Jimmy Rogers. He was also influenced by several other black bluesmen.

But it was Jazz that was Michael's first major influence. He first became exposed to it when he went to Art College. The main influence on him was a guy called Ed O'Donnell who was a trombone player with Ken Collier and who actually made a record. At the time Michael thought that records came from a parallel universe. "We had no idea that people like us made them, like I had no idea who wrote songs at that point - they just kind of appeared on the landscape. Ed was very much into the New Orleans, Kid Ory thing and he had a great band with an almost modern rhythm section of bass and drums. I used to borrow his rhythm section and go out as a modern jazz trio. But Ed was a major influence because I'd go back to his house and he'd play me Jimmy Rodgers and Leadbelly records, which was astonishing because this whole new world of music suddenly opened up to me."

Michael had to pay for his Art school education with his guitar. He would play with jazz bands, country and western bands - any kind of band there was. "I didn't care, I was playing four to five nights a week with anybody including dance bands."

After completing his Fine Art course Michael studied for a post-graduate qualification and then went into teaching. He secured the position of Lecturer of Photography at Bolton Art College and during his time there even found time to manage the College band.

Michael arrived in Hull from Bolton quite by chance. It was in September 1966, when he came to the city to visit his girlfriend, Andru Makin, and he never went back. He was to spend 5 years in the city. On his arrival, instead of teaching, Michael decided to become a professional musician and began playing the folk circuit. Even then he had not seen himself as a folk singer, he was a 'guitarist', but in those days the folk clubs were the only place where you could play an acoustic guitar. Nevertheless, he was soon making regular appearances at the Freedom Folk Club, later 'Phase Two', both clubs being based at Hull's Blue

Michael Chapman

Bell Inn and run by Barry Nettleton. He also toured the country and in 1967 spent the first of many summers performing in the folk clubs and pubs of Cornwall.

This had come about when he had walked into a folk club called the 'Courthouse' at Botallach. It was raining, he had no money to pay to go in and just enough petrol for the return journey home the next morning. 'I just wanted to get out of the rain and so I said to them that I didn't have enough money to get in but I'd play the guitar for half an hour. At the end of the night the guy asked me what I was doing for the rest of the summer, because they needed a another resident musician.' At the end of the week Michael got a share of what was taken at the door. 'I got more money than what I was being paid for running a department in an FE college! So I thought, I like this - lie on the beach all day, play a bit of guitar for an hour a night and get paid. I love it! Everybody then would go down to Cornwall for the summer, They'd be me and people like Ralph McTell and other folk musicians down there for the entire summer.'

Michael's early style of acoustic guitar playing had shown strong influences of bluesmen such as 'Big Bill Broonzy', but his playing soon went beyond this as he began to develop a distinctive folk-rock style all of his own. This development was perhaps helped by, back in Hull, occasionally sitting in with local 'electric' musicians with this loose arrangement of 'jam sessions' given the title, 'Michael Chapman's Electric Army of Friends'.

In 1968, while supporting the Who at Hull University they were so impressed by his performance that singer Roger Daltrey asked him if he would like to record an album for their label, Track Records. While this didn't work out, he was shortly afterwards signed to EMI's newly forming Harvest label. This had come about when someone acting as a talent scout for Essex

Music had walked into one of Michael's Cornwall shows and he had talked him into recording a 'guitar' album. "I wasn't writing songs, but I'd play anything on the guitar." Just before he was supposed to record the album Michael suddenly started writing and was able to turn the whole thing around. He convinced the record company that his first album, 'Rainmaker', should contain his new songs.

'Rainmaker', showed much promise and included such great tracks as 'Mozart Lives Upstairs' and the atmospheric title track 'Rainmaker'. Around this time Michael also made some of his first radio appearances, being interviewed on Radio 3 by Alexis Korner and playing a couple of songs which included 'No One Left To Care' and 'Been Down So Long'.

But it was with Michael's second album, 'Fully Qualified Survivor', that he really showed his true potential, containing so many great tracks, including the brilliant 'Electric Ladies and Ragtime', 'Rabbit Hills' and 'March Rain'. The album was to be his only UK chart entry - peaking at number 45, in March 1970. Hull's Mick Ronson and Rick Kemp both played on the album and it was Rock Broadcaster, John Peel's, album of the year. Michael made numerous TV and Radio appearances to promote the album, including guesting on the John Peel Show.

"By the second album I had more ideas about what I wanted and the songs were better because I could see a direction that I wanted to be going in. I started using different tunings too. This came about because of Ralph McTell. One soggy afternoon outside the 'Folk Cottage' in Cornwall - I think we were going to do some duets that night - he dropped his E string down to a D and, coming up through jazz, it was a thing that I hadn't seen. Ralph showed me dropped D tuning and I though, Aaah! All of a sudden things began to make sense and I took it from there."

Michael Chapman

In 1970, following the release of 'Fully Qualified Survivor', Michael Chapman became a band. Supported by Rick Kemp on bass and Richie Dharma on drums, this formidable threesome after just one week of rehearsals appeared on the Peter Cook and Dudley Moore TV Show, one week later playing as support to the legendary Ginger Baker's Airforce in front of an audience of 2000. That same year, the trio also played an absolutely brilliant show at Hull's Leo Shulz High school.

The eagerly awaited follow-up album, 'Window' was also excellent, containing such great tracks as 'Among These Trees' and 'In The Valley'. But later, when Richie Dharma joined the recording band 'Arrival', Michael and Rick Kemp went off and toured the USA as a duo. On his return Rick was recruited into 'Steeleye Span'.

Throughout the Seventies' and Eighties' Michael continued to tour, both as a solo artist and by putting various prestigious bands together. He played both the UK, and Europe where he was particularly popular and recorded his live album, 'Pleasures of The Street' in Germany. He also appeared twice on BBC television's legendary rock programme, 'The 'Old Grey Whistle Test' and performed in concert on the BBC radio programme 'Sight and Sound'. One of these performances, was with his band of the mid-Seventies' and was recorded at the Paris Studios where he played selections from his album, 'Savage Amusement'.

During the late 1980s Michael seemed to have a lower profile but today he remains as popular as ever on the small club circuit and every year makes at least one appearance in Hull. Indeed, recently Michael appears to have been rediscovered and his following seems to be growing, even amongst teenagers. He has latterly had his semi-biographical novel 'Firewater Dreams' published and recently completed new albums 'The Twisted

Road' and 'Americana'. He is now well on his way to having released nearly Thirty albums.

Michael is also apparently writing a second novel provisionally entitled 'Time Past and Time Passing' and has had most of his back-catalogue released on CD. An album of his BBC Radio sessions has also been released which includes excellent versions of 'The Hero Returns', 'Deal Gone Down' and the brilliant 'Among These Trees'. He has also had an album of some of his previously unreleased early recordings put out on CD, including tape recordings from the time of his arrival in Hull. Combined with all of this have been recent trips to play in the USA, a visit to Hong Kong and an on-line fan club. Michael's star is clearly once again in the ascendancy.

For me, Michael Chapman, like Leonard Cohen, has always had a quality about his songwriting. I remember playing his 'Fully Qualified Survivor' and 'Window' albums around midnight in 1970/71. Listening to tracks such as 'Among These Trees' or 'Kodak Ghosts' after some love affair had floundered, would give you the strength to carry on. Indeed, not only has Michael written some great songs, but for my money, he is among that very select group of people who have written a classic. His of course is the very haunting and timeless 'Postcards of Scarborough'.

MICHAEL CHAPMAN

Discography:

ALBUMS

'Rainmaker'	1969	EMI HARVEST SHVL755
'Fully Qualified Survivor'	1970	EMI HARVEST SHVL764
'Window'	1970	EMI HARVEST SHVL786
'Wrecked Again'	1971	EMI HARVEST SHVL798
'Millstone Grit'	1973	DERAM SML1105
'Deal Gone Down'	1974	DERAM SML1114
'Lady On the Rocks'	1974	DERAM
'Pleasures Of The Street (Live)'	1975	NOVA 622321
'Savage Amusement'	1976	DECCA SKLR5242
'Play The Guitar The Easy Way'	1978	CRIMINAL RECORDS STEAL 2
'The Man Who Hated Mornings'	1978	CRIMINAL RECORDS STEAL 3
'Life On The Ceiling'	1978	CRIMINAL RECORDS STEAL 5
'Looking For Eleven'	1980	CRIMINAL RECORDS STEAL 9
'Almost Alone'	1981	BLACK CROW CRO 202
'Michael Chapman Lived Here'	1982	CUBE GNAT1
'Original Owners'	1987	KOMA 788003
'Heartbeat' (CD)	1988	CODA
'Fully Qualified Survivor (CD)	1990	SEE FOR MILES SEE-CD-230
'Best Of Michael Chapman' (CD)	1990	C5 RECORDS C5CD 527
'Navigation' (CD)	1991	PLANET RECORDS SPANCD005
'Still Making Rain' (CD)	1995	MAKING WAVES SPIN
'Life On The Ceiling' (CD)	1996	EDSEL

'Dreaming Outloud' (CD)	1997	DEMON RECORDS FIEND796
'Rainmaker' (CD)	1997	REPERTOIRE REP4679WY
'The BBC Sessions 1969 –1973'	1998	STRANGE FRUIT (CD)
'Fully Qualified Survivor'	1999	REPERTOIRE REP4687WY
'The Twisted Road'	2000	MYSTIC RECORDS (CD)
'Growing Pains'	2000	Trojan Records
'Pleasures of The Street'	2000	Trojan Records
'Americana'	2000	Siren/Apropos
'Live In Hamburg'	2000	Mooncrest Archives CRESTCD06Z-UK

SINGLES:

'It Didn't Work Out'/' Mozart Lives Upstairs'	1969	HARVEST HAR5002
'Banjo Song'/'Dumplings'	1974	DERAM DM407
'While Dancing The Pride of Erin'/'The Man Who Hated Mornings'	1978	CRIMINAL Records
'Loving Dove'/ Steel Bonnets	1976	GAMMARecords
'Blue Season'/	1979	CRIMINAL Records
'Theme From The Movie of the Same Name'	1980	CRIMINAL Records
'East Coast'/White Night Starlight'		
'All Day And All Night'/ 'Geordies Down The Road'	1984	KONNEXION

Books:

'Firewater Dreams'	Rampant Horse Books	1997

| CHAPMANS' | 1968 -1969 | HULL |
| ELECTRIC ARMY | | |

Drum	Keith Stutt (East Coast Jazz Band)
Bass	Dick Heaton (That Feeling)
Vocals Guitar	Dave Richardson (William Cotton Blues Band)
Guitar/ Vocals	Michael Chapman
Potted History:	'MICHAEL CHAPMAN'S ELECTRIC ARMY OF FRIENDS'

A loose ensemble of musicians occasionally coming together for jamming and musical experimentation purposes. It clearly gave the chance for Michael Chapman to extend his music and take his songs further. Just like Bob Dylan had done, in crossing over from folk to rock, the sessions provided him with the opportunity to work within the rock genre which he clearly enjoyed and which with the release of his second album would culminate in him forming a more permanent band.

CHEAVOURS   circa 1964   **YORK**

Drums   Dave Crabtree

Bass   Pete Allen

Rhythm   Don Gargott

Lead   Paul Blanchard

Vocals   Chris Queminet replaced by
Alex Blaydon Hill

Potted History: 'THE CHEAVOURS'

A very popular group, the Cheavours could often be seen playing such York venues as the Boulevard Night-club and the Assembly Rooms. The group came second to York's 'Viceroys' in a heat of the 1964 National Beat Contest held at the Rialto Cinema. The Cheavours later evolved into the 'Small Sounds'.

CHECHAKOS	circa 1965	SCUNTHORPE

Drums   Steve Cox

Bass   Geoff Theaker

Lead   Greg Tomlinson

Potted History: 'THE CHECHAKOS

Another of the top Scunthorpe groups, Greg Tomlinson would go on to join Scunthorpe recording group the Dimples. Several of the early beat groups had unpronounceable names like the Chechakos. Harrogate for example had the Kokomos while another strangely named local group were the Magyars. The Chechakos went on to tour Germany and supported Van Morrison's 'Them' at the Drill Hall. They were certainly not the only Scunthorpe group to have a strange name, another was the Kraakans. This group included guitarists Steve Bird and Cliff Chappel. They lasted from 1961 until 1966 playing their final gig at the Queen Bess on New Years Eve.

CHEST FEVER   1968 - 1969   HULL

Drums   Dave Eastwood

Bass   Pete Bell replaced by John Bentley (Flesh)

Lead   Paul Shallcross replaced by Keith Hale

Organ   Roy Neave (Scene)

Vocals   Steve Parsons alias 'Snips' (Mutiny)

Potted History: 'CHEST FEVER'

Named after a track from the album 'Music From The Big Pink' by the 'Band', Chest Fever were a great professional sounding band with plenty of stage presence. In their time they supported several top groups including 'Free' and would often appear at the open-air Concerts held in Hull parks during the late Sixties'. 'Chest Fever' played excellent versions of songs such as the Rolling Stones 'Lets Spend The Night Together. But arguably their greatest moment was an absolutely brilliant version of Bob Dylan's classic 'Like a Rolling Stone'. From Bridlington, vocalist 'Snips, with his long cheese cloth shirt hanging down just above his knees, would stomp his stiff leg throughout the performance. As the song slowly built up to a crescendo the roadies would appear on stage. I particularly remember one with a head of bright ginger fuzzy hair wearing a caftan and bells, both he and the others roadies would dance themselves into a frenzy. Chest Fever's guitarist Keith Hale later went on to write some hit songs for Toyah Wilcox. After a few personnel changes the group changed their name to 'Nothineverappens'.

The Cheavours (York - 1964)

CHORDELLS   **circa 1963**   **BEVERLEY**

Guitar   Chris Lewis

Guitar   Tony Soames

Vocals   Connie

Potted History: 'THE CHORDELLS'

One of the very early Beverley groups, others included the Rogues and the Satalites. Tony Soames would go on to join several Beverley groups including the Penjants, Sedation and Rip Van Winkle.

CHOW'S MEN   *circa 1965*   **SCARBOROUGH**

Drums   Dave Pinkney

Bass   Danny Darley

Lead   Derek Cook

Keyboards   Derek Boyes

Potted History: 'CHOW'S MEN'

Formed by ex-members of the Tennesseans and managed by
Peter Pitts, Chow's Men were very busy in the Scarborough
area. Their sound was billed as 'Big, Bluesy and Exciting'. Local
gigs included the Scarborough Spa. Chows Men supported
several top groups included the Searchers and the Alex Harvey
Soul Band. This was before Alex Harvey's eventual rise to fame,
having spent most of the early Sixties' in Hamburg, like the
Beatles, perfecting his art. Derek Boyes went on to join York's
Escorts and later went down to London to join David Bowie in
his group the Buzz. The Buzz had a residency at the Marquee
Club at the height of the Swingin' Sixties' and Derek also
featured on some early recordings with Bowie. Most of these
recordings have recently been released on Bowie's 'London
Boys' CD.

CITIZENS	1963 - 1967	SHEFFIELD
Drums	Dave Bennet	
Bass	Richard Hodgson	
Rhythm	Alan Middleton	
Vocals	Graham Boone	

Potted History: 'THE CITIZENS'

A Sheffield   R & B group who played in Hull quite often, especially at the Gondola Club down Little Queen Street. Quite a few Sheffield groups played the Gondola, including the Citadels (who were managed by the Club's owner) and an outfit called Vance Arnold and the Avengers whose singer would go on to greater things. The 'Gondola' was the 'Mods' club and one New Years eve when the Citizens played there the Mods were fighting in Little Queen Street. Bar stools were being thrown through the club's windows and cars being turned over. Other marginally less violent local gigs the Citizens played included the Kon Tiki Club down Whitefriargate, the Beverley Regal and Hull University. One of the top stars the Citizens supported was Tom Jones, who they appeared with at the Rawmarsh Bath Hall. Stood alongside him, the group were surprised to find that apparently in reality he was not as tall as he was reputed to be and relied for a lift in height on his high-heel boots.   The Citizen's Manager, Mike Boone, remembers attending evening classes in plumbing and welding, where one of his classmates was future rock superstar, Joe Cocker (alias Vance Arnold). Mike recalls the teacher speaking solemnly to Joe one evening and advising him, 'You'll never meck any money out of singing lad, stick to the plumbing!' The Citizen's eventually changed their name to the Male Set.

The Clubmen

CLUBMEN	1960 –1964	YORK
Drums	Colin Carr	
Bass	Graham Cambridge	
Rhythm	David Bicknall	
Lead	Anton Betteridge	
Potted History:	'THE CLUBMEN'	

The Clubmen were named after the Vox 'Clubman' guitar owned by their lead guitarist. The group played mostly Top Ten numbers and featured at several residencies including the Londesboro' Arms (York), the Golden Lion (Selby) and the Wild Man Inn on the A64, near Tadcaster. Colin Carr had been asked to join the group in 1960 when he was a drummer in the Territorials. He wasn't that keen at first, having to attend rehearsals with his rope-tension side drum. But he eventually became interested and bought a second-hand drum kit for £14, he soon afterwards got hooked and almost 40 years later is still playing the same music. Colin remembers that there was a great group scene during the Sixties' in York, which lasted mainly from 1960-1967. He estimates that in 1963 alone there were around 50 groups in the City which meant that about 250 of York's teenagers were members of beat groups! The Clubmen stayed together for 4 years and a highlight of their career was playing for a week at York's Theatre Royal, where in the Royal Box, they provided the music for a stage play called 'Semi-Detached'. The play's leading man was future Dad's Army star, James Beck, alias 'Private Walker'. Colin Carr went on to join York group, Gerry B and the Rockafellas, whose singer was to become future TV comedy star Dustin Gee.

COASTAL EROSION   1968 - 1970   **WITHERNSEA**

Drums   Derek Wilkinson

Bass   Michael Milner

Lead   John Raper

Organ   Nick Belcher

Vocals   Alan Harriman

Potted History: 'COASTAL EROSION'

Coastal Erosion were a very popular Withernsea group managed by Richard Stead. They played 'progressive' rock music and featured three part harmonies. The group were named after the high level of coastal erosion affecting the East Yorkshire coastline. A highlight of their career was when they auditioned for a London Agent and were offered a Management and Recording deal. But apparently they turned it down because it meant turning professional! Coastal Erosion supported several top groups including 'Cupid's Inspiration and the Spencer Davis Group. Sadly, they disbanded in 1970 when drummer Derek Wilkinson was taken ill and died.

Coastal Erosion (Withernsea - 1969)

COASTERS   **1960 –1963**   **SCARBOROUGH**

Drums   Leslie Turner

Bass   Bob Ford

Guitar   Stephen Morley

Lead   Peter Liley

Potted History: 'THE COASTERS'

Named after the East Yorkshire coastline, the Coasters had their own signature tune. They, along with Jonty and the Strangers, the Moonshots, the Sherburn Panthers and Rikki and the Blue Stars, dominated the Scarborough music scene during 1963. When the Coasters split, Pete Liley went on to join the Moonshots and was later an early member of the Mandrakes.

COCK-A-HOOPS   1964 - 1967   BROUGH

Drums	Geoff Korklin replaced by Dave Stow
Bass	Tony Beastie replaced by Alan Robson
Rhythm	Dave Lockyer replaced by John Bartlet (Organ)
Lead	Martin Bridges (Martians)
Vocals	Barry Kennedy
Potted History:	'THE COCK-A-HOOPS'

Named after a track by Manfred Mann, the original members of the Cock-a-Hoops were Martin Bridges, Geoff Korklin and Tony Beasty. Martin Bridges had formerly led local instrumental group the 'Martians'. The Cock-a-Hoops were formed to play British R & B especially numbers by the Yardbirds. They played village halls and youth clubs and could often be seen performing on a Saturday evening at the Hull City Hall. They were also very popular on the other side of the Humber at such venues as the South Bank Jazz Club in Grimsby. In the summer of 1967, when group members Tony Beastie and Dave Lockyer went off to College to study to be Civil Engineers, soon afterwards the group folded. Martin Bridges then went down to London and secured a job with recording group 'Black Cat Bones' whose lead guitarist had been Paul Kossoff a future member of 'Free'. Unfortunately, Martin fell ill and had to come home. But he later returned to London and after unsuccessfully auditioning for 'Jon Hiseman's Coliseum' and performing at the Marquee Club, he secured the guitarist slot with recording group 'Pickettywitch'. Pickettywitch had a number two chart hit with their single 'That Same Old Feeling' and Martin appeared with the group on 'Top Of The Pops'. A Hank Marvin lookalike with long hair, he left Pickettywitch to pursue his guitar playing, today is believed to live in Spain.

| **COSSACKS** | **1962 - 1967** | **HULL** |

Drums | Ken Lee

Bass | Mike Walsham replaced by
Graham White

Rhythm | Steve Wiley replaced by Pete Raywood,
Glen Edson

Lead | Roy Thompson

Vocals/Guitar | Vic Harbord

Potted History: | 'THE COSSACKS'

One of the many groups I saw appearing at the 'Beat Nights' held in Hull's West and East parks during the summers of 1964/5. The Cossacks had a great name and did actually dress for the part on stage. They played Cliff Richard, Shadows and Top Ten numbers. The group performed both in and out of town and their gigs included the Kon Tiki Club, 49 Whitefriargate Hull, and such large venues as the Brid Spa and Hull's Locarno Ballroom. At one point the Cossacks had the chance to go places and received some good offers, but it meant turning pro and unfortunately, Roy was serving his apprenticeship and Steve was studying for University so it never quite came off. The group later changed their name to 'Vic and the Strangers'.

The Cossacks (Hull - 1964)

COTTON PICKERS 1957 - 1961   HULL

Drums   Rod Nicholson

Bass   Rod Stubbs

Guitar   John Robinson

Guitar/Vocals   Malcolm Bradley

Vocals/Banjo   Jim Shann

Potted History: 'THE COTTON PICKERS'

Like the Beatles, a group who would grow out of skiffle and into rock 'n' roll. Jim Shann had originally started out with another skiffle group called the Kingston Five when he was just 14. The members of this outfit included Jim Shann first on tea-chest bass, and eventually banjo, mandolin and vocals, David Young on washboard, Leslie Palmer and George Freeman on guitar. They also had a part time singer called Eric Morfitt. The name of the group came from the pub were they played, the Kingston Hotel, down Cumberland Street. The Kingston Five played there twice a week for free. But eventually they got other gigs around the clubs, mainly in East Hull and managed to get regular gigs at the Bull Pub on Beverley Road and the Lady Le Gross, in Beverley.

Jim Shann went to work at Rosedowns and Thompson where other employees had formed a skiffle group called the 'Cotton Pickers'. They were in the V.A. and had a regular gig at Hull's Halfway House on Spring Bank West. Jim had by now taught himself to play the guitar and banjo and was soon snapped up by this rival skiffle group. Other Hull skiffle groups around this time include the Blackjacks and the Aces. None of the Cotton

Pickers were really proficient but Jim recalls that at the time you didn't have to be. Their vocalist, Malcolm Bradley, could sing like Lonnie Donegan and the group were influenced by the Vipers and similar American sounding groups.

The Cotton Pickers didn't have a group van as such and transport of equipment to gigs was usually by bus. One evening when the group had a gig out at Beverley, they boarded one of the new two-door East Yorkshire buses at Paragon Station and moved down to the back of the bus. It was raining and the bus was soon full. When the time came for the group to get off, they made their way to the back door off the bus but found that they couldn't get the tea chest bass through it as there was a vertical bar halfway across the exit. The only way for the group to get the Tea Chest bass off the bus was for everyone else standing on the bus to get off, which they did, in the pouring rain! Skiffle groups with tea chests basses were banned from East Yorkshire Buses after that!

The Cotton Pickers were paid the princely sum of two pounds, ten shillings for their sessions at the Halfway House. One evening, after playing there, a well dressed man complimented the group and asked them if they played anywhere else. Thinking that they might be getting another gig, they exaggerated the number of places they played and how much they got paid. A couple of weeks later, the Cotton Pickers got a letter from the local Tax man, asking them to call in to see him, since he had been told just how much they were earning as a group. The Cotton Pickers must have been the first group in Hull to pay tax! The group eventually evolved into rock 'n' roll outfit the Tornadoes.

The Cotton Pickers

The Kingston Five

179

COUNTERPOINTS circa 1964   **YORK**

Drums   Geoff Gill replaced by Derek Waugh

Bass   Colin Whotton

Rhythm   John Fielder

Lead/vocals   Dick Thorpe

Vocals   George Hall

Potted History: 'THE COUNTERPOINTS'

The Counterpoints played R & B and were voted into 7th position in York's 'Favourite Local group' pop poll published in a 1964 edition of the Ousebeat magazine. Out of town gigs included Driffield's Town Hall. The group later changed their name to the Crawdaddies. Geoff Gill went on to join the Viceroys and later became a member of hit recording group the 'Smoke'. John Fielder joined another York recording group the Roll Movement.

CRAWDADDIES   *circa 1965*   **YORK**

Drums   Derek Waugh

Bass   Colin Whotton

Lead   Dick Thorpe, John Vickers

Vocals   Jim Hall

Potted History: 'THE CRAWDADDIES'

Formed out of the Counterpoints, the Crawdaddies were a very popular R & B group on the York scene. They were resident at the Kings Manor Hotel and took their name from the Richmond club where the Rolling Stones and the Yardbirds had first started out, the 'Crawdaddy'.

CRESTAS	1960 - 1966	HULL

Drums   Mike Kitching replaced by
Dave Bradfield (Mariners)

Bass   Pete Cannon replaced by Tim Myers

Rhythm   Mike Harris replaced by Henry Temple
(Aces)

Lead   Bill Dall replaced by Mick Ronson
(King Bees)

Vocals   Pete Morris replaced by
Norman Beharrel, Johnny Hawk,
Eric Lee, Malcolm Hunt

Potted History: 'THE CRESTAS'

The Crestas history can be traced back to the 'Solids' who also featured Jack Gilchrist and Charles Erickson. The Crestas first appeared on the scene around 1960 and they retained the same line-up for several years. When Johnny Hawk joined the group they were for a while known as 'Johnny Hawk and the Crestas'. Early in 1964 Bill Dall left the group and Johnny Hawk let it be known that the Crestas were looking for a lead guitarist. On talking to his friend Johnny Griffiths, who was the leader of local outfit the 'Mariners', he told Johnny of a guitarist he might be interested in. The Mariners were finding it difficult to get gigs and Johnny Griffiths thought that a young guitarist in his band deserved better. So Johnny Hawk went along to see the young guitarist at work and after the show was introduced to Mick Ronson. When Mick joined the Crestas the group played mostly Top Ten material. Ex Aces singer, Eric Lee also soon afterwards joined the group and for a while the Crestas featured two vocalists up front. This then was the classic line-up of the Crestas with Johnny Hawk and Eric Lee on vocals, Mick Ronson on lead guitar, Tim Myers on bass and Mike Kitching on the drums. But eventually there were further changes in line-up with both Johnny Hawk and Mike Kitching leaving and Dave Bradfield joining on the drums.

The final line-up of the Crestas in 1966, featured Malcolm Hunt on vocals. Regular local gigs by this time included the Beverley Regal and the Halfway House. That year the Crestas also supported top British Bluesman John Mayall at the Skyline Ballroom. When the Crestas finally split Mick Ronson suggested to drummer Dave Bradfield that they should go down to London and turn pro. But having already had mixed experiences as a member of pro group the 'Batmen', Dave wasn't too sure and suggested that if Mick found a band and they needed a drummer, then he would join him later. So Mick went down to London on his own and joined a recording band called the 'Voice' and later when the original drummer left, he telephoned Dave inviting him down to audition, which he did successfully.

The Crestas (Hull - 1964)

CRUSADERS   1963 - 1964   **HULL**

Drums   Harry Dunn

Bass   Geoff Mortimer

Lead   Andy Woonton

Guitar/   vocals   Ronald Mitchell (Astronauts)

Potted History: 'RICKY KNIGHT AND THE
                   CRUSADERS'

Ricky Knight and the Crusaders were the second local beat group I saw playing live at one of the 'Beat Nights' held in Hull's West and East Parks during 1964. Ricky Knight was also the first vocalist I saw make their entrance on stage by making a six foot leap over the drum kit! The Crusaders were formed a long time ago, in a far distant galaxy when rhythm guitarist Andy Woonton and bass guitarist Geoff Mortimer of the original Ricky Knight and the Crusaders were looking for a new lead guitarist to join them. They had visited St John's Church Hall on Hull's Newbridge Road, to check out Bob, the lead guitarist in the Astronauts Beat group. They liked what they saw and asked him to rehearse with them. Somehow during the conversation it was assumed that they also wanted fellow Astronaut Ron Mitchell to also join them and so he went along to the rehearsals as well. Bob and Ron were accepted and Ron took over the name 'Ricky Knight'. The Crusaders began playing youth club dances and other similar gigs, but Bob soon left and Andy took over on lead guitar and Ron took over on rhythm guitar and lead vocals. When Harry Dunn joined the group on the drums, the classic line-up was complete.
Ron recalls that the local scene at the time was brilliant. It was the age of the first 'teenage market' where products were being

185

created and packaged for this emergent socio-economic group - everything was brand-new and hadn't been done before. For the first time, teenagers had their own culture and that included and perhaps hinged around the music. 'If you were in a group then you were someone special. For instance, you were even allowed to sit at the very back of the Coffee House (opposite the old Bladons) with the intelligentsia i.e. University students. The order of seating would be those with no O' levels at the front followed by O' levels, followed by A levels, followed by University students and groups.' The Crusaders played R & B and featured several Buddy Holly songs in their repertoire. They soon became very popular on the local scene and took over from Dev Douglas as the resident group at the Linzi Coffee Bar in Skipsea during the summer of 1964. The group tended to concentrate on dance venues including youth clubs and dance halls such as the Majestic, the Kevin Ballroom and the Bridlington Spa. They also played many of the Teen clubs including the Kon-Tiki Club in Whitefriarsgate and Club Bohemia in Driffield. Ron recalls that there was a lot of rivalry between the local groups at this time, most of it friendly. He remembers that during one period of the band's development (or was it decline?) that they were upset to hear that one of their supporters admitted that the Rats were actually scruffier, dirtier and generally more outrageous than the Crusaders were!!! In the early days they earned very little but had a lot of fun! But the Crusaders were fortunate to be spotted, while playing in the village of Sproatley by the Chichester Constable's of Burton Constable Stately Hall. The Constables agreed to manage the group and were responsible for getting them to grow their hair really long and to dye it 'blond'. There was then a change of name to the 'Hullaballoos' and the group would go on to tour the USA and make records.

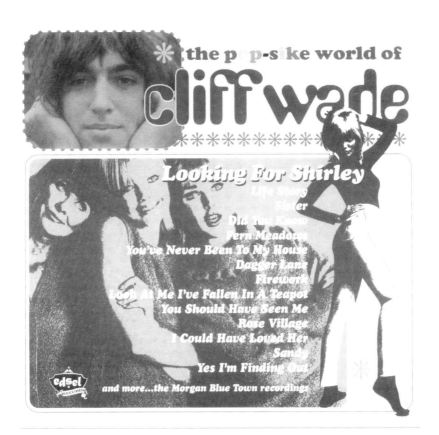

the pop p-sike world of

cliff wade

Looking For Shirley
Life Story
Sister
Did You Know
Fern Meadows
You've Never Been To My House
Dagger Lane
Firework
Look At Me I've Fallen In A Teapot
You Should Have Seen Me
Rose Village
I Could Have Loved Her
Sandy
Yes I'm Finding Out
and more...the Morgan Blue Town recordings

edsel
RECORDS

187

Cliff Wade

CUCUMBER	circa 1968	YORK

Drums   Steve Jackson

Bass   John Lockran

Lead   Cliff Wade

Potted History: 'CUCUMBER'

A temporary outfit joined by Cliff Wade on his departure from top York recording group the 'Roll Movement'. Cucumber's inaugural gig was at York's Enterprise Club. The group didn't really last long, with Steve Jackson joining Red Dirt and Cliff Wade going solo releasing the single 'You've Never Been To My House.' This was recorded at Morgan Studios in London along with 20 or so other tracks. Cliff would eventually go on to work as a copyist in Morgan Studios where former York 'Viceroy' and 'Smoke' member Geoff Gill had become a record producer. After dealing with the various studio clients by day Cliff and other former members of the Smoke including Mal Luker, would be involved in after midnight recording sessions producing tapes and records under various names. One of these names was Fickle Pickle who would have a hit record in the Netherlands. By 1974 Cliff and Geoff had moved to 10cc's Strawberry Recording Studios in Manchester where Cliff continued to record and write songs. He also took to the road and toured with various artistes including Jenny Darren. Cliff would eventually have two of his songs recorded by Jenny and these in turn would be picked up by Canadian rock star Pat Benetar who would record his song 'Heartbreaker'. Tina Turner also recorded one of his songs and another entitled 'Bulldog' was recorded by 'Curly Watts' of Coronation Street fame. Today, Cliff continues both to write and record and has recently had a substantial number of his early songs released on CD.

The album is called 'Looking Out For Shirley – The Pop Sike World of Cliff Wade' and is released on the Edsel label.

'You've Never Been To My House' c/w 'Sister' Morgan Blue Town 1969

Ian King and The Classics (Scunthorpe - 1964)

CULT   **circa 1967**   **YORK**

Drums   Richard Atkinson

Bass   Mick Gossop

Rhythm   Pete Mathews

Lead   Owen Wroot

Vocals   Mick Miller (Misfits)

Potted History: 'THE CULT'

Mick Miller was formerly the vocalist with the Misfits who had evolved into the Roll Movement. The Cult's first gig was at the Imperial Hotel in York. Mick Miller went on to join the Screen and later 'Matchbox'.

CYCLONES   **circa 1966**   **SCARBOROUGH**

Drums   Roger Milner

Bass   Mick Noble

Rhythm   Richard Sargent

Lead   Roy Chilton

Vocals   Colin Larn (Deccanairs)

Potted History: 'THE CYCLONES'

The Cyclones played their own versions of pop songs, all of the members were still at school. Roger Milner and Richard Sargent went on to play with the very popular late Sixties' Scarborough group, 'Lazy Poker'.

DECCANAIRS   **circa 1965**   **SCARBOROUGH**

Drums   Colin Larn

Bass   Stephen Brewster

Rhythm   Michael Stephenson

Lead   Michael Dove

Potted History: 'THE DECCANAIRS'

One of the youngest of the Scarborough groups, all of the
members were aged between 13 and 15. The Deccanairs catered
for the younger teenage market and played at parties, youth
clubs, etc. Colin Larn went on to become vocalist with the
Cyclones.

DELTONES	circa 1963	SCARBOROUGH
Drums	Bob Powell	
Bass	Richard Widdows	
Guitar/Vocals	Dennis (Del) Hitch	
Piano	Roger Dean	
Sax	Derek Hood	
Sax	Barry Hampshire	
Potted History:	'DEL MARTYN AND THE DELTONES'	

The Deltones played R & B. One of their earliest appearances was at Scarborough's Gaiety Cinema Beat Contest. Richard Widdows went on to join Scarborough groups the 'Panthers' and Group 29.

Many of the early beat groups like the Deltones included the word 'Tones' in their name. While nationally we had outfits such as 'Shane Fenton and the Fentones' and Helen Shapiro's banding group the 'Trebletones', locally we had the Semi-Tones (Beverley), the Flintones (Scarborough), the Truetones (York) and the Stereotones (Hull).

DIMES	**circa 1965**	**HULL**

Drums   Glen Petty (Yorkies)

Bass   Dick Whittles

Rhythm   Mike Smith

Lead   Les Wasling (Moonrakers)

Vocals   Ray Goodwin

Potted History: 'THE DIMES'

Several of the early beat groups eventually crossed-over onto the cabaret and WMC circuit, the Dimes were one such band. They wore 'smart' tuxedos and gold lame bow ties. Vocals, Ray Goodwin, was considered to sound like Elvis and the group featured a fair amount of rock 'n' roll material in their act, also R & B, and ballads. Dick Whittles and Mike Smith went on to join the Unnamed and Glen Petty became a member of the Skysounds.

DIMPLES	1964 - 1967	SCUNTHORPE
Drums	Stuart Smith	
Bass	Johnny Johnson replaced by Craig Austin (Imps)	
Lead/Vocals	Greg Tomlinson (Chechakos)	
Guitar/vocals	Terry Wincott	
Guitar/vocals	John Gladwin	
Potted History:	'THE DIMPLES'	

Named after the John Lee Hooker number, the Dimples were formed by Terry Wincott and John Gladwin on leaving school. They soon became very popular in the area and supported many top groups including the Pink Floyd. It wasn't long before the group had turned pro and signed to Don Arden's Galaxy Agency which was based in London's Carnaby Street. Arden's stable of stars at this time included the Small Faces, the Move and the Nashville Teens.

The Dimples soon took to the London lifestyle and were resident at London's infamous Madison Hotel in Sussex Gardens were they became hotel-trashing pioneers. They had regular gigs at several top London clubs including the Marquee, the Flamingo and other major London blues haunts. They also played on the College Circuit, at Mecca and Top Rank Ballrooms and had gigs at Newcastle's Club A-Go-Go and Quay Club.

The Dimples first live radio gig was at the Tiles Club in Oxford Street where they appeared on 'Ready Steady Radio' with Pete Murray. Their live TV debut was on Granada Television's 'Scene At Six Thirty'.

Don Arden got the group a deal with Decca Records. Decca forced them to record the single 'Love of A Lifetime' for which the Dimples wrote the B-side. The record was produced by Tony Clark (the Moody Blues Producer), but it was totally unrepresentative of the group's style and failed to chart. The Dimples had already made a bad career decision because they had turned down the chance to record 'Hi Ho Silver Lining', which later became a big hit for Jeff Beck. It wasn't the first or even last bad decision that Dimple members, Terry Wincott and John Gladwin made. Because even while at school, they had refused to allow future Michael Jackson 'Thriller' co-writer, Rod Temperton to join their band. Keeping up with the changes happening musically the Dimples decided to undergo various personnel changes and evolved into psychedelic harmony soul band 'Gospel Garden' .

One story about the Dimples relates to an evening around bonfire night in 1967 when they appeared at the Skyline Ballroom supporting the Pink Floyd. After the gig they followed the Floyd in their van along the old A63 out of Hull. Racing side-by-side, the Dimples and the Pink Floyd's rival transit vans became locked in mortal combat as a massive barrage of penny bangers, rockets and other assorted incendiary devices were launched at each others vehicles. Through open windows and sliding doors, flaming missiles and exploding gunpowder ignited the hair and flesh that cowered within, to an accompaniment of screams of pain and terror. As the groups napalmed each others battle wagons, the rumble continued the full length of the carriageway with seemingly no regard whatsoever for the sanctity of human life, or the unfortunate plight of other innocent road users caught in the crossfire. In the end there was no real outcome and no clear victor, but miraculously all parties survived and were soon sharing a celebratory feast at the infamous 'Norman's' greasy spoon transport café. A place which itself was also a serious health risk.

The Dimples (Scunthorpe - 1965)

Discography:

Singles:

'Love Of A Lifetime' c/w 'My Heart Is Tied To You'	Decca F12537	1966

Albums

'Dimples/Imps'	V9 Music	CD2000

DIONNE FIVE   circa 1960   HULL

Drums   Brian Hague

Bass   Pete E Green

Lead   Pete Green

Vocals/vocals   Dave Tenney replaced by Keith Tucker

Potted History: 'THE DIONNE FIVE'

Named after the Canadian star Dion Quins, the Dionne Five contained the nucleus of future local R & B outfit the 'Sunsets' and also Dave Tenney, who would change his name to Dev Douglas and go on to become a minor recording star.

DISTANT JIM   Circa 1969   HULL/SCUNTHORPE

Drums   Steve Chapman

Bass/Vocals   Craig Austin

Lead/Vocals   Les Nicol

Potted History: 'DISTANT JIM'

Craig Austin and Les Nicol formed Distant Jim after the break up of Scunthorpe recording group 'Methuselah'. Basing themselves in London they teamed up with former Juniors Eyes drummer Steve Chapman whose position had been filled by Hull's John Cambridge. Throughout 1969 Distant Jim were writing their own original material and performing at Klooks Kleek and other now long forgotten North London venues. During the psychedelic mayhem that ensued, a single for Dutch label Negram, as well as an album were somehow recorded at Morgan Studios by ex York Viceroy and Smoke member ('My Friend Jack Eats Sugar Lumps') producer Geoff Gill. Because of gross obscenity the single was apparently banned in the UK and released only in Holland where it failed to do well. The B-side 'Cosmarama' also apparently had its moments. Consequently, the album (if it was actually ever finished?) was never released and after a brief period of total insanity the trio split. Craig Austin became the 'Loonpant King' and is now writing and producing for V8 music. Les Nicol joined Coast Road Drive, Leo Sayer, Dana Gillespie and American Glamrockers Magnet.

When Craig Austin got the idea of designing pairs of trousers with huge flares and no pockets everybody thought that he was crackers. Nevertheless, disillusioned with the music business he and partner Stuart Knox went into production. They sold their first pair of 'Loon Pants' at the 1970 Isle of Wight Festival from the back of a mini-van. There were 300 pairs in the initial batch and they sold out within a couple of days. From being poverty stricken in bands for years, Craig went home with pockets over-flowing with wads of cash.

Distant Jim (Hull/Scunthorpe - 1969)

DISTURBANCE	circa 1967	HULL

Drums	John Etton
Bass	Ray
Keyboards	Zak The Bolt replaced by 'The Prof' (Paul Sutton)
Lead	Morgue
Guitar/Vocals	Rick Holgate
Potted History:	'DISTURBANCE'

This group really lived up to their name and made use of loud feedback, distortion, Go Go dancers, lighting effects, pitch blackness, sledge-hammered television sets, the works! The whole experience was an onslaught on the ears and the nervous system. Disturbance supported several top stars including P P Arnold. The group were big fans of the Move and took the name 'Disturbance' from the B-side of a Move single. One Saturday evening at the Hull City Hall whilst enthusiastically sledge-hammering a television set to pieces live on stage and then spraying it all over with paint, the group had the tricky problem of what to do with the wreckage. After much deliberation they gingerly carried the remains down to the side-entrance of the City Hall, hoping to leave it dumped in the doorway. But no sooner had they with much relief put it down than a passing Policeman came along and gesticulating with his thumb, advised them to 'Shift It!' Paul Sutton went on to join and mould local group the Variations into one of the top groups around.

DIZZY WHEELA	1968 - 1971	LOFTUS

Drums   Pete Jackson

Bass   Keith Tose

Rhythm   Mike McMaster

Lead   Graham Barker

Vocals   Robin Winspear

Trumpet   Howard Jackson

Tenor Sax   Keith Morrison

Potted History: 'DIZZY WHEELA'

This outfit were originally called the 'Minority Soul Band' and were formed in Loftus near Scarborough in 1967. After two successful years, in July 1969 they stopped playing for a while to develop a new image. Back on the road with their new name the band played the Beverley Regal and demonstrate what I said earlier about the violence to be had at this venue and the Hull City Hall. After the gig the group were attacked by a gang of youths and received abrasures, head wounds and black eyes, which they all sported for several weeks at their future gigs.

DOMINOES	circa 1964	YORK

Drums   Dave Johnson (Escorts)

Bass   Ricky Monfort

Guitar   Dave Kendal replaced by Mick Mills

Vocals   Gerry Stanard

Potted History: 'THE DOMINOES'

The Dominoes were yet another of the very popular York groups. They had originally been called the 'Hi-Fi's' but changed their name as everywhere they went there seemed to be yet another group called the Hi-Fi's. Dave Johnson and Dave Kendal had played with some of the last of the big bands of the late Fifties'. Dave Johnson had also begun his career playing with skiffle group Johnny Newcome and the Wabash Four. This group had appeared low down on the bill of some of the early rock 'n' roll shows held on the national cinema network which included the Rialto Cinema in York. This had also often included appearing alongside top York outfit the John Barry Seven. Dave had gone on to join the Derek Dudden Orchestra and then Steve Cassidy and the Escorts before joining the Dominoes. The Dominoes name had been chosen because the group (in the true rock 'n' roll lifestyle) would often in-between sets be sat backstage playing dominoes! The group became very popular and on stage began to develop a successful impromptu comedy routine. This was a big hit all around the West Riding. The group began to notice that a small party of Leeds University students would regularly turn-up at their gigs and that they particularly paid attention to the Dominoes comedy routines. The students later set-up their own comedy group under the name of the Grumbleweeds. Dave Johnson is still drumming.

DOUGLAS, DEV   circa 1963   **HULL**

Potted History: 'DEV DOUGLAS'

Real name Dave Tenney, a guitar/vocalist who after initially
playing solo around Hull's youth clubs (including Sidmouth
Street Youth Club) joined several local groups including the
Relations and the Dionne Five. But in 1963 he again went solo
and took up residency at the Linzi Coffee bar in Skipsea. Soon
afterwards he gained a recording contract. Basing himself in
London, he appeared on Television and released several records
including the song 'I Don't Know'. He also toured with several
pop package shows of the early Sixties' which featured many of
the early rock 'n' roll stars including Gene Vincent and Johnny
Kidd and the Pirates.

DROGOS   circa 1965   HUNMANBY

Drums   John Mainprize replaced by
               John Fairbank (King Bees)

Bass   Bob Fox

Rhythm   Derek Gill

Lead   Colin Bardsley

Vocals   Jock Scullen replaced by   Mick Bowen

Potted History: 'DROGOS TROLLS'

Originally called the 'Trolls', the group renamed themselves after they became resident at the Skipsea Beat spot 'Drogo's Den' and became known as 'Drogo's Trolls'. Managed by Peter Pitts, the group were very busy on the Scarborough scene.

When vocals Mick Bowen took a trip to London to visit two of the former 'Moonshots' he apparently met the Rolling Stones manager, Andrew Oldham. Oldham invited him to undertake a 'Singing test' in front of Mick Jagger, Keith Richards and Lionel Bart. All of them thought that Mick had a good voice but nothing appears to have come of it. He later went on to sing with 'Brave New World', while Derek Gill went on to play with the Mandrakes.

EASYBEATS   circa 1965   **YORK**

Drums   Stewart Batters

Bass   Derek Hughes

Lead   Dave Alderson

Vocals   Brian Fawcett

Potted History: 'BRIAN AND THE EASY BEATS'

The Easybeats were one of the top York groups. Local gigs included the Big Coach and the Boulevard Night-club on Tadcaster Road. Most of the original group members left to form the Gideon's Few. Brian fronted various line-ups of 'Easy Beats' for a further 3 to 4 years.

ELECTRAZ   *circa 1966*   **SCARBOROUGH**

Drums   Gordon Magson

Bass   Andrew Peter Justice

Lead   Roy Moore

Vocals   Andrew Newton

Potted History: 'THE ELECTRAZ'

The Electraz were a very young group who were on the scene for quite a while. They played Top Ten material and amongst others supported Liverpool recording outfit the 'Fenmen'.

ELITE	circa 1968	**WITHERNSEA**

Drums   Geoff Parrot

Bass   Mike Wright

Rhythm   Malcolm Todd

Lead/Vocals   Jay Dene

Potted History: 'THE ELITE'

Managed by Pete McLeod, the Elite were formed out of the C-Beats. Local gigs included the Beverley Regal. The Elite supported several top groups including Dave Berry and the Cruisers. The group had a nice line in flyers.

EMBERS   circa 1965   **YORK**

Drums   Pete Thompson

Bass   Ray Hill

Guitar   Dave Earnshaw

Vocals   Aidan (Jim) Boyle

Potted History: 'THE EMBERS'

The York 'Embers' had previously been know as the Vampires and were resident at the Clifton Hotel where they were very popular. Pete Thompson had come out of York group the Sunsets and the Pentagons to join the Embers.

ESCORTS 1960 - 1966 YORK

Drums	Dave Johnson replaced by Colin Berryman
Bass	Michael Goodrick
Lead	Michael McNeil
Keyboards	David Nellist replaced by Derek Boyes (Chow's Men)
Vocals	Steve Cassidy replaced by Sylvia Leon
Potted History:	'STEVE CASSIDY AND THE ESCORTS'

Steve Cassidy had started out with the stage name Sammy Brown and then changed it to Johnny April before eventually using his real name. As a schoolboy, he had been a member of a Leeds skiffle group called the Gambling Men. They played school dances and church halls in Leeds and York. Local impresario John Prendergast became much impressed by the group as they matured and turned towards more sophisticated material. He began to give them support spots on several package shows appearing at his cinema. Before he was 18, Steve had appeared on York bills with Michael Holiday, Cliff Richard and Adam Faith. By 1960 Steve's backing group had become the 'Escorts' and together they cut a couple of records for a London Company. Unfortunately, the discs were never released. But later in 1963 the group produced a single entitled 'Ecstasy' (a Marty Wilde composition) which was released on Ember Records and which gave then a Number One hit in Greece. The group appeared on Television's 'Ready Steady Go' to promote the record and it was played both on Saturday Club and Radio Luxembourg. Steve Cassidy left the band in 1965 and Sylvia

Leon and Derek Boyes joined as replacements. The group then went on a tour of France. During their trip, the band worked for six days a week, which consisted of eating, sleeping and playing. The cities the tour took in, included Paris, Orleans and Verdun. Back home the Escorts appeared on Television in Manchester and local gigs included Scarborough's Candlelight Club. The group were occasionally billed as Sylvia and the Escorts. On splitting Derek Boyes went down to London to join John Hutchinson on some of the early recording sessions with David Bowie.

E-TYPES	1963 - 1964	DRIFFIELD
Drums	John Hall	
Bass	Dick Theakston	
Rhythm	Bryan Wheeldan	
Lead	Dave Lawson	
Vocals	Dave Westaway	
Potted History:	'THE E-TYPES'	

The E-Types were a young R & B group who later changed their name to the Road Runners. There were many local groups around at this time named after cars. Hull had its 'Jaguars', 'Crestas', 'Zodiacs' and 'Mustangs', Driffield had its 'E-Types', Hutton Cranswick its 'Chevrolets', Bridlington its 'Corvettes', Scunthorpe its 'Cadillac's' and York its 'Escorts'.

EXECUTIVES   circa 1964   **GOOLE**

Drums/Vocals   John Harrison

Lead Guitar   Alan Knight

Keyboards   Robert Todd

Potted History: 'THE EXECUTIVES'

The ages of group members was between 14 and 17. The Executives played early Shadows numbers, Elvis and the Top Ten, including Manfred Mann's 5-4-3-2-1. Robert Todd left the group to play football for Liverpool while John Harrison and Alan Knight played together throughout the Sixties', in a succession of local bands including the Sunsets (Goole version), Gulliver's Dream and the Shades. Alan Knight remembers playing a club in Moorends where when they were just about to strike-up for the last spot there was a sudden mass rush by the audience for the exits and the place emptied leaving just the group and the bar staff. The Executives were fed-up and demoralised as they thought that the evening until then was going great. But the reason for the audience's sudden exit was nothing to do with their performance, it was simply that the club next door was technically classified as being in the next village where closing time was half-an-hour later!

EXODUS	circa 1967	BRIDLINGTON

Drums   George Cundill (Fabulous 006 and the Agents)

Bass   Barry Sharpless (Fabulous 006 and the Agents)

Sax   Brian Pashley

Trumpet   Graham Storey

Vocals/Organ   Len Foster (High Voltage)

Potted History: 'THE EXODUS'

Full name the 'Exodus Showband', five experienced musicians playing East Riding Clubs and dances. The Exodus supported many top groups at the Bridlington Spa including Ike and Tina Turner, Amen Corner and the Troggs. Local gigs included the Beverley Regal. The group played rock 'n' roll and Top Ten hits and were managed by Peter Foster. The Exodus were one of many groups to audition for Television's weekly talent show 'Opportunity Knocks'. They later changed their name to the 'Blue J Showband' and eventually evolved into 'Kaleidoscope' who were the resident band at Tiffany's (Mecca) in Scarborough. One of their most memorable evenings was at Whitby Floral Hall. Len Foster was a talented rock 'n' roll singer/piano player and the group revolved around him. That evening on stage at the Whitby Floral Hall, he discovered a recently tuned Grand Piano and all his dreams were immediately fulfilled. He apparently near wrecked the instrument with a rockin' rendition of 'Nut Cracker' by B. Bumble and the Stingers. Later members of the group included Dave Hammerton of the Avengers and Ray Stannard and Ian Phillips of the Zircons.

FABIANS	1963 - 1967	HULL
Drums	Derek Mason	Mike Wright
Bass	Gary Davidson	Malcolm Caws (Rivals)
Rhythm	John Small	Pete Townsend
Lead	Mike Peterson	Mike Peterson
Potted History:	'THE FABIANS'	

The Fabians were popular at both clubs and dances. Local gigs included Hull's Kon-Tiki Club and appearances at the Hull Parks Beat Nights. Featuring four-part harmonies, the Fabians repertoire included such numbers as 'Blue Moon'. In 1965 the group produced an EP of themselves at the Malconi Recording Studios on Hessle Road in Hull. The original band folded in 1965 and a new line-up in 1966 auditioned for 'Opportunity Knocks' but they too were finished by 1967. Later members Barry Donald and Tony Auld went on to form 'Sugar 'n' Spice' while John Small joined the Small Four and later the 'Little People' before eventually moving to the USA.

The Exodus

FALCONS   **1958 - 1963**   **GOOLE**

Drums   Alan Roberts replaced byKen Wilde

Rhythm   Dean Cresta replaced by John Lawson, Peter Raywood

Lead   John Aire replaced by John Lawson

Keyboards   Rob Thornton

Vocals   Allan Vaux

Potted History: 'DEAN CRESTA AND THE FALCONS'

Guitarist Pete Raywood first saw this group performing at a local dance in Yorfleet Village Hall in 1959 and couldn't believe what he was hearing - it was magic, quite unlike anything he had ever heard before, but he had to wait another three years before being able to join them. The Falcons played Top Ten, Chuck Berry and Elvis numbers and their original line-up featured Saxophonist Doc Holiday. They were resident every Saturday evening at the Tavern Pub in Goole. Other local gigs included Goole's Old Drill Hall.

Several of the local beat groups around this time, like the Falcons, named themselves after some of the early guitars. These included the Gretsch 'Falcon' series (Hull and Goole), the Gretsch 'Tennessean' (Scarboro'), the Vox 'Clubman' (York) and the 'Burns' Beat Combo (Hull). I suppose we were lucky not to get the Columbuses, the Hofners, the Futuramas, or even the 'Solid' or 'Lucky Sevens'.

FALCONS	1963 - 1969	HULL
Drums	Gavin Wignal	
Bass	Nev Moore (Zircons)	
Rhythm	Wally Boulton	
Lead	Rodney Boulton	
Keyboards	Wally Scarah	
Potted History:	'WALLY AND THE FALCONS'	

The Falcons played Top Ten, rock and R & B. At one time they were managed by Michael Moore. On the scene for many years, they were resident at the Ferryboat Inn in Hessle which like the Halfway House in Hull was a big promoter of local beat groups. Other regular gigs for the Falcons included the Hull City Hall. The group eventually changed their name to the Rennison Six with the addition of Harry Fussey and Laurie Rennison. Bass player Nevil Moore had originally played an Hofner 500/1 'Violin' bass made popular by Beatle Paul McCartney. Nevil bought the guitar from Cornell's of Spring Bank Hull, for the princely sum of £57.10. His amplifier was a Vox AC3O. While with the Falcons he moved on to a Fender 'Precision' bass and a Vox AC5O amp with split-speaker cabinet especially built for him by Keith Herd. Fellow guitarist, Rod Boulton, played a 'Gretsch 'Red Falcon' (Wally also used a 'Falcon' which probably accounted for the group's name). The 'Red Falcon' had a great sound and today would be worth a lot of money. Nev Moore considers that the reason why there were so many great sounding groups around Hull at this time was because many were using top quality guitars and amplifiers.

FIVE TRAX 1963 - 1965 **HULL**

Drums Chris Horsley

Bass Ken Lambert

Lead Steve Warner

Vocals Paul Clough

Potted History: 'THE 5 TRAX'

The Five Trax were one of the top local R & B groups. They made regular appearances at the Beverley Regal, Hessle Town Hall and the Beverley Road Baths. They also played out of town at such venues as Scarborough's Condor Club. At one stage the group would finish their set with a Smarties jingle which was very popular at the time. The Five Trax were involved in an early 'Battle of the Bands' when they came second to arch R & B rivals the Gonx at a local Beat Contest held at the Locarno Ballroom in Hull.

FIX   **circa 1965**   **YORK**

Drums   Dave Vickers

Bass   Ian Hall (Poachers)

Rhythm   Greville Osborne

Lead   John Pearson

Vocals   Brian Parkin (Fossils)

Potted History: 'THE FIX'

The Fix came together late in 1965 and were one of the new wave of York groups of the mid-Sixties'. They played such gigs as the Zarf Club and the Londesborough Arms where they were resident. Brian Parkin had previously sang with the Fossils while Ian Hall had played bass with the Poachers. Ian went on to become a member of top York group of the late Sixties' the 'Screen' and Dave Vickers joined 'Little Dedication'. Towards the end of their career, the Fix in a moment of madness, changed their name to the Baskerville Mood!

FLESH   **1969 - 1970**   **HULL**

Drums   Keith Stutt (Bird's Groove)

Bass   John Bentley replaced by Trevor Bolder
(Chicago Style Blues Band)

Lead   Ian Bolder

Lead   Keith 'Ched' Cheesman

Potted History: 'FLESH'

Formed out of the Jelly Roll Blues Band, this is the second identified sighting of the 'Bolder' brothers on the local scene. Trevor Bolder would go on to join Hull group the Rats from where he would graduate to becoming a member of David Bowie's 'Spiders From Mars'. John Bentley would join local 'good time' group 'Chest Fever' and later become a member of hit recording group 'Squeeze'.

FLINTONES   1962 –1963   **SCARBOROUGH**

Drums   John Smith

Bass   Paul Farnell

Rhythm   Dave Wakeley

Lead   Morris Stephenson

Vocals   Mick Blackburn

Potted History: 'THE FLINTONES'

The Flintones were one of Scarborough's earliest beat groups. Their name was clearly a pun on the 'Flintstones'. The group won their way through two rounds of the 'People' Newspaper's National Talent Contest and did apparently receive offers to turn pro.

FLYAWAYS   circa 1963   **HULL**

Drums

Bass   Malcolm Barnett

Lead   Mike Barnett

Potted History: 'THE FLYAWAYS'

The Flyaways were originally a three piece group playing instrumentals like the Shadows. They dressed in 'space age' clothes typical of the time. The group eventually evolved into a duo playing the pub/club and 'Opportunity Knocks' circuit.

FOOT-TAPPERS	circa 1964	BEVERLEY
Drums	Les Foster	
Guitar	Barry Donald	
Organ	Norman Cowey	
Potted History:	'THE FOOT-TAPPERS'	

This group were probably named after the 1963 Shadows hit 'Foot-Tapper', although there was plenty of foot-tapping going on by this time. The Foot-Tappers were the resident group at the Haworth Arms in Hull. One evening they played at a talent contest in Walkington on the same bill as top Beverley group the Strollers. The Strollers were so impressed by the keyboard skills of Norman Cowie that they asked him to join them, which he did. Beverley produced many fine groups during the 1960s including the Strollers, the Penjants and the lesser known, Limited Company. It also spawned talented rock/blues guitarist Laurie Burnett, a contemporary of Mick Ronson and offered regular rock venues including the Memorial Hall, the Beverley Regal, Hodgson's Ballroom and the Beverley Youth Centre.

FOSSILS circa 1964 **POCKLINGTON**

Drums Wally Johnson

Rhythm Ken Molineaux

Lead Pete Storm

Vocals Brian Parkin

Potted History: 'THE FOSSILS'

The Fossils were formed by students at Pocklington School. A very young group they took their 'rock' seriously. The Fossils played R & B and also tried to write their own material. Brian Parkin later went on to sing with York outfit the Fix.

FOUR ACES   circa 1963   **HULL**

Drums   Adrian Gatie

Bass   John Paterson

Rhythm   Henry Temple

Lead   Brian Gatie

Lead   John Robinson (Tornadoes)

Vocals   Eric Lee (Tornadoes)

Potted History: 'ERIC LEE AND THE FOUR ACES'

A couple of 'Tornadoes' joining forces with the 'Aces'. Regular local gigs included the Majestic Ballroom. After slimming down to a four-piece the group evolved into Hull's first recording group of the 1960s the 'Aces'. Henry Temple left the group to join the Crestas.

FOUR CENTS	1960 –1964	SCUNTHORPE

Drums	Toyne Tomlinson
Bass	Tony Davis
Lead	Paddy O'Connor
Vocals	Mike Nicholls
Piano	Mel Oliver
Other Members:	Jimmy Ryder (Lead), Dave Markee (Lead)
Potted History	'NICK JAMES AND THE FOUR CENTS'

Nick James and the Four Cents were yet another of the popular Scunthorpe groups. An early gig was playing a 'Beatnik Ball' at the Brigg Corn Exchange.

Paddy O'Connor later joined the 'Turnabouts' and Mel Oliver played keyboards with the reformed 'Worrying Kind' at Scunthorpe's Sixties' Reunion Mega Gig held in 1999.

Another Scunthorpe group from this period was Ian King and the Classics. Members included Don Lee on Drums, Rod Clark on Bass, Eddie Ashworth on guitar and Ian Matthews MacDonald on Guitar/vocals. They were resident at the Priory Hotel Beat Club. Ian left the group in 1966 to take up a job in a Carnaby Street Boutique. He went on to join Pyramid, Fairport Convention and Matthews South Comfort.

GAZELLES	1961 - 1963	HORNSEA

Drums   Dave Harrison

Bass   Robin Taylor

Rhythm   Mike Donald

Lead   Tony Capes

Potted History: 'THE GAZELLES'

The Gazelles played Top Ten hits and R & B. They joined the Variety Artiste Association to get gigs on the local clubs but also got their own gigs through self-publicity. The Gazelles were for a while the resident band at the 'Trees' Country Club in North Ferriby where many other local groups including the Strollers would become resident. Two of the Gazelles later formed the Relations who featured future recording star Dave Tenney.

GEMINI'S	1960 - 1965	HULL

Drums   Dave Bradfield replaced by Keith Stutt

Bass   Mike Ward replaced by Jess Boot

Rhythm   Dave Hare replaced by Chris Fairbanks (Organ)

Lead   Geoff Smelt Replaced by Kev Clifford

Vocals   Geoff Drake

Potted History: 'THE GEMINI'S'

Originally, called Geoff Drake and the Gemini's, the Gemini's were an R & B group formed by school friends Dave Bradfield and Geoff Drake. Dave Bradfield had wanted to be a drummer in a band ever since first hearing the 'Shadows'. He would tap the ends of two of his mum's large knitting needles on the top of the family's old fashioned valve radio set, playing along to songs on Pick of the Pops. The young Gemini's appeared at Youth Clubs and had a regular gig at the Liberal Club, Beverley Road, Hull for which they were paid in bottles of pop and crisps. One evening while playing at the Club, 16 year old drummer Dave Bradfield was approached by the Batmen who where appearing at the Mayfair Cinema (which was nearly opposite). They enticed him to turn pro and join them on a tour of France. The later line-up of the Gemini's still fronted by Geoff Drake, included such numbers as 'St James Infirmary' and James Brown's ' I'd Go Crazy' in their repertoire. Wally Scarra (Ye Barons) and ex-Rats Brian Buttle and Robin Lecore also later joined the Gemini's. But by 1966 the group had evolved into the more 'way-out', 'Birds Groove'.

| GENGHIS KHAN | circa 1965 | PICKERING/ |
| | | SCARBOROUGH |

Drums	Rick Barber
Bass	Ben Harland
Rhythm	Mark Hick
Lead/Vocals	Dave Brown
Piano	Pete Storm
Vocals	'Malc' Jackson

Potted History: 'GENGHIS KHAN'

Genghis Khan were Pickering's top group and were managed by Jimmy Robson. They played strictly blues material. Gigs included local village halls around North Yorkshire. The group marketed themselves as 'Genghis Khan, The Powerful Name, The Powerful Sound, The Real Blues Scene'. Dave Brown's favourite local outfits of this time included York's Vampires, Bridlington's Avengers and Scarborough's Moonshots. Dave would go on to form Big Change.

GIDEONS FEW   1965 - 1968   **YORK**

Drums   Mick Mathews

Bass   Derek Hughes

Guitar   Dave Alderson

Vocals   Mick Fallon

Potted History: 'GIDEONS FEW'

The Few were one of the top York groups of the second half of the Swingin' Sixties. Formed out of the Easy Beats, Gideons Few were busy on both the local and national scene for several years. They toured the country and made several visits to Wales, they also had a residency at Butlins. In 1965 the group gained publicity for themselves by playing non-stop for 10 hours in an attempt to achieve a world record. The event was held at York's Zarf Club. Their manager of the time, W H Thornton actually got a mention of it in the March 1966 edition of top music magazine 'Beat Instrumental'. Gideons Few supported many star groups including the Pretty Things and the Moody Blues. Towards the end of their career they had their management taken over by Top Promoter Syd Hartness and they toured Germany, Switzerland and France but eventually not achieving that ultimate recording contract disbanded. In 1972 Derek Hughes went on to join American Underground Rock legends the MC5.

GIRLFRIENDS	1965 - 1967	HULL

Drums	Hilary Morgan replaced by Maureen Scholes
Bass/Vocals	Lesley Saxil-Nielsen replaced by Betty Beaumont
Lead/Vocals	Linda Harrison replaced by Margret Wedgner,
Organ/Vocal	Karen Baker replaced by Merle Pryor, Marion 'Rusty' Hill
Vocals	Mandy Smith
Potted History:	'MANDY AND THE GIRLFRIENDS'

Mandy and the Girlfriends were Hull's first all girl group of the 1960s. Very popular locally, the Girlfriends also toured the American bases in Germany. The Girlfriends were one of the first Hull groups to record a demo tape in Keith Herd's Willerby Studio. The session included the track 'You Can't Destroy My Love'. In 1966 the Girlfriends auditioned for Television's weekly talent show 'Opportunity Knocks'. However, despite being successful and on the books of a London agent there were several changes in line-up during their existence. On disbanding, Girlfriends, Margaret Wedgner, Merle Prior and Betty Beaumont joined with Linda Thompson to form the 'Honeys'. Leslie Saxil-Neilson, Marion 'Rusty' Hill and Linda Thompson formed 'Girl Talk'. Leslie later went on to join a band in Germany called the 'Losers Showband' with whom she toured with the likes of Ray Charles, the Everley Brothers and Ricky Nelson. The Girlfriends recently played some reunion gigs.

GONX   1965 - 1966   **HULL**

Drums   John Cambridge (Hullaballoos)

Bass   Steve Powell

Rhythm   Dave Carmichael (Riverbeats)

Lead   John Rowe replaced by Mike Tyson
                 (High Numbers)

Vocals   Dave Gardener

Potted History: 'THE GONX'

The Gonx got their name from a small weird looking cuddly toy (Gonk) which was very popular at this time. The group includes one of the first identified sightings of John Cambridge on the local scene who was later responsible for introducing Mick Ronson to David Bowie. The Gonx played R & B and made regular appearances at the Hull City Hall, the Beverley Regal and the Barracuda Club,. They also worked for Scarborough agent Peter Pitts, playing the resort's Cricketers Arms, Condor Club, YMCA and Spa. The Gonx were one of the top local R & B bands whose main local rivals were the Five Trax. A highlight for the Gonx was winning a Beat Contest at the Locarno Ballroom in Hull, where their rivals, the 'Five Trax, came second. The Gonx supported several top groups including the Four Pennies, but by early 1966 they had evolved into the short-lived 'Attack' with Dave Carmichael leaving to join newly forming soul band 'Plague 66'.

Mandy and the Girlfriends (Hull - 1965)

The Gonx (Hull - 1965)

Gospel Garden (Scunthorpe - 1967)

GOSPEL GARDEN   1966 - 1968   SCUNTHORPE

Drums   Steve Cox

Bass/Vocals   Craig Austin (Dimples)

Rhythm/Vocals   Terry Wincott (Dimples)

Lead/Vocals   Geoff Eaton Tindall

Vocals   John Gladwin (Dimples)

Potted History: 'GOSPEL GARDEN'

Gospel Garden had evolved out of the 'Dimples'. They played
Tamla and soul type material especially numbers by the
'Impressions with lots of harmonies. The group were heavily
influenced by the 'Fifth Dimension's, 'Magic Garden' album
which was written by classic songwriter, Jimmy Webb. They
were also influenced by Curtis Mayfield but gradually began to
feature an increasing amount of material by vocals John
Gladwin.

The group were originally jointly managed by Club Owner
Peter Stringfellow, promoter Sid Hartess and crazy American DJ
'Chicken Fat Charlie'. However, tight arrangements and
complex harmonies soon attracted the attention of pop star and
A and R man Dave Dee and their Management was taken over
by producer Steve Rowlands at Double-R productions. Double-
R were at this time also managing top recording group the Herd.
The band's busy gigging schedule was now mainly London 'In
Crowd' venues such as the Speakeasy, Blazes, Sybillas, Scotch of
St James, the Revolution Club the Marquee, the Flamingo, and
the 100 Club. As well as this they played the University circuit,
Northern mod clubs such as the Twisted Wheel, the Mojo, the

Broken Wheel, Golden Torch, Castleford Bowl, the Jazz Workshop and endless other drug-fuelled all-nighters throughout the land. Gospel Garden were also the first white band to play Paddington's notorious Q (Cue) club. After a gig at the Speakeasy, Gospel Garden actually had their performance praised by several top stars who had been in the audience including Herman of the Hermits and Graham Nash of the Hollies.

A short spell followed with Robert Stigwood negotiating a TV advert featuring the band being chauffeur driven in the ill-fated Humber Sceptre. Needless to say this was a total flop and was hastily withdrawn from our screens, the Humber Company almost immediately going bust! By this time, the band was pretty wild looking and claimed to do 'wappy' things such as spend the early hours of the morning sitting in deckchairs on one of Scunthorpe's traffic islands taking in the night air! The group were then picked to share the bill on the first ever televised psychedelic flower power festival up in Newcastle along with Scarborough's 'Mandrakes'. Some of the concert was the next day shown on the Tyne Tees Television programme 'Six Five'. Meanwhile they had gained a record deal with Polydor's little-known 'Camp' label and were offered several 'bubblegum' numbers to record, which they disliked and kept changing the arrangements to. Eventually, they released the single 'Finders Keepers'. Unfortunately, popular as the band were performing live the record failed to chart and Gospel Garden's management, in their infinite wisdom decided the group's name wasn't commercial enough and ordered a total makeover with the group evolving into heavy rock band 'Methuselah'.

Many local groups of the Swingin' Sixties' have tales to tell of their life on the road, many tales are often unprintable! Gospel Garden had more tales than most. At a gig at Brandesburton Village Hall in 1967, at some point in the set, their drummer would perform a rather tasteless striptease. On this particular evening, he got down as far as his underpants and fearing removal of this last remaining item of clothing, at the critical moment and just in the nick of time, the local village bobby leapt on stage with his cape, draped it over Steve and his offending parts and hauled him off the stage. As far as can be remembered the gig was abandoned and the Gospel Garden never got paid. Barefaced cheek!

Discography:

'Finders Keepers' c/w 'Just A Tear' 1968 CAMP 602 006

GROUP 29　　　　　circa 1964　　　　**SCARBOROUGH**

Drums　　　　　Dave Ayres

Bass　　　　　Richard Widdows (Deltones)

Rhythm　　　　　Brian Sharpe (Sonics)

Lead　　　　　Steve Morley (Coasters)

Vocals　　　　　Bill Cryer

Potted History:　　　'GROUP 29'

Probably the 29th group to be formed in the Scarborough area. Group 29 played R & B and appeared regularly at various Scarborough venues including the Condor Club, the Gemini Club and the Cricketers Arms. Their ambition was to become the best group in the Scarborough area. Brian Sharpe went on to join the Iguanas while Dave Ayres became a member of the Kerbsiders.

HAMMER	1968 - 1970	HULL

Drums   John Howden replaced by
                   Russ Aisthorpe

Bass   Stan Saye (Ways 'n' Means)

Lead   Chris Ramsdale replaced by Geoff Tindle
                   (Gospel Garden)

Sax   Darrly Adams

Vocals   John Parker (Peighton Checks)

Trumpet   Ian Gray replaced by Rod Temperton
                   (John D Puhliant)

Potted History: 'THE HAMMER'

The 'Hammer' had evolved out of 'Roger Blooms Hammer'. A professional band, they gigged all over the country, played the infamous Top Ten Club in Hamburg and toured Denmark. By mid 1969 the group were down to a four-piece of Aisthorpe, Saye, Parker and Temperton and changed their name to Spreadeagle. Keyboard player Rod Temperton went on to join 'Jessie (Jessie Litton) and the Gang', and then after answering an advert in the Melody Maker joined 'Heatwave' who had a big hit with the song Rod wrote for them 'Boogie Nights'. After moving to America he also amazingly co-wrote 'Thriller' with Michael Jackson plus several of the songs off Jackson's 'Off The Wall' Album. Often seen performing with Quincy Jones, today he lives in Los Angeles, and is one of the highest earning songwriters of all time.

HARVEY	1968 - 1969	EAST RIDING
BROOKES		
SKUTTLE		

Drums   Ken Markham

Bass   Pete Scarfe replaced by Bruce Kirton

Organ   Paul Lloyd replaced by Mike Freebean

Lead   Dave Smith

Vocals   Harvey Brookes

Potted History: 'HARVEY BROOKES SKUTTLE'

Originally called 'Harvey Brookes Sack of Woe'. A busy professional band who toured Denmark and played support to lots of top groups at the Brid Spa, including 'Dave Berry and the Cruisers'. The group eventually evolved into 'Roger Blooms Axe'. I remember attempting to audition for 'Harvey Brookes Skuttle', turning up in the village of Long Riston one summer evening in 1968. I was toying with the idea of changing to the bass and had bought an extremely heavy 'wooden' electric bass guitar manufactured by 'Fenton Weil'. It weighed a ton and looked like a tree trunk with iron girders for strings, it also played like one. Thankfully, I never had to use it in anger, for after being politely 'examined' and looked over by various members of the band, I didn't (as a short haired, thin, boyish looking 16 year old) appear to fit the image they were looking for and never had to get my bass out of the van.

HENRY STREET JAILERS	circa 1965	COTTINGHAM

Drums	Mike Kitching (Crestas)
Bass	Adrian Gatie (Aces)
Lead	Tony Gosling (Small Four)
Lead	Pete Green (Mods)
Vocals	Val Buffrey (Scorpions)
Potted History:	'THE HENRY STREET JAILERS'

The membership of the Henry Street Jailers reads like a potential supergroup with the various members having, even by this time, probably over 25 years experience of the local group scene between them. Despite gigging locally the group would appear to have suffered from 'arrested' development'.

HERBIES ii's circa 1967 SCARBOROUGH

Drums Ernie Dickenson

Bass John Pearson

Guitar Graham Hopwood (Iguanas)

Guitar Tom Ward (Kerbsiders)

Potted History: 'HERBIES ii's'

Herbies ii's were one of the popular Scarborough bands of 1967. The group concentrated on close harmony numbers especially songs by the Beach Boys. They gigged at local village halls and supported several top groups at Hull's Skyline Ballroom including the Kinks. The group didn't last long and Tom Ward went on to join the Purple Mist.

HIGH NUMBERS   **1965 - 1966**   **HULL**

Drums   Robb Welton

Bass   James Stewart

Rhythm   Mike Tyson

Lead   Steve Howden (Gondoliers)

Vocals   Stewart Inness

Potted History   'THE HIGH NUMBERS'

The High Numbers played rock and soul music. Their vocalist, Stuart Inness, was 6' 7" tall. A 'mod' group they appear to have had a very short life. Their name was probably stolen from that other mod band, the 'Who', whose original name was also the 'High Numbers'. Steve Howden and Robb Welton later joined the 'Night People' while Stewart Inness became a DJ.

HIGH VOLTAGE   **circa 1967**   **BRIDLINGTON**

Drums   Roger Scales

Bass   John Lawn

Rhythm   David Berriman

Piano   Leonard Foster

Potted History: 'HIGH VOLTAGE'

Originally called the 'Unknowns', High Voltage played the Top 10 at clubs and dances including the Beverley Regal. They also supported the Alan Price Set at the Brid Spa. Talented piano player Len Foster later formed the Exodus.

HONEYS	1967 - 1968	HULL

Drums   Linda Thompson

Bass   Betty Beaumont

Lead   Margaret Wedgner

Organ   Merle Prior

Potted History: 'THE HONEYS'

The Honeys included three ex-members of 'Mandy and The Girlfriends'. Busy gigging locally, a highlight of their career was touring the American Army bases in Germany. Barry Donald, and Tony Auld of the Fabians joined the Honeys shortly before the group split. Later, together with Margaret Wegner they formed 'Sugar 'n' Spice'.

HORNETS	**circa 1961**	**YORK**
Drums	Ron Illing	
Bass	Barry Wood	
Lead	Ron Goodall	
Vocals	Gerry Harrison	
Potted History:	'GERRY B AND THE HORNETS'	

In the late 1950s, drummer Ron Illing was playing in a skiffle group but was shortly afterwards called up for his National Service. When he came out two years later he formed the 'Hornets'. Typical gigs at the time included York's Whitehouse Pub. The Hornets played early rock songs such as 'Poetry In Motion'. The group wore maroon jackets, white shirts and black bow ties. Gerry wore a pink suit and white 'winkel-picker' boots. Most of the groups members went on to form the Rockafellas.

HULLABALLOOS   1964 - 1966   HULL

Drums   Harry Dunn

Bass   Geoff Mortimer

Lead   Andy Woonton

Guitar/   Ronald Mitchell (alias Ricky Knight)
Vocals

Potted History: 'THE HULLABALLOOS'

While the Aces were the first Hull group of the 1960s to sign a recording contract, it could be said that the Hullaballoos were the first Hull recording group to really receive the 'star treatment'.

The Hullaballoos were born out of 'Ricky Knight and the Crusaders'. The Crusaders had been fortunate to be spotted by the Chichester Constables of Burton Constable Stately Hall, while playing a gig in the village of Sproatley. Liking what they heard, the Chichester Constables agreed to manage the group and set about changing their image. The first thing they did was to get them to grow their hair really long, especially for the time and then to dye it blond. Now appearing like four blonde 'Mop Tops' the name of the group was changed to the 'Hullaballoos'. John Chicester Constable then arranged for various A and R men to come and see the group (who rehearsed in a riding stable at Burton Constable Hall which was later also used to stage all-night rock concerts) and they eventually signed a recording contract with EMI and the American label 'Roulette Records'.

The Hullaballoos made their first recordings in the autumn of 1964. This was at EMI's Abbey Road studios (before Abbey Road was really made famous by the Beatles) and Malcolm Addey (producer for the Shadows) produced them. The group recorded around 12 tracks during the session, amongst which were covers of songs such as Party Doll, Learning The Game, Rave On, That'll Be The Day and I'm Gonna Love You Too. They also recorded a number of original songs few people in the UK had at this time heard.

A tour of the USA was then arranged for the group and they took their Road Manager, Michael Moore (wearing his trademark Deer Stalker hat) with them. Following in the Beatles footsteps, when the Hullaballoos arrived at New York's Kennedy Airport, unbeknown to them the hype had really been built up about them on local radio stations and there were fans, photographers and reporters waiting there to see them arrive. Just like the Beatles, Rolling Stones and Animals a few months earlier, they were driven to their hotel in limousines and given a police escort.

The following day the Hullaballoos appeared on 'Murray the K's Radio Show at the Fox Theatre in Brooklyn along with Ben E King, the Shirelles, the Drifters, the Zombies, the Nashville Teens, the Shangri-Las, and Patti La Belle and the Bluebells. The group played a three number spot.

The Hullaballoos also recorded at various times in New York for Roulette Records using one of the many independent US studios. The first time was in the January of 1965 and also again in the Easter of that year.

Ron Mitchell (Ricky Knight) suggests that it is easy to distinguish between the Abbey Road and the US recordings by the warmth and the roundness of the bass and rhythm guitars. The US recordings also had this sound, which was the Hullaballoos sound, but it was equalised out in an abortive

The Hullaballoos (Hull - 1965)

253

attempt to get the popular 'clangy' Beatles sound of the times and therefore the US recordings tend to be extremely thin in these areas.

Ron also points out that all the recordings in those days were 'live' in as much as all instruments were played and recorded and all vocals were sung and recorded at the same time on 4-track monaural machines - not for them the luxury of 24 track stereo decks. Similarly they did not enjoy the services of a musical producer such as George Martin and Ron feels that at times this shows.

The Hullaballoos formed part of the 1960s 'British Invasion' of America, they visited the States three times. On their first visit in December 1964 they stayed for six weeks, but because of visa problems, a planned tour had to be cancelled and their performances were limited to the Fox Theatre in Brooklyn and various TV appearances on top shows such as Shindig and one appropriately titled 'Hullabaloo'. In March 1965 the Hullaballoos went back to the US for further TV appearances and soon afterwards they returned again for a stay of about six months. This was in May 1965 and this time they played the Paramount Theatre in Times Square, more television shows and a six week tour with Gene Pitney's 'Shower of Stars'. Brian Hyland was also on the tour. The Hullaballoos then headlined on their own tour of dance hall size venues. The tours took in a line from New York to Savannah in Georgia, across to Memphis, up to Bismarck North Dakota and back to New York - basically the East Coast and Mid West with a swift visit to LA and Hollywood. Screaming girls would crowd outside theatres where the Hullaballoos were playing and they would often be mobbed as they tried to escape. The group also made further appearances on popular American television shows 'Shindig' and 'Hullabaloo'.

The Hullaballoos released three singles in the UK (all of which failed to chart) and four singles in America. Their first single, 'I'm Gonna Love You Too' reached No. 56 in the US charts while their second 'Did You Ever' crept to No. 74. They also recorded a album with the cover featuring a picture of the group standing on the staircase of Burton Constable Hall. A further album was produced of them live on the Hullabaloo TV show. Both albums featured several Buddy Holly covers.

The group also appeared on TV in Britain on pop shows such as 'Thank Your Lucky Stars'. Despite their apparent success, the Hullaballoos were never as popular in this country as they were in America. Their last single 'Learning the Game' was only released in the USA where it peaked in the Singles Chart at 121. Ronald Mitchell (Ricky Knight) left the band in 1965 "disillusioned" and was replaced by Michael Wayne from London (who was later a member of 'Juniors Eyes' like Hull's John Cambridge). But the rot had clearly set in and with further changes in line-up (which included John Cambridge joining on the drums) it wasn't long before the group disbanded altogether.

In the 1970s, Debbie Harry of Blondie, who as a teenager had liked the Hullaballoos Hollyesq version of 'I'm Gonna Love You Too' so much, that she recorded it herself. Sting of the Police is also thought to have got the idea for dying his hair blond from the Hullaballoos. Most of the Hullaballoos original recordings were recently re-released on CD.

Some of Ron Mitchell's (Ricky Knight's) favourite memories of those times include meeting many of his musical heroes - names that had previously been only on a record label were accepting the Hullaballoos as peers. The Hullaballoos particular liked their appearances in New York with the Hollies when they performed together at the Paramount Theatre in Times Square. Allan Clarke, the Hollies singer and drummer Bobby Elliot were apparently both fun loving guys and before the show both of them were crawling about on the darkened concert hall floor locked in mortal combat with the Hullaballoos. Each of them had powerful toy guns and were shooting crazy foam at one another. What Allan Clarke didn't realise was that there was a New York cop stood guiding the stage door, and when he shot his crazy foam at Ron Mitchell, it missed and the whole lot shot down a stairwell and landed on the cop. Ron quickly made himself scarce but Allan was unaware of where the foam had landed and only became aware of it when he looked up from the floor to see a large irate 'foam covered' New York cop looming over him.

One of Ron's most indelible memories is of seeing Diana Ross at the NBC Television Studios. He recalls that in those days the groups would spend three days filming and rehearsing before the actual live television show. When the Hullaballoos turned up for the first day of rehearsals, the Supremes were running through their numbers for the show. As the Hullaballoos entered the studio, Diana Ross looked up from the microphone and for one moment her eyes met and stayed with Ron's and he remembers her as being 'sensuality personified'!

Ron recalls that one of the funniest moments in touring America was on the Gene Pitney 'Shower Of Stars' Tour. On the day in question the tour bus had dropped off the entourage of pop stars and returned to Chicago for its fortnightly servicing. The driver had arranged to pick up the pop stars later that day at a meeting place down a certain street on the outskirts of Chicago. Unfortunately, the driver was late in returning and the entourage of stars stood in a queue patiently waiting. These included Gene Pitney, Brian Hyland, the Ronettes, Bobby Goldsboro, the Hullaballoos and Gary Lewis and the Playboys. Gradually, the locals began to notice that there was a host of pop stars in their presence and a crowd began to gather. The crowd gradually grew larger and larger and eventually the Chicago Police were called. Quickly reviewing the situation it appeared to the police that the ones causing the problem must be the four 'blond' mop tops from England. So they arrested the Hullaballoos and took them down to the local Court House where apparently the various members ran amok until they were eventually released.

Another great memory Ron has is of the Peppermint Lounge in New York (home of the Twist) when he played rhythm guitar in a scratch band with assorted members of the Nashville Teens and the Zombies.

But perhaps the gig that stands out most in his memory is when the Hullaballoos played at the McCormick Place in Chicago - the Hullaballoos set up in the orchestra pit while the support bands were playing. When the time came for them to appear on stage they came up in total darkness and just as they hit the opening guitar lick to the blues-rocker 'Talkin' 'Bout You', the spots came on and the audience erupted! "We played out of our skins that night - we were so loud that when we got off the stage we couldn't hear a thing. Somebody once said that nobody should be louder or having more fun than the band - it's true!"

The Hullaballoos (Hull - 1965)

Discography:

Singles:

'I'm Gonna Love You Too' c/w 'Why Do Fools Fall In Love'
1964   COLUMBIA DB7392

'I'll Show You How To Love' c/w 'Did You Ever'
1965   COLUMBIA DB7558

'Don't Stop' c/w 'I Wont Turn Away Now'
1965   COLUMBIA DB7626

'Learning The Game'
1965   COLUMBIA (Only released in the USA)

Albums:

'England's Newest Singing Sensations' 1965 Roulette R25297

'Hullaballoos On Hullabaloo' 1965   Roulette R25310

'Hullaballoos & Hullabaloo' (CD) 1995   BLACKMAIL REP4593

(The CD combines all of the tracks from The Hullaballoos two albums and also includes all of their singles)

Beware/I Couldn't Get Along Without You/Did You Ever/If You Don't Know By Now/Can't You Tell/Party Doll/I'll Show You How To Love/Every Night/Why Do Fools Fall In Love/Wouldn't You Like To Know/Who Do You Think You're Fooling/I'm Gonna Love You Too/I Won't Turn Away Now/Rave On/I Got This Feeling/Better Change Your Ways/You Were There/Never Ever Will/Learning The Game/Don't Stop/My Heart Keeps Telling Me/That'll Be The Day/Don't Cha Know/It's About Time!

HUTCH   1961 - 1970   SCARBOROUGH

Potted History: 'JOHN HUTCHINSON'

Singer, songwriter, guitarist John Hutchinson, better known as 'Hutch' began his rock career as a member of the Tennesseans, a powerful three piece R & B group well ahead of their time. In 1965 he left the Tennesseans and moved to Sweden where he had a solo hit record with the Bob Dylan song 'It Ain't Me Babe' and became known over there as the Swedish 'Donovan'. Returning to England in 1966, Hutch rejoined the Tennesseans until they finally split. He then went to London where he heard from Marquee Club owner Harold Pendleton that a guy named David Bowie was looking for a guitarist. He first phoned, and then met Bowie, who impressed by Hutch's Swedish clothes invited him to join his newly forming backing group the 'Buzz'. The Buzz had a residency at London's Marquee Club at the height of the Swinging Sixties' and they appeared with Bowie on Television's Ready, Steady, Go. They also recorded several songs with Bowie most of which are included on the album 'London Boys'. After the Buzz broke-up Hutch went to Canada and on his return was asked by David Bowie to join him and Bowie's then girlfriend. 'Hermione Farthingale', in an outfit called 'Feathers'. This made its debut at London's Round House in 1968. They then performed on the local College circuit and also played a gig at London's Middle Earth Club. Hutch also appeared with Bowie and Farthingale in the short promotional film 'Love You Till Tuesday' which was later released on video. After a further gig at the Roundhouse supporting the Who, Hermione Farthingale left Feathers and Bowie and Hutch continued as a duo for a few more gigs including a short tour with Marc Bolan's T Rex. During this period Hutch also recorded several demo tracks with Bowie including the particularly memorable song 'Life is a Circus' written by an American group called Diijo which Hutch later performed on stage. He also sang the part of 'Ground Control' to David Bowie's 'Major Tom' on the first recording of the future hit 'Space Oddity'! Which Bowie had purposely written for them to perform as a duo. But due to financial pressures Hutch had to leave Bowie and return to Yorkshire. He was then very busy on the local scene, playing acoustic guitar and performing with bass support, Leonard Cohen numbers and songs such as the Beatles 'Blackbird' and an haunting version of the Joni Mitchell number 'Michael From Mountains'.

In 1973, David Bowie recalled 'Hutch' back into his ranks inviting him to join the Spiders From Mars (playing 12 string guitar) on their 1973 'Aladdin Sane' Tour of Japan. He also appeared with David Bowie at Ziggy's legendary final 'live' appearance, which was filmed at the Hammersmith Odeon by D A Pennebaker who had directed the great Bob Dylan movie 'Don't Look Back.' In the mid 1970s Hutch formed his own original group called 'Hutch and Its Easy' this group featured another ex-Bowie member, drummer John Cambridge. The group made several TV appearances in the North East. After this disbanded, in 1979 Hutch formed the highly acclaimed 'American Echoes' who released the single 'Las Vegas' and they too made both radio and television appearances with the record becoming Dave Lee Travis's 'Record of the Week'. Today, Hutch can be seen performing both home and abroad with regular gigs in York and Scarborough.

Discography:

'Space Oddity'	'The Marquee 30 Legendary Years Album' Polydor
American Echoes	'Las Vega' c/w 'I Can't Believe It' Mercury/Blueport -
Video:	'Love You Till Tuesday' Polygram 040 313-2

Bowie and Hutch (1968)

John Hutchinson

IDES OF MARCH 1965 -1967   **HULL**

Drums   Steve Pollard

Bass   Trevor Parker

Lead   Paul Leslie

Vocals   Mike D'Arcy

Potted History: 'THE IDES OF MARCH'

Originally know as the Rascals, the Ides of March appeared on
Television's weekly talent show 'Opportunity Knocks'. They
didn't last long, which was probably good, as there was already
a more nationally know group called the 'Ides of March' by this
time.

IGUANAS   1965 - 1967   SCARBOROUGH

Drums	John Hall replaced by Ernie Dickinson
Bass	John Pearson
Rhythm/Lead	Bri Sharpe replaced by Graham Hopwood
Keyboards	Sandy Johnson (The Methods)
Vocals	Geoff "Monster Mad" Pearson
Potted History:	'THE IGUANAS'

The Iguanas were formed in 1965. Geoff Pearson came from the duo - the Sundowners to join them. The group soon became popular and were booked into the Cricketers Arms, Scarborough for 32 weeks. They also appeared at Youth Clubs, WMCs and dances. The Iguana's played a regular gig at New Town Billingham and at the Brid Spa where they supported such groups as the Nashville Teens, the Small Faces and Long John Baldry. They also played at the Scarborough Spa where they supported the North East's top band the 'Blue Chips'. Graham Hopwood later joined Herbies ii's and John Hall emigrated to South Africa. Geoff and John Pearson formed the Mark Slade Set which proved even more popular than the Iguanas This comprised of Geof Pearson (vocals), John Pearson (Bass), Sandy Johnson (Organ), Calvin Turner (Drums). Geof says that they were the first group to use an electric pianonetter and later a Vox Continental electric keyboard. The Mark Slade Set catered for a more sophisticated age group. They became the regular band to play at the Five Acres Restaurant, East Heslerton and the customers rolled in and it became 'the' place to be. The group split in the mid 1970s.

IMPACT   circa 1967   **HULL/YORK**

Drums   John Costello

Bass   Jed Vivian

Lead   John Green

Keyboards   Steve Major

Potted History: 'THE IMPACT'

The Impact was a great 'mod' sounding name. The Hull version of the Impact didn't last too long with some of its members going off to form West 28 Street. Another version (adding an 's') of the Impacts was from York and they were around for quite a while. A five piece combo they were fronted by Adrian Kaye. They later changed their name to the Corvettes and played such York venues as the Imperial. The group were apparently known for their wild stage performances!

IMPS	1964 –1966	SCUNTHORPE

Drums   Chris Ellerton

Bass   John "Boot" Ancliffe replaced by Craig Austin

Rhythm   Bill Gibson

Lead   Craig Austin replaced by
Greg Tomlinson (Chechakos)

Vocals   Fred Havercroft replaced by Iain Matthews

Potted History: 'THE IMPS'

The Imps played Chuck Berry, Hollies, Cliff Bennett, Mersey Beat and R & B numbers. They got their gigs usually by word of mouth/hustling and through various agents. Local gigs included the Scunthorpe Jazz Workshop and local pubs and clubs around the area. The Imps were named after the 'Lincoln Imp' but they eventually changed their name to the 'Craze' after discovering that there was already a Lincoln group called the Imps. Craig Austin and Greg Tomlinson later joined another Scunthorpe recording outfit, the Dimples. Iain Matthews, who was originally from Barton-on-Humber, moved to London and after a succession of groups formed recording band Matthews Southern Comfort. They produced a brilliant haunting version of the Joni Mitchell song 'Woodstock' which was a huge hit, putting Joni's version well into the shade. Later, Iain moved to the USA where he both recorded and produced groups. Today he can be seen performing with Plainsong. After a very successful Millennium Mega Gig reunion concert (the second and third ones also sold out) the Imps, together with various members of the Dimples produced a absolutely stunning studio album of Sixties' classics. Many of the tracks sound better than the originals. The CD was available from V8 Music.

The Dimples/Imps   V8 Music   CD   2000

The Imps (Scunthorpe - 1965)

The Incas (Scarborough - 1965)

The Incas (Scarborough - 1965)

INCAS	1964 - 1967	SCARBOROUGH

Drums   Ken Thomas replaced by Dave Rose (Moonshots)

Bass   Graham Trousdale replaced by Pete Little, Pete Hargreaves

Rhythm   Bob Woodyatt

Lead   Brian Thompson

Vocals/Harmonica   Chris Bagnall

Other replacement members WEM Brookes (in London) Graeme Flinton (in London)

Potted History: 'THE INCAS'

The history of the band goes back to 1963 when they were known as the 'Blue Stars'. The Incas were born in 1964, they became well known over both North and East Ridings and local gigs included the Scarborough Spa. After playing with the Pretty Things they changed their style of playing and began including songs such as Jimmie Reed's 'Shame' and Howling Wolf's 'Smokestack Lighting' in their repertoire. Pete Little then became their Road Manager. The Incas were winners of the 1964 Hornsea Beat Contest and also appeared at the legendary 2 i's coffee bar in London. In March 1966 they were voted the top band in Scarborough. Later that year, while playing in Hornsea, at the Floral Hall, they met ex-pirate radio DJ Mike Berry. Berry persuaded them to make a demo-disc of a song called 'Outside World'. This proved a great success and in October 1966, after being offered a recording contract, most of the band went down to London, but Dave Rose and Pete Hargreaves decided to stay on in Scarborough. In London, replacement members were found in Graeme Flinton from Scarborough and Londoner Wem Brooks. The Incas then recorded the song 'One Night Stand' which was written for them by the Small Faces. It sold 15,000 copies. Unfortunately, the band arrived back in Scarborough in February 1967 and disbanded. Chris Bagnall joined the 'New Religion' previously known as the 'Ox'. In December 1967 Chris joined the 'Spell'. On 12 March 1969 the Incas came together again for a one night stand at Scarborough's Candlelight Club. During the 70s and 80s Chris and Bob Woodyatt formed and toured the clubs as a duo. Sadly, Chris Bagnall died in 1988 and Brian Thompson died in 1993. Bob Woodyatt is today joined with Ian Fletcher and they sing around the pubs.

Discography:

'One Night Stand' c/w 'I'll Keep Holding On'
Parlophone R5551   1966

INSECTS circa 1963 **HULL**

Drums   Bob Welton

Bass   John Tomlinson (Davy Jones and The
   Buccaneers)

Lead   Mick Ronson

Potted History: 'THE INSECTS'

Several groups in the early Sixties had the idea of naming
themselves after 'creepy crawlies'. The Beatles had originally
cribbed their name from one of their heroes, Buddy Holly and
the 'Crickets'. The 'Insects' in turn was probably a crib on the
'Beatles'. The Insects were a group formed by local teenagers
and included the first identified sighting of Mick Ronson on the
group scene. John Tomlinson left the outfit apparently due to
lack of work and took up a job at a holiday camp. Mick Ronson
moved on to the Mariners.

JAGUARS	1963 - 1965	HULL
Drums	John Pearson	
Bass	Allen Bowes	
Guitar	Pete Shally	
Guitar	Jim Kitching	
Potted History:	'THE JAGUARS'	

While also popular on the clubs, local dance gigs included the Beverley Regal and the Ferryboat Inn at Hessle. The Jaguars sported matching Burns guitars and were managed by one of the fathers of a band member. They were yet another local group to produce a demo disc at the Malconi Studios on Hessle Road. The Jaguars supported Jimmy Powell and the Five Dimensions when they appeared in Hull, a group who around this time featured a young 'Rooster haired' Rod Stewart on harmonica and vocals.

JELLY ROLL   *circa 1967*   HULL

Drums   Keith Stutt

Bass   John Bentley

Lead   Ian Bolder

Lead   Keith 'Ched' Cheesman

Potted History: 'THE JELLY ROLL BLUES BAND'

Named after famous blues piano player Jelly Roll Morton this band contained the first sighting of the Bolder brothers on the scene. Local gigs included the Beverley Regal. The group later changed their name to 'Flesh'.

JOHNNY BALLAD GROUP	1963 –1968	SCUNTHORPE

Drums	Frank Coult
Bass	Mal Evans
Rhythm	Barry Garner
Lead	Johnny Robinson
Piano	Mel Oliver
Vocals	Johnny Dobbs
Other Members:	John Hill (Lead)
Potted History:	'THE JOHNNY BALLAD GROUP'

This group was formed by some of the former members of the Cadillacs. Other Scunthorpe groups at this time included the Dimples, the Imps, the Nightriders and the Checkakos.

The original Johnny Ballad Four consisted of Frank Coult, Mal Evans, Johnny Dobbs and Barry Garner. They supported Little Richard when he appeared at the Scunthorpe Drill Hall in 1964. Despite being huge fans of Little Richard, that night they found him to quite arrogant and he even turned up without any amplifiers and had to borrow theirs!

KARAELIUS	*circa* **1970**	**HULL**

Drums   Frank Preston (Variations)

Bass   Ray Hussey   (Variations)

Organ   Nigel Dalton   (Variations)

Lead   Paul 'Prof' Sutton   (Variations)

Potted History: 'KARAELIUS'

Karaelius was the new name for the 'Variations' after the tragic death of vocals Noel Carroll. The new group was named after the 'Karaelius Suite', a favourite piece of music. They were very busy on the local scene but never really recaptured their former glory. Paul Sutton later toured with the Michael Chapman Band and I saw both him and Michael gigging at the Newcastle Mayfair with the rest of the band including Ainsley Dunbar on Drums and Clem Clempson on bass. The 'Prof' also appeared on Michael Chapman's live 1975 album 'Pleasures of The Street' and has also recently recorded again with Michael on the album 'Dreaming Outloud'.

KAREMA 4   **circa 1968**   **HULL**

Drums   Dave Bradfield (Gary Landis and the Set)

Bass   Robin Taylor (Skysounds)

Lead   Alan Morris (Objeks)

Vocals   Janet Hassan (Skysounds)

Potted History: 'KAREMA 4'

Formed by very experienced musicians on the local scene. The
'Karema 4' were resident at the Cave Castle Hotel and at the
Hull Locarno Ballroom. They also auditioned for television's
'Opportunity Knocks'. Vocals, Janet Hassan, had previously
sang with Hull groups Purple Haze, Twiggy's People, and the
Variations. Whilst a teenager at school she had also written the
lyrics for a potential 'Twist' record and sent them off to London
to musical Impresario 'Norrie Paramor. After a few weeks she
received a request from 'Norrie' asking to see the music.
Unfortunately, she didn't follow it up!

KEITH HERD RHYTHM GROUP   1963 - 1965   HULL

Drums   Calvin Winetroube

Bass   Alan Turner, Tony Luke

Keyboards   Keith Herd

Vocals   Keith Kelly

Potted History: KEITH HERD RHYTHM GROUP

Keith Herd began his musical career at the age of five and by the time he was 17 could play six instruments. The Keith Herd Group had evolved out of 'Keith Kelly and the Crowd' and were managed by Cleethorpe's agent Mark Yale. A very popular and busy group on the local scene, this version of the Keith Herd Group also included recording artist Keith Kelly. In 1966 Keith Herd set-up his 'Fairview Studios' in Willerby and for over 30 years has been responsible for recording each new wave of local groups who attempt the often 'perilous' journey on 'the road to rock'. Keith Herd also wrote many songs in the Sixties' including some with Barry Paterson and Rick Kemp and he often got local outfits to record them. In 1968 The Keith Herd Group evolved into Johnny Small and the Little People

KELLY KEITH   **1960 - 1965**   **SELBY/YORK**

Potted History: 'KEITH KELLY'

Keith Kelly had originally started out with York's 'John Barry Seven' and had then gone solo. After hanging out at the legendary '2 i's Coffee bar in London (where groups like the Shadows were spotted) he too, also gained himself a recording contract. He then made several records which were released on Parlophone. A couple of these were minor chart successes. He also appeared on some of the early Television 'rock' shows including the 'Six-Five-Special' and 'Saturday Club'. (The Six-Five-Special had actually been televised from Hull's Continent Theatre on Anlaby Road, in 1959). After his initial success Kelly returned to Hull where he took Cleethorpe's agent, Martin Yale as his manager and joined the Keith Herd Group on vocals. Martin Yale through London Agent Bunny Lewis later heard a song entitled 'Laurie' which he was convinced Kelly should record. Yale then managed to get Kelly a contract to release it on CBS. Unfortunately, the record failed to chart.

Discography:

'Tease Me' c/w 'Ooh-La-La'
Parlophone R4640   1960
'Listen Little Girl' c/w 'Uh-Huh'
Parlophone   R4676   1960
'With You' c/w 'You'll Break My Heart'
Parlophone R4713   1960
'Cold White and Beautiful'
Parlophone R4797   1961
'Save Your Love For Me' c/w 'Laurie'
CBS 201794   1965

KERBSIDERS   circa 1966   HUNMANBY

Drums   Dave Spink

Bass   Mick Metcalf replaced byLes Crockett

Lead   Tom Pickersgill

Guitar/Vocals   Tom Ward

Sax   John Pitts

Potted History: 'THE KERBSIDERS'

The Kerbsiders played Kinks, Elvis and Chuck Berry songs. Other members included Dave Ayre. Tom Ward went on to play with 'Beat Cult', 'Herbies ii's and the Purple Mist. The Kerbsiders supported the Hullaballoos at the Scarborough Spa and also the McGill Five, whose record 'Mockingbird Hill' I remember buying from Boyes. This wasn't the original record but a recording on 'Cannon Records', a label on which you got six 'sound-a-like' tracks for only 1/6d!

KING BEES   1963 - 1965   HULL

Drums   Trevor Marriot

Bass   John Thundercliffe replaced by
                 Brian Hairsine (Batmen)

Rhythm   Ralph Taylor

Vocals   Alan Coldbeck

Potted History;   'THE KING BEES'

The King Bees had one of the most recognisable group vans in
Hull. Bill Wyman of the Rolling Stones gave them their name,
probably backstage at the Hull City Hall when the Stones
appeared there in 1963. When he had heard their original name,
'Alan Dean and the Soundtracks', Bill thought that it sounded
so terrible that he suggested that the group change it to the
'King Bees'. Not that this was a very original name as there were
seemingly dozens of groups called the 'King Bees' at that time,
including one in Scarborough, one in Grimsby and one with
David Bowie in it! The band originally played R & B and were
resident for a while at the 'Kon Tiki' Club, Whitefriargate. Mick
Ronson was also for a very short time a 'member' of their line-
up. The King Bees turned professional at the end of 1964.
Perhaps in response to the 'Hullaballoos' success in growing
their hair long and dying it blond, The King Bees claimed to be
the first local band with 'short hair, dyed black'! The King Bees
played regularly at the Beverley Regal, Hessle Town Hall Beat
Nights and had out of town gigs as far away as Manchester's
Cavern Club. The group also tried writing their own material
and made a demo disc of cover versions at the Malconi Studios
in Hull. They sent copies of the disc to several London Record
companies but it failed to arouse interest. Alan Coldbeck, on

vocals had a 'talking blues' style of singing and had also been a member of the Rascals and the Mods before, sadly, he was killed in a car crash.

The Kraakans (Scunthorpe - 1964)

LAZY POKER　　　**1969 - 1970**　　　**SCARBOROUGH**

Drums　　　　　　Roger Milner (Cyclones)

Bass　　　　　　　Pete Warwick

Lead　　　　　　　Richard Sargent (Cyclones)

Keyboards　　　　Denis Jaconelli

Vocals　　　　　　Paul Murray
　　　　　　　　　Pete Rennison

Potted History:　　'LAZY POKER'

Lazy Poker played strictly commercial numbers as well as blues and soul. Paul Murray and Pete Rennison were finished by the summer of 1969 which left a four-piece. Pete Warwick became lead vocalist with Denis Jaconelli on backing vocals. Richard Sargent remembers that there were so many good groups around in the late 1960s and the Peter Pitts Agency in Scarborough managed most of them. Lazy Poker were playing at least 4 nights every week at village halls at Pickering, Malton, Kirbymoorside and Whitby. The highlights of their career included supporting 'Marmalade' and 'Three Dog Night' at Brid Spa in August 1969. Lazy Poker had an incredible following in the Scarborough area. Richard remembers playing a gig at the 1st Scarborough Scout Group Hut at Northstead, Scarborough in September 1969. He was late in arriving and they were due on in 10 minutes. When he got there, there were so many people that the place was full and they weren't letting any more in. About 50 people were outside being turned away. Richard say's that it was 'incredible'. It took him 20 minutes to convince the doorman that he was a member of the band before he let him in!

LIMITED COMPANY   circa 1967   **BEVERLEY**

Drums

Guitar   Stan Leach

Guitar   Paul Bullock

Potted History: 'LIMITED COMPANY'

A Beverley group who included several Beatle numbers in their set and had great harmonies. Local gigs included the Beverley Youth Centre.

LISTEN circa 1969 **HORNSEA**

Drums Gary Burroughs (Pink)

Bass

Lead

Potted History: 'LISTEN'

This is the group future recording engineer Gary Burroughs formed on leaving the Pink. One of Listen's claims to fame was playing support to two ex-members of 'Methuselah' at Hornsea Youth Club. The two people in question had recently formed a folk duo and this was one of their tentative first gigs. The duo were billed as 'Blondel'. Listen's drummer would go on to join 'Blitzkrieg'.

**LITTLE
DEDICATION**   circa 1967   **YORK**

Drums   Dave Vickers (The Fix)

Bass   Colin Whotton (The Crawdaddies)

Rhythm   Paul Hurworth

Lead   Kel' McKensie

Vocals   Mick Thompson

Potted History: 'LITTLE DEDICATION'

Colin Whotton had been a member of the Crawdaddies and the
Counterpoints before joining Little Dedication. Local gigs
included the Tramways Club in York and St Peters Youth Club
in Scarborough.

LITTLE PEOPLE   **1968 - 1969**   **HULL**

Drums   Mike Heap

Bass   Rick Kemp

Organ   Keith Herd

Lead   Steve Trice (Small Four)

Vocals   John Small (Small Four)

Potted History: 'JOHNNY SMALL AND THE LITTLE
                    PEOPLE'

This band underwent various name changes including calling
themselves the 'Johnny Small Society'. The group appeared on
Television's weekly talent show 'Opportunity Knocks'. Keith
Herd's Willerby based Recording Studio has over the years
produced demo tapes for thousands of local bands.

LOCOMOTION   *circa 1968*   **EAST RIDING**

Drums   Robin Welton (Night People)

Bass   John Illingworth (Society)

Rhythm   Chris Ford (Society)

Lead/ Vocals   Steve Howden (Night People)

Potted History: 'THE LOCOMOTION'

Prior to this, Steve Howden had been playing with London based recording band the 'Ricochets'. Busy on the local scene, one of the highlights of Locomotion's career was standing in for the 'Yardbirds' when they failed to turn up for their gig at the Brid Spa. Unfortunately, they nearly missed it as they were one of many local bands to be refused to be allowed in to the gig they were playing. After setting their gear up on the stage at the Spa they had gone outside for a breath of fresh air and on their return the bouncers refused to let them back in, due to the way they were dressed! They only managed to make an appearance by someone hearing them hammering on the back doors of the Spa. Other stars the group did support include Geno Washington. Steve Howden left the band to turn professional with York based recording group the 'Roll Movement'. The Roll Movement had themselves played in Hull several times during 1967 supporting both the Allan Bown Set and Geno Washington at the Skyline Ballroom. Later members of Locomotion included Dave Marshall.

LUCIFER   circa 1970   **HULL**

Drums   John Hobson (Dusty Morning)

Bass   Fred Norton (Spanish Leather)

Rhythm   John Lewis (Spanish Leather)

Lead   Paul Jenkins

Vocals   'Tusker'

Potted History: 'LUCIFER'

A group who played their own original progressive rock music. By 1970 a new wave of top rock bands were appearing on the national scene, several with some very influential first albums. Their music would soon be termed 'Heavy Rock'. Black Sabbath were one of this new wave of groups and that year they released their extremely influential first album, its darkness and apparent devil worshipping scenario probably accounted for local band, 'Lucifer's' name. Other influential albums in the same vein around this time included Uriah Heep's 'Very 'Eavy, Very 'Umble', soon to be followed by Deep Purple's 'In Rock' album which featured the classic, 'Child in Time'.

McCOYS	1963 - 1966	SELBY
Drums	Paddy Hannon	
Bass	John Queenan	
Rhythm	Bernard Middleton	
Lead	Mike Soar	
Vocals	Maurice O'Neil	
Vocals	Liz Jackson	
Vocals	Bridie Corabally replaced by Joan Cooper	
Potted History:	'THE McCOYS'	

The McCoys were the beat group that musically put Selby on the map. Fronted by a long-haired, bespectacled, singer going by the name of 'Tosh', the McCoys played R & B, Top Ten and rock 'n' roll. They had quite a following along the East Coast. The boys had originally started up on their own but added the girls to enable them to do a greater variety of numbers. Very popular at the Brid Spa, one of the highlights of their career was playing on the same bill as Little Richard. They also supported several other top groups including the Mersey Beats, Freddie and the Dreamers, and Screaming Lord Sutch and the Savages. The McCoys eventually disbanded due to members getting married and musical differences. Mike Soar and Joan Cooper switched to folk music and Mike, became quite successful. Today, he still manages the Selby Folk Club. Maurice O'Neil has also recently returned to singing.

The McCoys (Selby - 1965)

MAGPIES	1965 - 1969	HOLDERNESS
Original line-up		1968/69 line-up
Drums	Jim Thetford, Pete McLeod	Wayne Nicholls
Bass	Ralph Thetford	Paul Stevenson
Rhythm	Dave Hodgson	Tony Wardill (Organ)
Lead	Stan Bemrose	Stan Bemrose
Vocals	Roger Bloom	Rodd Alexander

Potted History:'THE MAGPIES'

The first identified sighting of Roger Bloom on the local scene. Local Agent Pete McLeod was also at one time a member of the Magpies. Busy in the local area, out of town gigs included the Belle Vue Club in Filey. The later 1968/69 line-up of the group tended more towards the WMCs. Roger Bloom went on to release two singles with his recording group, Roger Blooms Hammer.

MAGPIES	circa 1965	HUTTON CRANSWICK

Drums   Martin Taylor

Guitar   Graham Thompson

Guitar   Howard Teal

Guitar   John Blewitt

Vocals   Scott Barron

Potted History: 'THE MAGPIES'

The Hutton Cranswick version of the Magpies were originally formed to play four or five songs in shows forming part of the "Happy Wanders Concert Party'. These shows were organised by Jean and Melvyn Hopps of Hutton Cranswick. The group played about six shows on a tour taking in Beverley, Hutton Cranswick and Brandesburton. Their repertoire included songs such as 'Glad All Over', 'The Cruel Sea', 'A Groovy Kind Of Love' and 'Bits and Pieces'. Some members of the group are still active on the local music scene.

MAIDEN PRAYER circa 1968   SCARBOROUGH

Drums   Paul West

Bass   Gordon Adams

Rhythm   Stuart Wharton

Lead   Pete Winship

Potted History: 'MAIDEN PRAYER'

One of the many young groups who formed during their final year at school. Like many starting out on 'the road to rock', they couldn't quite decide on a name and within a period of a month had gone from 'Creative Innocence' through to 'Squelch' before finally settling on 'Maiden Prayer'. In the meantime there had been various comings and goings of band members. But at last the group got off the ground with a gig at the local school youth club and later gigs in Scarborough.

MAJESTICS   **circa 1963**   **HULL**

Drums   Jim Simpson

Bass   Brian Buttle

Lead   Frank Ince

Vocals   Benny Marshall

Potted History: 'PETER KING AND THE MAJESTICS'

The Majestics were originally known as 'Rocky Stone and the Stereotones' but changed their name when 'Benny' Marshall joined the band. They started out playing just chart material with no attempt to be original. But after joining Cleethorpe's agent, Martin Yale their musical direction changed. With the rising popularity of R & B, Yale suggested that the group should adopt a much rawer, earthier sounding name such as the 'River Rats' or simply 'Rats' and at the same time change their musical direction to R & B. The group took his advice and changed their name to the Rats.

MAJORITY 1965 - 1971 **HULL**

Drums Don Lill (Mustangs)

Bass Ken Smith (Mustangs)

Rhythm Bob Long (Mustangs)

Lead Roger France (Mustangs)

Vocals Barry Graham (Mustangs)

Potted History: 'THE MAJORITY'

Formerly known as 'Barry Graham and the Mustangs', the Mustangs had turned professional in 1965, changed their name to the 'Majority' and now under top management moved to London. They were resident for a while at several prestigious London clubs including 'Dolly's Club, the Pickwick Club and the 'Playboy Club'. These club audiences would often include members of top rock groups including the Beatles, and the Majority soon wowed them over. Paul McCartney actually once praised the Majority's rearrangement of 'Ticket To Ride' in a national pop paper.

Because of their great four-part harmonies the group were often billed as the British 'Beach Boys'. They became a popular attraction at the debutante balls of the Swingin' Sixties' and were even invited to Paris to play in front of the late Duke and Duchess of Winsor.

Soon after their arrival in London the Majority had secured a recording contract with Decca Records and between 1965 and 1968 released a string of 8 singles. Their first release 'Pretty Little Girl' was voted a 'certain hit' on Television's 'Juke Box

Jury', but true to JBJ form, it wasn't! Apart from recording in their own right the Majority also provided the backing on several Barry Ryan singles including the 1968 near chart-topping classic 'Eloise'. They also played on Ryan's first album, supported him on tour and appeared with him on Television's Simon Dee Show. The group also supported the Beach Boys on tour, which commenced at the London Palladium. In 1968 they played on the same bill as the Byrds. The Majority also made several Television appearances themselves including 'Ready Steady Go'. They were also the group selected to play at the opening night of London's legendary 'Revolution Club' whose members included such luminaries as Jimi Hendrix.

Despite the Majority's apparent success their records were a series of chart misses and both Roger France and Don Lill left the band in 1968 (with Don Lill for a while managing the Rats). The Majority's 1968 single was their last to be released in Britain and in 1970 the group, with only two of their original members remaining, changed their name to 'Majority One'. Basing themselves in France they released a further single. But eventually singer Barry Wigley emigrated to Australia and the group was no more.

What the history of the Majority clearly demonstrates is that despite the fact that you have a great sound, a recording contract, are releasing regular singles, have songs written for you by successful songwriters, are playing premier venues and being seen on Television, then you can still miss out on that ultimate success which consolidates you as a rock 'n' roll star.

A few of the Majority's singles have recently been re-released on compilation albums. The track 'One Third' was included on both the albums 'Diggin' For Gold' and 'The Freak Beat Scene'. 'All Our Christmases' can be found on 'The British Psychedelic Trip, Vol 4. Also, a previously unreleased track entitled 'Time

The Majority (Hull - 1968)

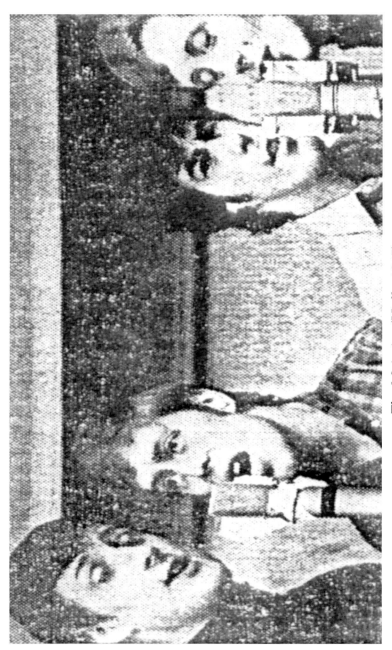

The Majority (Hull - 1965)

Machine Man' has just resurfaced on the CD, 'Psychedelia Vol 4'. The quality is not too good as it was recorded from a crackly unreleased acetate. The group also recently had the track 'One Third' played on BBC North's Top Radio programme 'Sixties Souvenir' and even after all these years it still sounded quite good, if only!

Discography:

'Pretty Little Girl', written by Carter-Lewis of the Ivy League, c/w 'I Don't Wanna Be Hurt No More' July 1995, Decca F12186

'Little Bit of Sunlight', written by Ray Davies of the Kinks, c/w 'Shut Em Down In London Town' Oct 1965, Decca F12271

'We Kiss In A Shadow, written by Rodgers and Hammerstein, c/w 'Ring The Bells, written by Ray Davies of The Kinks, 1966, Decca F12313

'Simplified', c/w 'One Third' 1966, Decca F12453

'To Make A Man' c/w 'Tears Wont Help' Oct 1966, Decca F12504

'I Hear A Rhapsody' c/w 'Wait By The Fire' Feb 1967, Decca F12537

'Running Away With My Baby', c/w 'Let The Joybells Ring' 1967, Decca F12638

'All Our Christmases', Written by Bee Gees Barry and Robin Gibb c/w 'People' 1968 Decca F12727

'Glass Image' c/w 'Friday Man' 1970, London 2534 (Majority One)

MALE SET   **circa 1967**   **SHEFFIELD**

Drums   Dave Bennett

Bass   Richard Hodgson

Lead   Alan Middleton

Vocals   Graham Boone

Potted History: 'THE MALE SET'

The Male set evolved out of Sheffield group the Citizen's. Local gigs included the Beverley Regal.

The Mandrakes (Scarborough - 1969)

MANDRAKES   1965 - 1971   SCARBOROUGH

Drums	Mick Stephenson
Bass	John Standidge replaced by Mick Cook, Derek Gill
Bass/Rhythm	Keith Griffin
Lead	Rob Southwick, Pete Lilley, Rich Hodgson, Allan Black
Vocals	Allen (Robert) Palmer
Other Members:	Maggie, Angela Holmes- Dixon, John Cambridge
Roadies	Rex (Boris) Barker, Andy Barker, Dave Johnson
Potted History:	'THE MANDRAKES'

This group has occasionally been confused with a recording outfit called 'Mandrake Paddlesteamer' but the two are totally unconnected. The Mandrakes were a Scarborough based group with a great sound, they played almost weekly in Hull throughout the Sixties'. In their time, the Mandrakes supported many top stars including Jimi Hendrix, Fleetwood Mac, Traffic, the Who, Amen Corner, Jeff Beck, Fairport Convention, the Move, Geno Washington, Soft Machine, the Tremolos, and many more. Their vocalist, Allen (Robert) Palmer, would go on to become a international rock star.

The Mandrakes were formed in 1965 when all of the original members were in their final year at school. The group initially practised in a chicken hut and their equipment, like so many young groups consisted of just one amp, a microphone, a set of drums and some cheap guitars. The Mandrakes first gig was at St. Peters Youth Club in Scarborough. Their singer was apparently quite shy at this time and spent some of the early gigs lingering behind the PA cabs. The Mandrakes early manager was Ron Gillet (who was the former manager of the Moonshots) and he had first heard about The Mandrakes while giving Allen Palmer a lift home after accidentally knocking him off his bike on the sea front at Scarborough. Despite humble beginnings, the Mandrakes began to quickly gain popularity and within months of forming were playing some of the top Scarborough venues including the Spa and Olympia. Several people on the local scene, including the manager of the Scarborough Spa, had noticed that even at this early stage of their career, the group had something extra, to that of many of their contemporaries. Some of the early songs played by the Mandrakes at this time included the Who's 'Substitute' and the Wilson Pickett track '6345789' on which Allen Palmer allowed Rob Southwick to sing the lead vocals.

In 1966 the Mandrakes, supported the Who at Leeds City Hall. Sandy Sargent, the featured dancer on Ready, Steady, Go! was there and she joined them on stage performing alongside Allen Palmer for one of their numbers. The same year, while playing at one of their regular gigs at a club in Rotherham, screaming fans virtually wrecked the place trying to get to the group backstage.

That year the Mandrakes also played several dates at the Brid Spa including supporting Jimi Hendrix. Backstage with Hendrix, Pete Liley remembers him being quiet and unassuming and he even asked if he could play on Pete's guitar, which he did. Pete also remembers the young Palmer being totally focused knowing exactly what he needed to do.

The Mandrakes (Scarborough - 1965)

305

The Mandrakes (Scarborough - 1968)

Despite their growing success, Pete left the band in 1966 and Rich Hodgson was recruited from Filey group, the Urge after Allen Palmer had been to check him out while playing at St. Peters Youth Club.

In 1967, the Mandrakes supported Jimi Hendrix again, this time at the Skyline Ballroom in Hull. On stage they could be heard playing tracks like the Beatles 'Fool On the Hill', the Bee Gees 'New York Mining Disaster', and Status Quo's 'Pictures of Matchstickmen'. The Mandrakes had begun to gain a reputation for being able to play a song better than the original version. Robert Palmer or Allen as he was then known also did a pseudo 'James Brown impersonation on stage and the Mandrakes were fast becoming known as one of Yorkshire's top Semi-pro groups. That year the group were captured on film by Tyne Tees Television, while playing in Whitley Bay at one of the first Flower Power Festivals. They appeared alongside Scunthorpe's 'Gospel Garden' and a four minute clip of the Mandrakes was the next day shown on the North East Television programme 'Six Five'.

In May 1968 the Mandrakes made a demo tape at Keith Herd's Studio in Willerby. The songs written by Allen Palmer were entitled 'Baby-sitting' and 'It's the Hardest Thing in the World'! The one-day session cost £12.50 and the resultant demo tapes were sent to record companies, Fontana and Apple, but nothing appears to have come of it. Around this time Allan Black joined the band on 12 string guitar after being poached from Bridlington group, the Mutiny. By this stage of their career, the Mandrakes had tired of playing village hall dances and were concentrating more and more on performing at Universities, clubs and other similar type rock gigs where they felt that their music was more appreciated. They were also being seen less and less in Scarborough.

In 1969 the Mandrakes undertook a four week tour of Denmark where they were a big hit. The tour took in 15 dates including 6 nights in Copenhagen. The group also starred in a 15 minute sound film made by their second manager, Brian Cooke and a former Hungarian TV cameraman. Shooting took place at the Skyline Ballroom in Hull in March 1969 and while being used to promote the Denmark Tour the film was made to be shown at the Hull Arts Festival. Both Allen Palmer and Allan Black recorded some flute music for the film, which they gave the title 'The Thief'. On stage the Mandrakes were now performing songs such as the Beatles 'Dear Prudence' , Family's 'Mr Policeman' and 'See-Through Window' and Traffic's 'Heaven Is In Your Mind'. Allen Palmer was also at this time influenced by the vocal inflections on Free's 1968 album 'Tons of Sobs'.

Around this time various members of the Mandrakes and Hull's Rats held secret rehearsals with a view to forming a potential local supergroup called 'Teeth' . But it didn't really work and in the end they didn't do it.

In the summer of 1969, the Mandrakes played alongside the 'Allan Bown' group at the Skyline Ballroom in Hull. Allan Bown was looking for someone to replace their singer 'Jess Roden'. Allen Palmer was interviewed by Bown's Road Manager at Redcar. He then attended a one-day audition at Ronnie Scott's Club in London, and they decided to take him on. The Mandrakes had such a strong fan base in Hull, especially at the Skyline Ballroom and the Civic Hall in Cottingham, that when Palmer made his last appearance at the latter, there was an attempt by local girls to kidnap him as they didn't want him to leave. But Allen Palmer gave up his job as a Process Engineer at the Scarborough Evening News and played his last gig with the Mandrakes at Scarborough's Penthouse on 23 July 1969. In October 1969 the first release of an Allan Bown record to feature Palmer was entitled 'Gypsy Girl'. He also recorded an album

The Mandrakes (Scarborough - 1968)

The Mandrakes (Scarborough - 1967)

with the band but had to use his middle name 'Robert' because Allan Bown didn't want two 'Allan's' (Allen) in the band. In 1970 Palmer joined 'Da Da' who also featured Elkie Brookes on vocals. Together they later formed 'Vinegar Joe' before eventually making it as solo artists. Robert Palmer is seldom seen in Scarborough nowadays!

After Robert Palmer had left the group, with him being such a difficult act to follow, the Mandrakes decided to take on a female vocalist. First, local folk singer/guitarist Angela-Holmes Dixon joined the band (sadly she died recently) but after she left was replaced by a girl called Maggie. Former Rats drummer, John Cambridge also joined the band after leaving David Bowie. The Mandrakes for a short while changed their name to 'Zoffany' - changed it back to the Mandrakes and then disbanded. On the break-up of the Mandrakes Rich Hodgson moved to London where while being employed for the BBC during the day, worked backstage at rock concerts at the Rainbow Theatre during the evening, alongside former Mandrake Roadie, Andy Barker. Meanwhile Allan Black formed a band called 'Milk Train' which toured forces bases in Europe. This became 'Rinky Dink and the Crystal Set' and they secured a contract with EMI cutting an album and a couple of singles before splitting. The Mandrakes Manager, Brian Cooke, was set up in business as a Photographer by Chris Blackwell (Island Records) - His company, 'Visualeyes', produced many famous album sleeves including those by Traffic, Heads Hands and Feet. He successfully built the company up and sold out. Keith Griffin joined the RAF and rose to the rank of Wing Commander flying Phantom F4 fighters before quitting to join Cathay Pacific as a pilot. The Mandrakes Roadie, Andy Barker, went on to Roadie for Ashton, Gardner and Dyke, then Aerosmith before returning to Hull as a Publican.

In December 1994, The Mandrakes came back together for a one-off reunion gig at the 'Stage Door' in Scarborough. Robert Palmer was expected to show but apparently, due to problems, at the last minute, was unable to attend. The Mandrakes were due to once again get back together for one more time, for a reunion 'Millennium' gig, and — who knew?

I remember in the summer of 1969 seeing Robert Palmer performing for probably one of the last times ever with the Mandrakes. This was at an Open Air Free Concert in Hull's East Park. His brilliant solo rendition of 'Suzanne', that day, turned me on to becoming a life-long Leonard Cohen fan. I'd never heard of Leonard Cohen before this (even though John Hutchinson had also been featuring Cohen songs in his set). The song 'Suzanne' haunted me for weeks, until finally I found a copy of the songbook 'The Songs of Leonard Cohen' and I duly learnt to play each song chord by chord.

An after-note is that the Reunion gig has now taken place and ... nope, Robert Palmer did fail to show, to front the Mandrakes for that proverbial 'one more time', but that as they say, is 'rock 'n' roll'. Nevertheless, despite being both a singer and a guitarist short, the remaining Mandrakes performed well, tackling the same songs they played in the Sixties', songs which lesser groups of that day would have left well alone, but they took them on and won. The songs included excellent versions of Traffic's 'Feeling Alright' and the Beatles 'Strawberry Fields Forever.' It was easy to see why the Mandrakes were so good, when having a drummer as excellent as Mick Stephenson, the guitar skills of Rich Hodgson and Pete Lilley and the excellent 'second' vocals of Rob Southwick.

The Mandrakes (Scarborough - 1969)

MARINERS 1963 - 1964 **HULL**

Drums Malcolm Dixon replaced by
Dave Bradfield (Batmen)

Bass Ron Ryan

Rhythm Johnny Griffiths

Lead Mick Ronson (Insects)

Potted History: 'THE MARINERS'

The Mariners were a young inexperienced R & B group who at
times found it difficult to get work. It has been reported that
Mick Ronson played his first gig with the Mariners on
November 3 1963 when they supported the Keith Herd group at
Elloughton Village Hall. The Mariners were paid the princely
sum of 10 shillings for the gig. Other local venues the Mariners
played included the Duke of Granby in Hessle. The group
would sometimes gig as a three piece and former Gazelle, Robin
Taylor, also at one time appeared with the group.

MARTIANS	1961 - 1964	HULL

Drums   Glen Petty

Rhythm   Steve Smith

Lead   Martin Bridges

Potted History: 'THE MARTIANS'

The Martians were the youngest group in Hull during this period with the oldest member of the band being just 14. I saw them play several time during the Saturday morning children's matinee at the ABC Regal Cinema in Ferensway. Bespectacled lead guitarist Martin Bridges could play the guitar behind his head at 13 (later copied by Jimi Hendrix). Martin had first shown an interest in the guitar when he was just nine and his parents had decided that he should be taught properly and for four years he studied under a tutor. The Martians tended towards instrumentals and were particularly influenced by the Shadows and the Ventures. Martin Bridges also wrote his own instrumental which he featured on stage entitled 'Chinese Echo' and he was certainly a talented guitarist for his years. When Martin moved to Brough the Martians split and he went on to form R & B group the Cock-a-Hoops. The remaining members of the band formed the Yorkies who featured future Rats member, Geoff Appleby.

MATCHBOX   circa 1968   **YORK**

Drums   Sid Locker (Pete Latta Group)

Bass   Pete Shaw (Roll Movement)

Lead   Eric Wragg (The Screen)

Organ   Dave Davis (The Thunderbolts)

Sax   Keith Kiddy (The Screen)

Vocals   Mick Miller (The Screen)

Potted History: 'MATCHBOX'

The first gig by this potential York Supergroup was at the Milton Rooms in Malton. Matchbox supported top American stars Reparata and the Delrons at the Bridlington Spa.

MATHEW AND SON	1967 - 1969	HULL

Drums   Dave Morris

Bass   Johnny Pat

Guitar   Tony Gosling replaced by Steve Powell

Vocals   Linda Harrison

Potted History: MATHEW AND SON

After several years of trying for the big-time, these experienced musicians settled for a regular income by becoming resident group at Hull's Locarno Ballroom. Tony Gosling later ended up playing with the Mecca House Band 'Eddie Gray and His Shades of Grey'. They were the first 'Light' band to use the new BBC Pebble Mill Radio Studio when they recorded for the Sam Costa Evening Programme for BBC Radio.

METHODS	1964 - 1965	SCARBOROUGH
Drums	Kelvin Robertson	
Bass	John Davis	
Organ	Sandy Johnson	
Rhythm	Trevor Wallis	
Lead	Derek Cook	
Bongos/Vocals	Roger Brophy	
Potted History:	'THE METHODS'	

'Kings of the 'Bongo Beat' the Methods originally started out as the 'G Men' before changing their name. The group gigged regularly in Scarborough appearing at such venues as the Candlelight Club. In 1963 they entered the Tyne Tees Beat Contest competing against top groups from the North East. The Methods were managed by Peter Pitts and were the first local group to play at the Futurist Theatre where they had the privilege of supporting the Rolling Stones. Dave Brown left Scarborough's 'Panthers' to join the Methods as their vocalist, and former 'Moonshot, Dave Rose, also joined the group for a while. Later, Sandy Johnson went on to join the Iguanas.

The Methods (Scarborough - 1964)

METHUSELAH   1968 - 1969   SCUNTHORPE

Drums   Mick Bradley   (Sorrows)

Bass   Craig Austin   (Gospel Garden)

Rhythm/   Terry Wincott   (Gospel Garden)

Lead   Les Nichol   (ABC)

Vocals   John Gladwin   (Gospel Garden)

Potted History: 'METHUSELAH'

Methusulah were formed out of Scunthorpe group Gospel Garden and featured whiz-kid guitar player Les Nicol, arch rival of Mick Ronson on lead guitar. Terry Wincott quotes Methuselah as being "a loud 'heavy rock' band". The group were managed by Steve Rowland at Double-R management and signed a three-album deal with Elektra Records. Songwriter Kenny Young ('Under The Boardwalk') was drafted in by label boss Jac Holzman to produce their first album of John Gladwin originals. The album was entitled 'Methuselah', and the group weren't happy with it, partly because the producer put the bass and drums on the same track, and they couldn't be separated in the mix. Elektra boss, Jac Holzman flew to Britain to see Methuselah at work in the studio. Inexplicably the album was never released in the UK and when nothing happened in the States, the band went on to record a much better second 'double' album, which unfortunately was never released. However, by this time 'proverbial' musical differences had begun to split the band. On stage to quieten things down during their set, Terry Wincott and John Gladwin had begun to perform a duet. Using acoustic guitars they would play folksy type songs. This proved so popular that they decided to leave the band and strike out on their own as a duo. Taking their recording connections with them they eventually gave themselves the title, the 'Amazing Blondel'. Craig Austin and Les Nicol meanwhile based themselves in London and formed psychedelic trio 'Distant Jim' with former 'Juniors Eyes' member Steve Chapman on the drums.

Discography:

'Finders Keepers' c/w 'Just A Tear'
CAMP 602006   1968
'Matthew, Mark, Luke and John'
Elektra EKS 74052   1968

The Amazing Blondel

Methuselah (Scunthorpe - 1968)

MINORITY SOUL SOUND	1967 - 1968	LOFTUS

Drums	Pete Jackson
Bass	Keith Tose
Rhythm	Mike McMaster
Lead	Graham Barker
Vocals	Robin Winspear
Trumpet	Howard Jackson
Sax	Keith Morrison
Potted History:	'THE MINORITY SOUL SOUND'

Based in Loftus near Scarborough, the Minority Soul Sound were very busy throughout the East Riding. Many people thought them purely a soul band and this eventually prompted them to change their name to 'Dizzy Wheela' as they played a wide range of music.

MISFITS	circa 1964	YORK

Drums   Dave Williams

Bass   Pete Shaw

Rhythm   John Cartwight

Lead   Cliff Wade (The Beautiful Delilahs)

Vocals   Mick Miller

Potted History: 'THE MISFITS'

One of the Misfits earliest gigs, or 'bookings', as they were then so quaintly called, was at York's SS Empire, which was a former theatre/music-hall. Cliff Wade remembers that most of the audience that night were dressed like 'Teddy-boys' and would, seemingly oblivious to any music, all walk around the dance floor, up to 4 in a row in a big clockwise circle. Anyone who fancied a fight would start anti-clockwise and deliberately bounce shoulders with on-comers. The sole object of the evening seemed to be to show how hard you were, and the inevitable punch-ups were always accompanied by the Empire's manager appearing with two large dogs to break it up. Other less violent gigs the Misfits played included the Burns Hotel. Cliff Wade had originally begun his music career with the fantastically named 'Beautiful Delilahs' playing lead guitar and vocals. He remembers being very proud of his long hair, leather Cuban heeled boots, bell-bottom jeans and waistcoat. The Misfits eventually evolved into the Roll Movement.

The Misfits (York - 1964)

MODS	1964 - 1966	HULL

Drums   Brian Sleight (Sunsets) replaced by
Pete McLeod (Magpies)

Bass   Pete Green (Sunsets)

Rhythm   Phil Jenkinson (Sunsets) replaced by
Ron Wilkinson (Texans)

Lead   Peter Green (Sunsets) replaced by
Michael Brooks (Rivals)

Vocals   Rod Ellis (Sunsets) replaced by
Alan Coldbeck (King Bees)
Roger Bloom (Magpies)

Organ   Bob Cranswick (Skysounds)

Sax/Trumpet   Chris Fairbanks (Rats)
Ian Gray

Potted History: 'THE MODS'

Born out of 'Tony Martin and the Sunsets', the group became 'Tony Martin and the Mods' and later just the 'Mods' when Roger Bloom took over on the vocals. The original 'Mods' were an R & B group who had a strong following in Hull. They were resident at the Gondola Club down Little Queen Street. Among the many top groups the Mods supported were the Rolling Stones and the Overlanders at the Palace Theatre in Manchester. That night the Mods remember that they had to negotiate with the Stones over which R & B numbers they were going to play and Stones guitarist, Brian Jones actually borrowed a plectrum off them. The Mods also supported Peter and Gordon at the

Coventry Theatre and featured on the first gig by the Easybeats on their arrival in Britain from Australia. This was in East Grinstead and was arranged by no less a personage than Robert Stigwood. The Mods also supported many other top rock stars at the Gondola Club, including the Pretty Things and Joe Cocker, and later also supported the Small Faces.

Martin Yale, who was responsible for getting the Rats their Recording contract, also asked the Mods if they fancied recording a song, by Chris ('I'm A Yesterday Man') Andrews, but they had the good taste to turn it down! The Mods were managed by Yale's Cleethorpe's Agency, through which they worked for Manchester's Kennedy Street Enterprises who gave them many of their prestigious supports. Pete Green, on lead, left the band in December 1965, and later, ex King Bee, Alan Coldbeck, took over on vocals for a while. But by late 1966 the Mods had almost a completely new line-up and soon afterwards changed their name to Roger Blooms Hammer. If one follows their history there is a direct link between the original Mods and mega star Michael Jackson via future keyboard playing member Rod Temperton.

Tony Martin and the Mods recently reunited for a short tour with Mandy and the Girlfriends.

Tony Martin and The Mods (Hull - 1964)

MONDAY MORNING GLORY BAND	1969 - 1970	SCUNTHORPE

Drums	Alan Beasty
Bass	Martin Street
Lead	Andy Boyd
Keyboards	Ray Johnson
Vocals	Dave Waterland, Ian Stranaghan
Brass	Alan Browes, Colin Brailsforth
Potted History:	'THE MONDAY MORNING GLORY BAND'

The Monday Morning Glory Band were formerly known as the 'Worrying Kind'. They were Influenced by American groups the 'Electric Flag' and 'Blood, Sweat and Tears'. The group signed a recording contract with Mercury Records, turned pro and played the London scene.

MOONRAKERS   1964 - 1965   **HULL**

Drums   Ashley Hillaby

Bass   Dennis Smith

Lead   Leslie Wasling

Vocals   Mandy Smith

Potted History: 'MANDY AND THE MOONRAKERS'

Mandy and the Moonrakers were very busy on the local scene, including gigs at the Beverley Regal and the Hull Parks Beat Nights. They eventually folded in 1965. Mandy then went on to form all girl group 'Mandy and the Girlfriends' with brother Dennis initially taking responsibility for managing them.

MOONSHOTS   1963 - 1965   SCARBOROUGH

Drums   Dave Rose

Bass   Paddy Wilkins

Rhythm   Phil Peacock

Lead   Pete Liley

Vocals   Mick Rowley

Potted History: 'THE MOONSHOTS'

The Moonshots were so popular that they were the first Scarborough group of the 1960s to have a fan club. They would also often be mobbed by screaming fans. The group were managed by Ron Gillet and they played at all of the top Scarborough venues including the Olympia and the Spa. The Moonshots supported and mixed with many of the top groups including the Rolling Stones and the Kinks. They would often ask permission to borrow the star group's gear as their own amps were so small. Permission would usually be granted providing they didn't play any of the tunes that the star group were playing. The Moonshots became so popular that they were actually featured in top teenage pop magazine of the time 'Mirabelle'.

Pete Liley considers that, It was the luck of the draw who made it at that time and who didn't. A lot of the bands the Moonshots supported weren't often really any better than them, they just got the break. Despite being so popular, in 1965
the Moonshots decided to split as some of the members felt that they had gone as far as they could in Scarborough and that to stand any real chance of 'making it' they needed to base

themselves in London. The group played their last gig, at the Scarborough Spa in 1965. On breaking-up Pete Liley, who had an apprenticeship as a Monumental Mason, decided that he didn't want to turn pro and joined newly forming local band 'Beat Cult', and later became a member of the Mandrakes. Dave Rose joined the Methods and later the Incas. Meanwhile, Mick Rowley and Phil Peacock went to York to join the remaining members of the 'Viceroys'. The new band then changed their name to the 'Shots'. The line-up of the Shots included Mick Rowley (vocals), Phil Peacock (Rhythm), Geof Gill (Drums), Mal Luker (Lead and Keyboards) and John "Zeke" Lund (bass).

Millionaire and entrepreneur Alan Brush discovered the 'Shots' supporting P J Proby. Brush offered to manage them and secured them a deal with Columbia Records. The group then moved to London and Columbia released their 1965 single 'Keep A Hold Of What You've Got Now Baby'. Unfortunately, the record failed to take off and Brush's interest waned. Sadly, Phil Peacock left the band and returned to Scarborough and was killed in June 1968 when his car rang through the railings into the sea on the Marine Parade.

The Moonshots (Scarborough - 1964)

The Moonshots (Scarborough - 1965)

MORVANS	circa 1964	**YORK**

Drums   Johnny Morrell

Bass   Bill Tunnah

Rhythm   Pete Bland

Lead   Mick Colley

Vocals   Keith Bellman

Potted History: 'THE MORVANS'

One of the earliest York groups, the Morvans had developed out of rock 'n' roll and featured a Honky Tonk piano player. They also played Shadows numbers and inspired many other York teenagers to join beat groups.

MOSAICS	1964 - 1966	FILEY

Drums/vocals Alec Cammish

Bass Phil Blowman

Rhythm Peter Tindall

Lead Maurice Martinson

Potted History: 'THE MOSAICS'

A Filey based band whose name was chosen in a competition held at Filey YMCA where they first performed. So keen were the Mosaics not to let their audiences down, that for a winter gig at Flamborough Village Hall the group spent two hours hacking their way through a snowdrift to travel the six miles there. When cold, wet and frozen, they finally arrived, they found a note on the village hall door, saying that the gig had been cancelled! The Mosaics played their last gig at St George's Hall, Eastfield, Scarborough in March 1966 where they were supported by the Cyclones. Most of the band members then went on to form new group the 'Urge', Maurice Martinson joined the Purple Mist.

Apart from the Voodoos, the Mosaics, Unit IV and the Vikings, Filey's other contributions to the 'beat scene' included the Belle Vue Club which was often played by Jonty and the Strangers, the Mandrakes, Mark Anthony and the Avengers, Hutch, the Urge and the Magpies; The Brigg Cinema which was played by star groups such as the Searchers and Gene Vincent and also local groups such as the Mandrakes and the Strollers; Filey Pavilion where such groups as Screaming Lord Sutch played; and for apparently one week only the 'Violet Beat Club' down Rutland Street!

Filey also has the claim to fame that the Beatles stayed there in 1964 at the Hylands Hotel following their concert at the Futurist Theatre in Scarborough. Not that they were welcomed with open arms, because rumour has it that when the Beatles reached Filey and couldn't find their hotel, they stuck their long-haired heads out of their van window and asked a local eccentric directions as to where the hotel was. The man is claimed to have looked at their long hair, shook his head sadly, and said, 'I'm sorry lads, but I'm not going to tell you, because they'll never let the likes of you in there!'

Despite this the Beatles eventually found their hotel and rumour soon spread around Filey that the Beatles were staying at Hylands. Some local Covent School girls went to see if they could get the Beatles autographs. Amazingly, the Beatles invited them up to their hotel room which was at the rear of the building. When they walked into the room all four Beatles greeted them and Ringo, who was having a wash at the sink, shouted to one of the girls, 'Here you are Chuck, do you want this!' He then threw her the tablet of soap he had been using to wash with. Needless to say, along with their autographs, the girl in question still has that piece of soap!

MUSTANGS	1961 - 1965	HULL

Drums   Tony Jackson replaced by
Don Lill (Phantoms)

Bass   Ken Smith

Rhythm   Bob Long

Lead   Roger France

Vocals   Barry Graham

Potted History: 'BARRY GRAHAM AND THE
MUSTANGS'

Rob Long and Kenny Smith formed the Mustangs in 1961. Their repertoire consisted almost entirely of Shadows-type material and they chose their name to match their style, after the title of a Shadow's tune. Early in 1963 the original Mustangs split with Barry Graham and Roger France joining as replacements. Later that year the new line-up reached the national finals of a beat competition run by the Rank Organisation, being placed fourth out of 4,000 groups. The Mustangs sound also began to change with them featuring more and more R & B. In 1964 the group turned professional and gigged throughout Yorkshire. By September of that year the group's sound changed again as they experimented with four-part harmonies. Enthusiastic audience reaction convinced them that they had at last found their true idiom.

The Mustangs had one of the best looking group vans in the area with their name boldly emblazoned on both sides. They wore tailored suits and had short hair in an attempt to achieve the gimmick of 'respectability'. On-stage the band would wow their audiences with their great harmonies.

Don Lill joined the group in November 1964 and they pooled their resources and took a day-trip to London where they made a demo recording of the Four Season's hit 'Sincerely'. By the end of the year the Mustangs had become one of Yorkshire's top groups. After hearing their demo disc, musical impresario Norrie Paramor invited them to take part in a recording session. A visit to Hull was then made by their future Manager to see them play live and they were signed on the spot.

Early in 1965, the Mustangs played their last gig in Hull. This was at the Continental (Palace) Theatre on Anlaby Road. Soon afterwards, to avoid confusion with an American group called the Mustangs, the group changed their name to the 'Majority' and moved to London.

Barry Graham and The Mustangs (Hull - 1964)

The Mutiny (Bridlington - 1968)

MUTINY	circa 1968	BRIDLINGTON

Drums   Paul Jenkinson

Bass   Ken Giles

Guitar   John Lewis

Guitar   Allan Black

Vocals   Steve 'Snips' Parsons

Potted History: 'THE MUTINY'

The Mutiny flared briefly from 1967/68, they had evolved out of the Bridlington group 'Spanish Leather' who featured Steve 'Snips' Parsons, one of the most eccentric rock products Bridlington ever created. The Mutiny were influenced by Bob Dylan, Jefferson Airplane, the Byrds and the Doors. Local gigs included the Seabirds Pub, the Ace of Clubs and various youth clubs. In 1968 a Rock Contest was held at the Gaiety Theatre in Scarborough and the Mutiny decided to enter. One member of the audience that day was Allen (Robert) Palmer and he was so impressed by Allan Black and his 12 string guitar playing that he invited him to join Scarborough's top group the Mandrakes. Allan Black had always been a huge fan of the Mandrakes and eagerly accepted his membership. The Mutiny soon afterwards disbanded and Snips went on to form 'Chest Fever', Ken Giles joined Red Dirt and John Lewis later joined 'Lucifer', not literally of course!

NAPOLEON TRUST	1967 - 1968	HULL

Drums	John Costello (Neutrons)
Bass	Gerald Vivien (Neutrons)
Lead	Martin Glover (Neutrons)
Lead	Brian Harberry
Organ	Kevin Towse (Neutrons)
Vocals	Dave Marshall (Shades of Blue)
Potted History:	'THE NAPOLEON TRUST'

Formed out of the Neutrons, the Napoleon Trust played regularly at the Beverley Regal and were frequent visitors to York where they played venues such as the Enterprise Club. The group's style was similar to the of the Small Faces. On stage they wore matching silk shirts. Among the top groups the Napoleon Trust supported were the Troggs who they appeared with at the Brid Spa. Martin Glover later became a member of the Third World and Dave Marshall joined the Variations.

NEUTRONS   **1964 - 1965**   **HULL**

Drums   John Costello

Bass   Gerald Vivien

Lead   Martin Glover

Organ   Kevin Towse

Potted History: 'THE NEUTRONS'

Born at a time of the Cold War and nuclear threat the Neutrons played R & B. They had gigs all around Hull. The group eventually changed their name to the Insex and later most members formed 'Wee Three'.

NEW RELIGION circa 1967 **SCARBOROUGH**

Drums   Calvin Turner

Bass   Colin Steele

Lead   Pete Hudson

Vocals   Chris Bagnall (Incas)

Vocals   Stewart Bedford

Potted History: 'NEW RELIGION'

The New Religion was a title previously used by soul band Jimmy James and the Vagabonds. Scarboro's 'New Religion' were reputed to have played their first few gigs dressed in Monk's Cowls! Not that I'm any stranger to a monks cowl myself, as I wore one at the Melody Maker Rock Contest in Leeds during the mid Seventies', but I gave it up as it began to become a habit!

New Religion were formerly known as the 'Ox' and their claim to fame is that they played as the opening act on the 1967 Stax Tour of the UK. This featured some of the legends of Soul music including Otis Redding, Sam and Dave, Arthur Conley, Eddie Floyd and Booker T and the MG's. It was Otis Redding's last visit to the UK before he was killed in a plane crash. One of the tour dates was at the Queens Hall, Leeds which was a major rock venue. The hall had seen concerts by Pink Floyd, Cream and the Who, who on that occasion were supported by Scarborough's Mandrakes. New Religion also played London's Marquee Club. Pete Hudson would go on to form the remarkably named 'Strawboa Fantasy'.

345

NIGHT PEOPLE   **1964 - 1966**   **HULL**

Drums   Robb Welton

Bass   John Dunlop

Rhythm   Ray Turner

Lead   Dick Flavell

Vocals   Phil Davies replaced by Steve Howden

Potted History: 'THE NIGHT PEOPLE'

Originally known as 'Sounds 4', the 'Night People' took their name from the Charlie Bird album 'Blues For Night People'. A Semi-pro group who while geared mainly towards playing the clubs and entertaining their audiences also played dances including the Hull City Hall, Beverley Regal and the Kon Tiki Club. The Night People had jazz/blues influences in the style of music they played and lead guitarist Dick Flavell was rated to be one of the best 'Beat instrumentalists' in the city at this time. The group played material by such artists as Otis Redding, James Brown and Ray Charles. They supported the likes of Long John Baldry, the Escorts and Jimmy Powell and the Five Dimensions.

NIGHTRIDERS   circa 1960   **SCUNTHORPE**

Drums	Toyne Tomlinson replaced by Pete (Fenwick) Johnson
Bass/Vocals	Pete Hornsby
Rhythm/Vocals	Mal Turner
Lead/Vocals	Jimmy Ryder
Potted History:	'JIMMY RYDER AND THE NIGHTRIDERS'

Formed in the late 1950s the Nightriders were Scunthorpe's first rock group. They rehearsed at the Youth Centre at the top of Doncaster Road and occasionally played gigs there. They also had gigs in Louth, Brigg, Cleethorpes and Scunthorpe's Drill Hall. But they really thought that they had hit the big time when they played a gig at Scunthorpe's Civic Theatre. The top stars they supported in the early Sixties' included Screaming Lord Sutch, Jimmy Justice, Terry Dene and Jet Harris and Tony Meehan. After various adventures and comings and goings the group changed their name to the Shantells and eventually joined up with recording star Jimmy Crawford.

Nothingeverappens (Hull - 1969)

NOTHIN-EVERAPPENS	1970 - 1972	HULL

Drums   Dave Eastwood replaced by Jim White (Sedation)

Bass   John Bentley (Chest Fever)

Lead   Roy Neave (Chest Fever)

Sax   Doug Houston

Vocals   Steve 'Snips' Parsons (Chest Fever)

Potted History: 'NOTHINEVERAPPENS'

A pro-band formed out of 'Chest Fever', Nothineverappens played mostly their own progressive rock material and were managed by Barry Nettleton and the Hull Brick Company. They gigged on the national circuit, playing such prestigious venues as City Halls and Universities, where they supported many top bands including Mott the Hoople and Family (with Family vocals Roger Chapman clearly influencing 'Snips' voice and stage presentation). They also played the top London clubs including the Marquee and upstairs at Ronnie Scott's Jazz Club. The group used props, smoke machines, lighting effects, theatricals and anything else to make a show. One of their typical gigs was at the Hornsea Floral Hall, it climaxed spontaneously with the entire audience headed by Snips and the band parading out of the building and disappearing down the road singing "The World is made of Sausage Meat", leaving a gob-smacked promoter and bar staff wondering where everyone had gone.

Unfortunately, after a couple of years on the road and despite much interest from the music business there was a realisation that sadly nothing was going to happen. The band split and Roy Neave began recording and producing generations of local bands at Keith Herd's Fairview Studios, in Willerby. Meanwhile vocals 'Snips' hung out in the London music scene and joined the Andy Frazier off-shoot of 'Free' called 'Sharks'. Later he joined the 'Baker-Gurvitz' Army which featured Ginger Baker of 'Cream'. He recorded several albums with this band and later one album and several singles on his own. In the 1970s the 'Nothins' bass player, John Bentley, joined recording band 'Squeeze'. He also appeared playing bass with the 'reformed' Rats at the Mick Ronson Memorial Concert held at the former Hammersmith Odeon. The tracks John played on that evening included 'I Feel Free' and 'It Ain't Easy' and they were recorded and later released on the Rats CD. In 1995, Steve 'Snips' Parsons got back together with another former member of 'Sharks', Chris Spedding and along with the ex-drummer of the 'Attractions' produced a new 'Sharks' album, 'Like A Black Van Parked On A Dark Curve' which is currently available on CD.

OBJEKS 5 circa 1965 **HULL**

Drums Dave Johnson (Carol's Knights)

Bass Frank Murphy (Carol's Knights)

Rhythm Vic Harbord (Cossacks)

Lead Alan Morris (Carol's Knights)

Potted History: 'THE 5 OBJEKS'

Formed out of Carol's Knights, a semi-pro group with great harmonies. They played mostly Top 20 numbers. Several groups around this period seemed to want to be 4 or 5 of something, such as Rotherham's 'Five Shades of Blue', York's 'Four Shades of Black', Scarborough's 'Four Just Men', Scunthorpe's 'Four Cents', Hull's 'Five Trax' and 'Four Aces'.

ODD ONES   circa 1964   **GOOLE**

Drums

Bass   Jeff Le Vogue

Rhythm   Jimmy Carol

Lead   Peter Raywood

Vocals   Dave Ramskill

Potted History: 'ODEIN AND THE ODD ONES'

One of the earliest and strangest named of Goole's bands.
Odein and the Odd Ones were resident at the 'Green Man' pub
in Hammerton. They played blues music and had gigs at both
Goole's Baths and Drill Hall. Brian Avery later joined the band
on keyboards. Pete Raywood went on to join Hull's 'Cossacks'.

OUSEBEATS	1965 –1967	YORK

Drums   Dave Leaper

Bass   Jim Russell

Guitar   Tony Lee

Leads   Mick Russell

Vocals   Ray Charles, Linda Russell

Potted History: 'THE OUSEBEATS'

The Ousebeats were one of York's top groups. Local gigs included the Boulevard Night-club and the Coffee House in Tadcaster. Out of town gigs included the Pavilion Theatre, Southdene, Filey and various venues in Scarborough. The group appeared on Television's 'Opportunity Knocks'. The two girl singers from this group (the Rowan Twins) later appeared on Top of The Pops.

OX   1966 - 1967   SCARBOROUGH

Drums   Dave McFegan replaced by Calvin Turner

Bass   Colin Steele

Rhythm   Clive Smith replaced by Gordon Williams

Lead   Pete Hudson

Vocals   Stewart Bedford

Potted History: 'THE OX'

The Ox were big fans of the Small Faces and the Who and they
named themselves after Who bass player John Entwhistle
whose nickname was the 'Ox'. The group was formed late in
1965 by old school friends but it didn't finalise its line-up until
June 1966 when Stewart Bedford (also an old school friend)
joined on vocals. The Ox were managed by Dave Cook. The
local live music scene in North Yorkshire was very active at this
time with many venues available for under 18's including Youth
Clubs, Village Halls, Olympia, etc., all of which featured a live
group more than once a week. The Ox played their first gigs at
Colley's Holiday Camp (just outside of Scarborough) where
they had a summer season out of the limelight. Their first major
gig in Scarborough was at the Olympia in October 1966 which
was the same night as the Incas farewell gig before they turned
professional and moved to London. The highlights of the Ox's
career were supporting the likes of the Small Faces and the
Troggs at the height of their popularity, at the Brid Spa. In Mid
1967 Gordon Williams left the group and Chris Bagnall
(formerly with the Incas) joined as 2nd vocalist and the name of
the band was changed to the New Religion.

PAGE THREE   1966 - 1967   HULL

Drums   Trevor Wilson (Trends)

Bass   Edward Ralph

Lead   Howard Marshall

Rhythm/Vocals   Geoff Prest (Trends)

Potted History: 'PAGE THREE'

Formed out of the Trends', Page Three were only on the scene for a short while. Local gigs included the Beverley Regal.

PANTHERS   *circa* **1964**   **SCARBOROUGH**

Drums   Dave Pinkney replaced by John Piper

Bass   Richard Widdows replaced by Tony Hick

Lead   Geoff Harrison

Organ   Tony Crewe replaced by Derek Boyes

Vocals   Sidney Beal

Other Members: Dave Brown

Potted History: 'THE PANTHERS'

The name, the 'Panthers', seems to have been very popular because Hull also had one. On the scene for quite a while, the group were originally known as the Sherburn Panthers. Tony Crewe was one of the first musicians on the East Coast to own an electronic organ and two of the group's members played Fender guitars. The early group included several instrumentals by the Tornadoes in their set. They played such local gigs as the Scarborough Spa. So good did the Panthers sound become that they won the final of the semi-pro section of Scarborough's Gaiety Theatre Band Contest. Johnathan Arthur Hartley, better known as 'Jonty', and formerly of 'Jonty and the Strangers' joined the group on vocals during their latter days. His first gig with them was at the Armley Baths Hall in Leeds.

PANTHERS   **1963 - 1965**   **HULL**

Drums   Dave Harvey

Bass   Bill Bolton

Lead   Dave Fowler

Vocals   Billy Shane

Potted History: 'THE PANTHERS'

This Hull version of the Panthers were originally called John D Hunter and the Panthers and they were resident at the Skyline Ballroom.   The group eventually changed their name to the 'Skysounds'. Drummer Dave Harvey turned professional and joined recording group the 'Garden Odyssey Enterprise'.

PEACEBREAKERS   circa 1968   **HULL**

Drums   Steve Markham

Bass   Bernard Dolman

Rhythm   Graham Drax

Organ   Steve Wilkinson

Vocals   Jim Berry

Potted History: 'THE PEACEBREAKERS'

I always thought that the Peacebreakers' was a great name for a group. This outfit had some very young members and at their early gigs they often had to borrow equipment from other bands. Local gigs included the Beverley Regal. Guitarist Graham Drax went on to join the 'Reflections'.

PEIGHTON CHECKS	1967 - 1968	SCUNTHORPE
Drums	Colin McArthur	
Bass	Paul Spiers	
Rhythm	Charlie Gillis	
Lead	Alan Tinkler	
Vocals	John Parker replaced by Graham 'Chalky' White	
Potted History:	'THE PEIGHTON CHECKS'	

The Peighton Checks were very popular on the local scene and were represented by the Pete McLeod Agency. Out-of-town gigs included the Mulberry Bush in Malton. John Parker left the band to join the Hammer. The Checks eventually disbanded when three of their members fell in love, one of them with 'Miss Hull'. The group's last gig was at York Technical College supporting the Allan Bown.

PENJANTS	1965 - 1967	BEVERLEY
Drums	John Burgess	
Bass	Tom Roantree	
Rhythm	Tony Soames	
Lead	Rod Turner replaced by Lawrence (Laurie) Burnett	
Sax	Colin Moore	
Vocals	Jerry O'Connell	
Potted History:	'THE PENJANTS'	

The Penjants were named after two of the members girlfriends, 'Penny' and 'Janesta'. They were formed during the early Sixties'. The various group members were all aged about 15 at this time and Jerry, Tom and Rodney were all in the same class at Longcroft School. The young Penjants rehearsed in an old hall down Lairgate. They gigged everywhere they could, including the Beverley Regal, Brid Spa and gigs in Hull and Scarborough. In 1966 the group fought their way through to the finals of the Yorkshire Beat Contest. The same year they also played support at Brid Spa to such groups as the Moody Blues and Jimmy James and the Vagabonds. Ace Beverley guitarist, Laurie Burnett, was later a member of the band. By 1967 the group were wearing caftans, psychedelic jackets and anything else they could find that was outrageous. One evening at the Brid Spa, after playing the first set as the Penjants, for the second set they evolved into the 'Scarlet Farmyard', which included taking on three new members. I remember one rainy winter evening in 1966 stood waiting for my brother on a cold, dark and empty Beverley Railway Station, while he auditioned for the vacant guitarist slot with the Penjants, which was eventually filled by Laurie.

The Penjants (Beverley - 1965)

PEOPLE	1968 - 1969	SCUNTHORPE
Drums	Trevor Mitchell	
Bass	Irving Blundell	
Lead	Steve Wright	
Keyboards	Dennis Donsdale	
Vocals	John Brady	
Potted History:	'THE PEOPLE'	

The People had a big following in the Scunthorpe area. They supported several top groups including 'Status Quo' and Marmalade. The People went into the local recording studios and produced a demo tape of an Allan Bown number entitled 'Sally Green'. Drummer Trevor Mitchell went on to set a drumming record. The group later changed their name to 'Kaleidoscope'.

PHANTOMS	1963 - 1964	HULL
Drums	Don Lill	
Bass	Steve Hodge	
Rhythm	Johnny Kemp	
Rhythm	Colin Havercroft	
Lead	Sid Gage	
Vocals	Irving Gordon (Sunsets)	
Potted History:	' THE PHANTOMS'	

A group formed in North East Hull by five members of the Young Presbyterians Youth Club who used to meet at St Ninians Church on Chanterlands Avenue in 1963. The Phantoms were one of the youngest groups in the City with Colin being only 14 and Sid Gage the oldest just 16. Sid was considered to be Hull's answer to Hank Marvin and indeed the Phantoms demonstrated their talent when they came second in the finals of the 1963 Hull Parks Talent competition held in the Guildhall. Local gigs included Hessle Town Hall. Colin and Steve eventually left the group because of pressing school exams. The remaining members were then joined by Irvin Gordon late of the Sunsets and their name was changed slightly to Dean Curtis and the Phantoms. A name which is considered to have been a split of 'Tony Curtis'. The 'Tony' staying with 'Tony Martin' and the Sunsets' and the 'Curtis' going with Dean and the Phantoms. Drummer Don Lill later joined the Mustangs who became recording group the Majority and Irving Gordon emigrated to Australia. I can't quite remember whether I saw this band or not. But if I did, as an imaginative 12 year old, I would have expected them to at least appear on stage with glowing white faces!

The Phantoms (Hull - 1964)

PINK	1969 - 1970	HULL
Drums	Gary Burroughs	
Bass	Richard Abbot	
Lead	Richard Burnham	
Keyboards	Steve Ryle	
Potted History:	'THE PINK'	

The Pink were a four-piece rock band based in various parts of Holderness. They supported several top groups including the 'Love Affair' and Geno Washington. Gary Burroughs left the Pink to form the rock group 'Listen' as lead vocalist. A short time later 'Listen' supported the 'Pink' and they were so impressed by Gary's vocals that they invited him to rejoin them in their newly forming rock band 'Blitzkrieg'. Richard Abbot went on to form 'Inspiration' and in the early 1970s was also a member of 'Harvest'. After 'Blitzkrieg' disbanded Gary joined very popular local group 'Weazel'. In the late 1970s he also worked as a tape operator in Keith Herd's recording studio and later set up his own studio. Over the years he recorded and produced many of the up and coming local bands.

PLAGUE 66   **circa 1966**   **HULL**

Drums	Kevin Corbett
Bass	Dick Heaton
Rhythm	Dave Jefferson
Lead	Dave Carmichael (Gonx)
Organ	Phil Mullet
Vocals	Tony Brown
Roadies	Steve and Dave Rowe
Potted History:	'PLAGUE 66'

Plague '66 began life in 1965 and were originally just called the 'Plague'. They rehearsed at Wheeler Street Youth Club and played their first gig there. Once on the road they began performing on the Youth Club and Village Hall circuit. Including gigs at Hessle Town Hall and St Peter's Youth Club in Scarborough. But as 1966 dawned their sound began to develop and they changed their name to Plague '66. Gigs began to increase and now included the Duke of Cumberland in Ferriby, the Queens Hotel in Withernsea and the Ferryboat Inn in Hessle.

Plague '66' became one of the most exciting groups in Hull during their relatively short existence and my favourite local group of the mid-Sixties'. As well as getting their own gigs they also worked for Pete McLeod and Scarborough Agent Peter Pitts and could by the middle of 1966 often be seen playing at the Hull City Hall and the Beverley Regal with other local gigs by this time including marketplace club 'Prohibition 66'.

The Plague (Hull - 1965)

The Plague (Hull - 1965)

The Plague (Hull - 1965)

369

Plague '66 (Hull - 1966)

Plague '66 (Hull - 1966)

371

Influenced by American labels   Stax, Atlanta and Motown Plague 66's music was 'Soul' including   Wilson Pickett's 'Land Of A Thousand Dances' and 'Midnight Hour', Otis Redding's 'Shake', James Browns 'I'd Go Crazy' and 'Papa's Got A Brand New Bag,' Junior Walker's 'How Sweet It is', Lee Dorsey's 'Ride Your Pony' and Arthur Conley's 'Sweet Soul Music'. They also played an excellent version of the Pretty Things/Bo Diddley's 'Mama, Keep Your Big Mouth Shut' and it was quite something to be at the Hull City Hall and hear the place reberate when the whole band joined in on the chorus of 'Hey, …. Hey Mama, …. Keep Your Big Mouth Shut, …. Keep Your Big Mouth Shut!' Despite not featuring brass their sound was authentic, alive and exciting.

Wearing turquoise blue psychedelic flares (made for them by fans Janis and Rose out of curtain material!) and some members with knee length fur coats, Plague 66's image was something across between the rebelliousness of the Rolling Stones and the excitement of a USA Soul Package. The group had an almost cult-like following and their name would mysteriously appear overnight on the walls and the shop windows of the City Centre. Their van was covered in their girl fans lipstick stained graffiti and a long white arrow was chalked along one side with the words 'Follow this!' written underneath. When 'Plague 66' arrived at a gig you just knew that there was going to be a happening. On stage Dave Carmichael, sported razor-cut pointed side-burns and a pear-shaped white Vox 'Tear Drop' guitar (as used at that time by Rolling Stone 'Brian Jones) and fellow guitarist, Dave Jefferson, matched it with his own white Vox 'Phantom'. Later the group featured two vocalists up front, one of whom would 'groove' in a pair of 'wellington boots while the other would stare contemptuously at the audience. Plague 66 were mean, moody and magnificent and might well have been the original 'Commitments'.

Organist, Phil Mullet was a trainee Humber Pilot, and having to work shifts found it increasingly difficult to find excuses to get nights off work to attend gigs. But so keen was he play with the group that he actually once purposely badly burnt his own hand to earn himself a three week sicknote. The same night, with one hand bandaged, he could be seen playing with the group live on stage.

Plague '66 often played out of town gigs including taking the ferry to New Holland for venues in Grimsby. On their return journeys they were one of many groups who would often risk their health by eating at the infamous 'Norman's' roadside café.

So popular were Plague '66 with the girls that at the end of a gig at the Whitby Spa, drummer Kevin Corbett had to be smuggled out of the building dressed in an 'amp' cover! Apparently an irate boyfriend in the audience had been reliably informed that Kevin had been 'befriending' his girlfriend.

The band underwent several important auditions including one at the legendary Marquee Club in London and another for Don Arden's Galaxy Agency, in Romford, Essex, who managed such top groups as the Small Faces. Unfortunately, nothing came of it. Much to the regret of their fans, not wanting to become 'Plague 67', on the stroke of midnight, New Years Eve 1966, the band changed its name to 'That Feeling'.

POACHERS   circa 1964   **MARKET WEIGHTON**

Drums   Graham Walker

Bass   Ian Hall

Rhythm   Chris Anderson

Lead   John Appleton

Potted History: 'THE POACHERS'

One of the many short-lived groups to spring up in the wake of Mersey Beat. The Poachers played local Youth Clubs. Bass guitarist Ian Hall graduated to playing bass with York outfit the Fix.

PURPLE MIST   **1967 - 1971**   **SCARBOROUGH**

Drums   Allen Turner

Bass/Vocals   Dave Simcox replaced by Ian Goodwill

Rhythm/Vocals   Tom Ward (Herbie's ii's)

Lead/Vocals   Maurice Martinson, John Ward

Other Members   Jimmy Meumier, John Harris

Potted History: 'PURPLE MIST'

The Hendrix influence hit the East Coast during 1967, while
Hull had its 'Purple Haze', Scarborough was slightly more
subtle with its 'Purple Mist'. The Mist supported several top
groups including Long John Baldry's Steam Packet, Jimmy
James and the Vagabonds, the Move and Jethro Tull. Tom Ward
remembers that the night they appeared with Jethro Tull they
were actually the Mist's support act. The Purple Mist had won a
'Battle of the Bands' contest for which the prize was topping the
bill at Manchester University. That night at the University, when
their support band took to the stage, they began playing
without their singer present. Then all of a sudden a scruffy
looking, wild haired bloke appeared on stage wearing a trench
coat and carrying a carrier bag. From out of the bag the scruffy
bloke brought a flute and the rest as they say is history! When
the Mist supported Long John Baldry's Steam Packet at the Brid
Spa, Tom Ward got speaking to their piano player. The piano
player said that he had just written a song called 'Your Song'
and he was taking it to London the next day to try to get it
recorded, the guy's name was Reg Dwight alias 'Elton John'. In
1968 Purple Mist sent a demo tape to the Robert Stigwood
Organisation who managed the Bee Gees and Cream. They

showed interest but nothing came of it. The band then took to featuring the 'Ukulele' in their act after local DJ Dave Marshall gave them one and Tom Ward would often sing a George Formby song! In September 1968 Purple Mist were the first group to play live on stage at Michael Corrigan's new Disco 35 in Scarborough which later became the 'Penthouse'. Other gigs included York's Beathive. A further highlight of Tom and John's time with the Mist was jamming with the Move's Roy Wood backstage at the Brid Spa. In 1969, for a short while Purple Mist changed their name to 'Friends' and then Tom Ward went solo. The group came back together in 1974 for a one-off reunion gig.

QUADRANT   **circa 1968**   **HULL**

Drums   Calvin Winetroupe (Skysounds)

Bass   Pete E Green (Mods)

Lead   Pete Green (Mods)

Organ   Bob Cranswick (Mods)

Vocals   Lynda Harrison (Skysounds)

Potted History: 'THE QUADRANT'

The Quadrant was formed by musicians who had been on the scene for quite a while. The group intended to perform good quality pop/Latin/jazz in Clubland. They played extensively throughout the West Riding as well as private functions locally. The group had the honour of supporting P.P. Arnold and Chris Farlowe when they appeared at Hull's Skyline Ballroom in 1968.

RANDON DESTINY	**1968 - 1969**	**YORK**

Drums	John Henry
Bass	Michael Cundall
Lead	John Hine
Trumpet	Dave Todd
Sax	Howard Welsh
Vocals	Pete Wilson
Potted History:	'RANDON DESTINY'

Randon Destiny were one of the popular York groups of this period. Typical local gigs included the Beathive on Dalton Terrace, the Assembly Rooms, the Enterprise Club and the Mulberry Bush in Malton.

RANGERS	1963 - 1964	HULL

Drums   John Kilvington

Bass   Tony Luke

Rhythm   Dave Webster

Lead   Ray Ellerington

Vocals   Chris Hogg

Potted History: 'SCOTT MADISON AND THE
                 RANGERS'

Promoted by Barney Coleham, the Rangers were very popular on the local scene playing venues such as the Majestic Ballroom. They also undertook a tour of the American Army bases in Germany. The group were extremely versatile, so much so that the Assistant Manager of the Skyline Ballroom, Malcolm Ladd, suggested that they be booked for the cabaret spot at one of the Skyline Ballroom's Saturday Evening Dinner Dances. These usually featured a 12 piece band playing to quite a middle aged audience. This was therefore seen as quite a risky venture, but nevertheless the Rangers were booked. On the evening of the Dinner Dance the Rangers opened their set with a rock 'n' roll number, then 'slid' into 'Moon River' and finally brought the house down with 'I'm Henry The Eighth I Am'! Scott Madison and the Rangers had the privilege of playing support to the Beatles when they played for the first time in Hull at the Majestic Ballroom in October 1962.

RASCALS	circa 1965	HULL

Drums	Trevor Marriott (King Bees) replaced by Steve Pollard
Bass	Trevor Parker
Lead	Paul Leslie
Vocals	Mike D'Arcy
Potted History:	'THE RASCALS'

Originally formed around 1960 as a Skiffle group, for a long time they were fronted by Johnny Lever and known as Johnny Lever and the Rascals. The group supported several recording stars such as the Remo Four and Tommy Quickly. A later vocalist with the Rascals was Alan Coldbeck of the King Bees. The group eventually evolved into the 'Ides of March'. In 1967 the 'Ides' appeared on Television's 'Opportunity Knocks'.

RATS **1963 - 1970** **HULL**

Drums James Simpson

Bass Brian Buttle

Lead Frank Ince

Vocals Peter 'Benny' Marshall

Piano Robin Lecore replaced by Chris Fairbanks
(Scorpions)

1967/70 line-up

Drums John Cambridge replaced by
Mick Woodmansey (Road Runners)

Bass Geoff Appleby replaced by
Keith Cheesman (Jellyroll BB),
Geoff Appleby, Trevor Bolder (Flesh)

Lead Mick Ronson

Vocals Pete 'Benny' Marshall

Potted History: 'THE RATS'

The Rats began life in 1963 as 'Peter King and the Majestics'. They
became the Rats in 1964 on a suggestion made by top local agent
Martin Yale. An R & B band managed by Barry Paterson and
Martin Yale's Cleethorpes Agency, they soon built a loyal fan
following around the area. Yale was responsible for helping the
Rats to sign a recording contract. He arranged for them to attend
London's Olympic Studios where they recorded several tracks

including the Chris Andrews song 'I've Gotta See My Baby'. This had been ear-marked as their first single but producer Bunny Lewis was more impressed by their version of the Willie Dixon number 'Spoonful'. Demos of the track were sent to all of the leading record companies. Probably because of the 'British Invasion' of pop groups touring America, Martin Yale managed to secure a deal with a small American record company called Laurie Records. They released the Rats recording of 'Spoonful' in that country, late in 1964. The record was finally released in the UK in February 1965. The track was later popularised by Cream. The B side of the record 'I've Got My Eyes On You Baby' was credited to 'Benny' Marshall who plays harmonica on the track with the Rats sounding very much like an early Manfred Mann. To promote the disc the Rats appeared on the Granada Television show 'Scene At Six-Thirty' and the BBC's 'Thank Your Lucky Stars'. Benny Marshall was also interviewed by Jimmy Saville on Granada Television's 'Pop Shop'.

I remember being pleasantly surprised when I rang Hull's own phone-in Tele-Disc service on 211411 and listened to the Rats playing 'Spoonful'. Unlike Hull's previous recording attempts of the early Sixties, the Aces and the Hullaballoos, the Rats record seemed much more progressive, looking towards the future rather than the past.

In June 1965 the group released their follow-up single on Columbia Records, which was entitled 'I've Gotta See My Baby'. This authentically captures the R & B sound of the time. The Rats promoted the record on the regional television show 'Discs A Go Go', but played the B side of the record (a poor mans version of 'House of The Rising Sun') entitled 'New Orleans' (which had also been released as a single in America on 'Rust' Records). They also played the great blues track 'Chicago Calling'. Mick Ronson didn't feature on either of these recordings as he wasn't a member of the band until 1966.

The Rats (Hull - 1965)

The Rats (Hull - 1969)

The Rats (Hull - 1966)

After the release of the records and several television appearances the line-up of the group changed. First, there was the addition of Robin Lecore on piano and then Chris Fairbanks on sax and trumpet. But by early 1966 Brian Buttle, Frank Ince and Robin Lecore had all left the group and for a while the line-up was original members Benny Marshall and James Simpson, joined by new members Mick Ronson and Geoff Appleby.

When James Simpson also left the group, Clive Taylor joined for a short while on drums. This line-up of the Rats spent a month resident in Paris at the leading French rock club, the 'Golfe Drouot' (Scarborough's 'Brave New World' would also later play there). On their return to England they spent a further week sleeping in the back of their van in London in an unsuccessful attempt to get some paid gigs in the capital.

By 1967 the Rats had their arguably classic line-up of Marshall, Ronson, Cambridge and Appleby. They built up a huge following in the Yorkshire area, being in big demand at such top venues as the Assembly Rooms in York. In 1968, with a change of management, the Rats for a short while changed their name to 'Treacle'. Despite much promise and rave revues Geoff Appleby got married and left the band and was replaced by Ched Cheesman. Early in 1969, John Cambridge also left the band to seek his fortune in London being replaced by former Driffield 'Road Runner' Mick 'Woody' Woodmansey. Down in the Smoke John joined recording group 'Juniors Eyes' who featured Tim Renwick later of the Sutherland Brothers and Quiver - whose hits including 'Arms of Mary'. John, through his, Juniors Eyes connections, met David Bowie. As a member of Juniors Eyes John recorded several radio broadcasts with Bowie including one on the Dave Lee Travis Show which was recorded on 20 October 1969. He later appeared on Bowie's 'Space Oddity' album with fellow Rat 'Benny' Marshall' also being featured, playing brilliant harmonica on the track 'Unwashed and Somewhat Slightly Dazed'. Later, John Cambridge suggested Mick Ronson as the guitarist for Bowie's newly forming 'backing group' the 'Hype'. John convinced Mick to join Bowie and the Rats eventually folded in 1970. Their first gig was a couple of days later when Mick and John appeared with Bowie on John Peel's Sunday Show recorded at the BBC's Paris studios on the 5 February 1970. When John left Bowie a month or so later, Mick Woodmansey was called up for service. Eventually most of the members of the Rats would be involved in 'Hype' and 'Ronno' then Ronson and Woodmansey together with bass player Trevor Bolder, would become the 'Spiders from Mars'.

After the break-up of the Spiders Geoff Appleby later rejoined his old mate Mick Ronson for a short period in the mid Seventies' when he toured with the Hunter/Ronson Band. He also played bass on 'Ian Hunter's' first solo album. Top Beverley guitarist Laurie Burnett was also called up for service with Woody Woodmansey's U-Boat, and recorded several tracks with them in the studios, but he was soon 'Man Overboard!' Meanwhile bass player Trevor Bolder was recalled for one last time by Bowie to record the album 'Pin-ups'. Bolder then produced a final 'Spiders' album and went on to join Uriah Heap and for a short while Wishbone Ash.

The good news is that all of the Rats recordings, both the original singles released when Mick Ronson wasn't a member and later tracks featuring him, which were produced in Keith Herd's Willerby Studio are now available on CD. Listening to tracks like 'Mick's Boogie' and 'Telephone Blues' one is transported back to the summer of 1969 and the Rats in full flow at one of the many free concerts held in Hull's parks.

Discography:

Singles:

'Spoonful' c/w' I've Got My Eyes On You Baby'
1964   Columbia DB7483

'I Gotta See My Baby' c/w Heading Back ('To New Orleans')
1965 Columbia DB7607

Albums:

'The Rise And Fall Of Bernie Gripplestone And The Rats From Hull'
1994   Tenth Planet Records (Vinyl)

'The Rats Angel Air Records (CD)
1998

'Bowie At The Beeb' BBC Records
2000

(This 2 CD set featured most members of the Rats including John Cambridge, Mick Ronson, Trevor Bolder, Mick Woodmansey and Benny Marshall)

RAYDENMICS   **1964 –1965**   **HULL**

Drums   Michael Moody

Rhythm   Dennis 'John' Moody

Lead   Ray Moody

Potted History: 'THE RAYDENMICS'

The boys from 15 Brisbane Street. All of the group members were aged between 11 and 15. The Raydenmics appeared at local talent competitions and youth clubs. They played mainly Shadows, Chuck Berry and Top Ten numbers. Equipment was at a premium and included a set of Beverley drums, one Vox AC15 amplifier (complete with Tremolo effect pedal) a mike and stand, one Hofner guitar and a Guyatone LG50 (formerly owned by a member of the Phantoms). In 1966, slightly better equipped they changed their name to the 'Shapes'.

REBELS 1963 - 1964 **GOOLE**

Drums Doug Draweley

Bass Jimmy Carol

Guitar Pete Raywood

Lead John Shipley

Potted History: 'THE REBELS'

While having a good sound this group were not very good at being 'Rebels'. Pete Raywood remembers the group's manager running off with his girlfriend. Pete went on to play with the Cossacks.

Another version of the Rebels came from nearby Scunthorpe and they were quite successful. They won Scunthorpe's 1965 'Battle of the Bands' competition. This group consisted of Andy Mayers on bass. Mick Graveling on lead, Keith Burdett on the drums and Rick Laughton on vocals.

RED DIRT   1969 - 1970   **EAST RIDING**

Drums   Steve Jackson (Cucumber)

Bass   Ken Giles (Mutiny)

Lead   Steve Howden replaced by
               Ron Hales (Sweet Sugars)

Vocals   Dave Richardson

Potted History: 'RED DIRT'

Steve Howden was prior to this with York recording band the 'Roll Movement'. Red Dirt initially called themselves 'Wellington Boot!' They soon joined a London Management Agency and secured a recording contract. The group released an album on Fontana in 1970 appropriately entitled 'Red Dirt'. Mint copies of the album are currently valued at £400! A limited edition (500 copies) 'Live' album entitled 'Diamonds In The Dirt' is also thought to have been pressed. After Ron Hales replaced Steve Howden the band changed its name to 'Snake Eye' and during the early 1970s they were managed by Barry Nettleton's Hull Brick Company. Snake Eye played national venues and supported many major rock acts. Steve Howden moved to America, later recording with a group called Jude.

Discography:

Album:

'Red Dirt'   1970   FONTANA STL 5540

Steve Howden (Red Dirt - 1970)

REFLECTIONS   **1969 - 1974**   **HULL**

Drums   Kevin Corbett (Scarlet Farmyard

Bass   Dave Carmichael (Childhood)

Lead   Graham Drax (Peacebreakers)

Potted History: 'REFLECTIONS'

Two former members of 'That Feeling' in a reflective mood. Reflections were busy both in town and out. Kev Corbett and Dave Carmichael had between them been members of some of the most influential local groups of the Swingin' Sixties'. These included the Gonx, Plague 66, That Feeling, the Variations and the Scarlet Farmyard.

RELATIONS   circa 1963   **HORNSEA**

Drums   Dave Bradfield

Bass   Robin Taylor (Gazelles)

Rhythm   Mike Donald (Gazelles)

Lead/Vocals   Dave Tenny

Other Members;   John Hutchinson

Potted History: 'THE RELATIONS'

The Relations featured two former 'Gazelles' and singer/guitarist Dave Tenny. Dave would later change his name to 'Dev Douglas' and move to London where he released several records including the song 'I Don't Know'. Unfortunately, non of his records reached the charts. He also made several television appearances and toured on various pop package shows with stars from the early Sixties'. He did however, much later, feature on the Bobby Blue hit 'Do You Wanna Dance' and in the 1980s did even better with the voice over part on the No. 1 hit 'Star Trekkin'.

RIP VAN WINKLE   1966 - 1968   BEVERLEY

Drums   Nigel Moxon, Barry Trousdale

Bass   Mike

Guitar   John Blizzard

Guitar   Robin Thornham

Lead   Tony Soames (Penjants)

Potted History: 'RIP VAN WINKLE'

A group which awakened to the sounds of rock music. Rip Van Winkle played regularly at the Beverley Regal. Other local gigs included Brandesburton Village Hall where they supported top Beverley group the Strollers. Tony Soames had come out of the Penjants to form Rip Van Winkle. Several members of this group were actually former pupils at Longcroft School in Beverley where various members of Beverley's top group, the Strollers, had also attended. Barry Trousdale could also honestly say that for a while he was also a 'Stroller' because for a few gigs he joined the group, filling in for Pete Cuthbert who had broken his wrist.

The Road Runners (Driffield - 1964)

RIVERBEATS	1963 - 1967	HULL

Drums   Brian Levitt

Bass   Eric Pascall

Rhythm   Graham Mundy

Lead   Tony Hadland

Sax   John Townsend

Vocals   John Reid replaced by Kevin Mulligan

Potted History: 'THE RIVERBEATS'

Like the 'Rats' a name linked to the 'River Humber'. Originally known as 'Jon and the Riverbeats'. The band played Top Ten and R & B. In 1963 they won a beat contest at the Skyline Ballroom in Hull with Robin Taylor standing in on the bass. The Riverbeats were busy gigging throughout the City for many years including pubs, dances and youth clubs. One memorable gig was supporting Zoot Money and the Big Roll Band along with the Tycoons at the Hull Art College dance. Zoot is quoted as saying that the Riverbeats were one of the best semi-pro bands he had ever heard. One of the band's worst moments was playing at a local youth club along with the 'Ides of March'. When drunken youths tried to get on to the stage there was nearly a full scale riot and on their way out the youths tried to tip the Riverbeats van over. Around 1965 there were some changes in line-up and later members included Dave Carmichael. In 1967 the Riverbeats supported the Small Faces at the Brid Spa and later that year some of the remaining members formed 'Night Starvation' who would support the Pink Floyd.

ROAD RUNNERS   1964 - 1969   DRIFFIELD

Drums   John Hall replaced by
Mick 'Woody' Woodmansey

Bass   Dick Theakston

Rhythm   Bryan Wheeldon

Lead   Dave Lawson

Vocals   Dave Westaway

Potted History: 'THE ROAD RUNNERS'

Originally an R & B group, the Road Runners were influenced by the sounds of Chuck Berry and Muddy Waters. They were previously known as the 'E' Types. A popular group they often played support at the Brid Spa. Other local gigs included the Beverley Regal, the Mandrake Club in York, the Condor Club in Scarborough and the Kon-Tiki Club in Hull. The Road Runners supported several rock stars including Jeff Beck, Zoot Money and the Troggs. The group were featured in the East Yorkshire Pop Magazine 'Beatcomber'. A later member of the Road Runners was drummer Mick 'Woody' Woodmansey who would go on to join David Bowie.

ROCKAFELLAS   1964 - 1966   **YORK**

Drums   Rob Illing replaced by Colin Berryman,
                 Rob Weldon

Bass   Barry Wood replaced by Murray Addison

Lead   Ron Goodall

Vocals   Gerry Harrison

Potted History: 'GERRY B AND THE ROCKAFELLAS'

Gerry B's name was a pun on a popular drink of the time
'Cherry B'. The Rockafellas were resident at the Wildman public
house on the A64 and were one of the top York groups. Their
gigs included Holiday Camps and wherever they played they
packed the venues out. The group eventually began to add
comedy to its repertoire and Gerry Harrison later went on to
build a successful career as top comedian Justin Gee.

ROCKING   circa 1965   **POCKLINGTON**
HELLIOTS

Drums   George Harper

Bass   Brendan Wilson

Rhythm   Adrian Wilson

Lead   David Yeats

Vocals   Barry Appleby

Potted History: 'THE ROCKING HELLIOTS'

The Rockin' Helliots specialised in R & B. Gigs included playing most places on the East Coast, including venues in Hull. The Helliots supported Billy J Kramer and the Dakotas at the Brid Spa. They later changed their name to the 'Sons of Witch'.

ROGER BLOOMS HAMMER   1966 - 1967   HULL

Drums	Pete McLeod (Mods)
Bass	Pete Green (Mods)
Lead	Mike Brooke (Rivals)
Sax	Chris Fairbanks
Trumpet	Ian Gray
Organ	Bob Cranswick
Vocals	Roger Bloom (Magpies)

Potted History: 'ROGER BLOOMS HAMMER'

Born out of the 'Mods', Roger Bloom's Hammer were a powerful sounding group who really tried for the big time. Managed by Pete McLeod, they played premier gigs and supported many top groups. The top gigs they played included appearing at the Tiles Club down London's Oxford Street and the groups they supported included Stevie Winwood's 'Traffic. RBH auditioned for Television's Opportunity Knocks and impressed show host, Hughie Green with one of the songs they played. The group then produced a demo tape at the Fairview Studios in Willerby which led to them signing a recording contract. Their single releases on CBS were 'Out of the Blue', followed by 'Polly Pan'. Both records were played over the airwaves by Pirate Radio Station 270. Despite this, with the lack of success with their singles, the original Roger Bloom's Hammer virtually disbanded in 1968 with most band members leaving. Replacement members Darryl Adams and Ian Gray stayed on for a while but eventually a virtually new line-up would go under the simpler title of 'Hammer'

Discography:

'Out Of The Blue', c/w 'Life's A Gamble'
1967   CBS   202654
'Poly Pan' c/w 'Fifteen Degree Temperature Rise'
1967   CBS

The Hammer (Hull - 1968)

ROGUES   circa 1963/64   **BEVERLEY**

Drums   John Burgess

Bass   Brian Cross

Guitars   Mike Coates

Vocals   Mike Booth

Potted History: 'THE ROGUES'

Formed by pupils at Beverley's Longcroft School. John Burgess went on to drum for top local groups the Penjants, the Strollers and the Scarlet Farmyard.

The Hammer (Hull - 1967)

ROLL MOVEMENT 1965 - 1968   YORK

Drums   Dave Williams

Bass   Johnny Fielder replaced by Pete Shaw

Rhythm/Trumpet   John Cartwright

Lead Guitar/Vocals   Cliff Wade

Potted History: 'THE ROLL MOVEMENT'

In the Autumn of 1965, Cliff Wade put together the Roll Movement. 'We were young, and we'd been playing paid gigs for years in various York bands. Hard to believe, but this time we did good, rock and soul, good looks, cool clothes - we had it all. Before too long we also had hundreds of loyal supporters (especially female ones) and we were supporting bands like the Who, Cream and Pink Floyd.'

The Roll Movement were formed out of the Misfits and were originally a 'Mod' band of the Swingin' Sixties'. They spent several years around York soon building up a reputation as one of the top groups in town. The group's early rehearsals took place in a local butcher's meat cellar where the group learnt to 'rock' in and out of the hanging carcasses. The Roll Movement's first gig was on the 10th December 1965 at York's Kings Manor Hotel. Once on the road, their sound began to develop after Cliff Wade watched how Manchester soul band 'St. Louis Union' combined guitar and sax to get a big sound. John Cartwright used to play trumpet in the Sea Cadets and Cliff Wade persuaded him to use his talent in their new line-up. 'We tried the same thing with guitar and trumpet. I would choose guitar chords carefully and emphasise certain notes to blend with John's trumpet, I think it worked well.'

The Roll Movement were very busy on the local scene making regular appearances topping the bill at such venues as the Assembly Rooms and the Boulevard Night Club. In 1966 the group took part in the Melody Maker Rock Contest and reached the semi-finals, which were staged in Brighton. Coach loads of fans made the trip to see them win their way through to the final. The final was held at the London Palladium where the Roll Movement eventually come second to the 'Eyes Of Blue' out of more than a thousand entries. By this time the group were being managed by promoter Syd Hartness who also managed Scunthorpe's 'Gospel Garden'. The group began to tour the country on the top national rock circuit with gigs at Newcastle's 'Club A-Go-Go', Blackpool's 'Twisted Wheel', Sheffield's 'Mojo Club' and the many and various top London clubs. Cliff Wade recalls that, 'The Mojo, like the Twisted Wheel were an elitist audience. It didn't matter how much real soul you were putting into your music, if it didn't appear fashionable in their eyes they were blind and deaf to it. As for the Mojo, yes, the sweat did drip from the ceiling and the price of coke (the drink!) was extortionate.' One night the Ike and Tina Roadshow turned up at the Mojo without a PA system and the Roll Movement lent them their's. Years later, Tina Turner would record one of Cliff's songs.

Around this time, Cliff Wade was almost coaxed into auditioning for the Spencer Davis Group as a replacement for Stevie Winwood, but he declined. The Roll Movement were then featured in a Scarborough newspaper when they took part in a sit-down protest at the closure of Pirate Radio Station 270. The Roll Movement had always been big fans of the Radio Station, so much so that early on in their career, in a moment of madness they had hired a fishing boat to personally take a crate of beer to the Radio 270 crew. As the fishing boat drew nearer, the North Sea went crazy and the mission had to be abandoned when Johnny Fielder went 'green around the gills'. Cliff Wade remembers that he felt too scared to be seasick!

The Roll Movement (York - 1966)

The Roll Movement (York - 1967)

It was only a matter of time before the group achieved a recording contract and after producing some demos tapes, they were eventually signed to the Go label. The group then recorded the single 'I'm out on my own'.

'Our first (and last release) 'Just One Thing' was a unmitigated failure. The London recording session was a rushed farcical affair. No band members were allowed to play on the record. Ken Goodman ('Puppet On A String' arranger) arranged two songs for a crew of seasoned session musicians over which I tried to place my bewildered vocals. After spending the night in London the next day I had to travel by train to Port Talbot in South Wales to meet up with the rest of the band for a gig. They never arrived. Our van had conked out on the M1, leaving me stranded in Wales without a penny or an explanatory phone call. Thanks to the support band's hospitality and a whip round, I was soon back in York to ponder whether I should dedicate my life to such a fruitless and frustrating occupation.'

'I'm Out On My Own', the B-side of the record was one of Chris Wade's earliest attempts at songwriting. Cliff considers that it conveys only a hint of how the Roll Movement used to sound. "Years later my Dad remarked on the song, that he never realised that I was feeling that way at 18. A lot of things were never realised."

The Roll Movement played at Hull's Skyline Ballroom several times during 1967 supporting both the Allan Bown Set and Geno Washington. But by the 'Summer of Love' with the failure of the single to chart, Dave Williams left the group to pursue a career as an Art Teacher and was replaced by Mike Candler. Then Pete Shaw left the group and Steve Howden joined switching duties between bass and lead with Cliff. But by the winter of 1967 interest and gigs were dwindling. Early in 1968 the group had a gig in Stoke.

'On the way home heavy snow and ice. Our van crashed into a dry-stone wall. "This is it! cried Syd Hartness, who was driving. We ended up crushed under our own equipment. No serious injuries, but I decided it was no longer worth risking life and limb for.'

'Let's leave it on a high, it's dawn, Roll Movement coaches pull into York from Brighton having won a place in the 1966 Melody Maker Beat Group Contest final. At this moment all things seem possible ....

Thanks to Denny and everybody else who made that moment happen. I still remember every single one of you.'

Cliff Wade.

Discography

'I'm Out On My Own'/'Just One Thing'   Go Records AJ11410   1967
'You've Never Been To My House' / 'Sister' Cliff Wade Morgan Blue Town 1968
'Looking For Shirley – The Pop Sike World of Cliff Wade' EDSEL EDCD707 2001

The Roll Movement (York - 1966)

RONNO   **circa 1970**   **HULL**

Drums   Mick Woodmansey

Bass   Trevor Bolder

Lead   Mick Ronson

Vocals   Benny Marshall

Potted History: 'RONNO'

The band formed directly after Mick Ronson had returned home after working with David Bowie and the Hype on the 'Man Who Sold The World' album. Mick basically changed the former Rats into 'Ronno' and they produced one single. However, within a matter of months he had been called back to rejoin David Bowie in London to work on his 'Hunky Dory' album. Mick took with him Woody Woodmansey and Trevor Bolder and the three of them were soon to become known as the 'Spiders From Mars'.

Discography:

'Fourth Hour Of My Sleep' c/w 'Powers of Darkness'
1970   Vertigo 6059 029

RONSON MICK   **1963 - 1970**   **HULL**

Potted History: 'MICK RONSON'

Mick Ronson was Hull's guitar hero. While there were many good guitarists in Hull and the East Riding, Mick Ronson didn't just play great guitar, he both performed and looked like a rock star. Known by his many local fans as 'Ronno' long before his rise to fame with David Bowie, Mick Ronson lived on the Greatfield Estate in Hull and worked as a Corporation Gardener for the Hull City Council. As a child he learnt to play both the piano and the violin. But with the coming of the Yardbirds and the Rolling Stones Mick's interest turned to the guitar. After quickly learning the instrument his first attempt at being a member of a   beat group appears to have been with the 'Insects' a group he formed with other local youngsters Bob Welton and John Tomlinson. From there he moved on to the lead guitarist position with R & B group the Mariners. After leaving them, for a very short while he joined the King Bees and then the Crestas. In 1966 after the Crestas folded, Mick moved to London where he joined a pro-recording outfit called the Voice. Shortly after joining the group, their drummer left and Mick telephoned ex-Cresta's drummer, Dave Bradfield inviting him down to audition for the band. The audition was held in Brighton, prior to the Voice's gig supporting the Yardbirds. Dave was successful and moved into a flat with Mick in London's Cavendish Square. The Voice played on the college circuit and Record Producer Mickie Most was at one point very interested in them. But Most's interest began to wane and one day when returning to their flat Mick and Dave found their gear waiting for them. Attached to it was a note informing them that the band had split and that their fellow band members had gone to live with the leader of a religious cult in the Bahamas. Dave Bradfield returned to Hull but Mick stayed on and joined another band, a soul outfit called the Wanted, but when this also split he too, reluctantly returned to Hull.

413

Back in his Greatfield Estate home, Mick joined the Rats. As a member of the Rats he played all over Yorkshire and Lincolnshire, his long blond hair getting progressively longer as the Sixties drew on. The Rats by the late Sixties' were featuring many 'Cream' numbers in their set and Mick would emulate Clapton's lead breaks, often playing with one arm in the air as he used feed-back and distortion. On stage he was using a 200 watt Marshall Amp with a Fender 'Telecaster' and later a Gibson 'Les Paul'. Backstage, in-between sets he could often be seen doing his 'Gardening' homework for his City and Guilds exams. Fond of wearing tie and dye 'Granddad' shirts and knee length boots he could easily be spotted at any gig. Around this time Mick was offered a lead guitarist slot with Scarborough's 'Mandrakes' and did actually attend a 'secret' rehearsal with Robert Palmer, but he declined to join.

By the time John Cambridge introduced Mick Ronson to David Bowie in 1970 he had already played lead guitar on arguably Michael Chapman's finest album, 'Fully Qualified Survivor'. John Cambridge together with a visit by David and Angie Bowie to Mick's Greatfield Estate home in Hull (later in the Seventies', Ian Hunter would also visit there) helped to convince him to join the newly forming band 'Hype'. The deal finally being clinched with the Bowie's over a meal of fish and chips at the Gainsborough Fish Restaurant in Carr Lane, Hull.

The Hype featured Mick Ronson on lead guitar, Hull's John Cambridge on drums and Tony Visconti on bass. Their first gig was at the BBC Paris Cinema in London, but soon afterwards they performed their first 'live' gig at the legendary Chalkfarm 'Roundhouse' supporting Country Joe and the Fish. That evening has been documented as the 'birth of Glam Rock'. They later also appeared at Hull University. When John Cambridge left the Hype, Woody Woodmansey took over on the drums and later that year they worked on Bowie's 'The Man Who Sold The

World' album. After which having made no money, they returned to Hull and reformed the Rats recruiting Trevor Bolder and changing their name to 'Ronno'. 'Ronno' recorded a single, 'The Fourth Hour of My Sleep' which unfortunately failed to chart. But after receiving a phone call from Bowie, Mick returned to London together with Woodmansey and Bolder, where they moved into Bowie's Haddon Hall apartments and began the recording sessions for Bowie's 'Hunky Dory' album with the group gradually evolving into the 'Spiders From Mars',

Mick was with the 'Spiders' throughout Bowie's classic 'Ziggy Stardust' period, appearing on that album and acting as the catalyst which established Bowie as a Rock Superstar. Mick was also credited with arranging the album and around the same time co-produced Lou Reed's album 'Transformer'. He also toured America and Japan with Bowie and the Spiders. Several memorable appearances were made with them on 'Top Of The Pops' and 'The Old Grey Whistle Test'. In 1973, when Bowie claimed live on stage at the Hammersmith Odeon that he 'didn't' want to tour anymore, Mick began a short solo career, recording two well produced albums. He also appeared with Bowie as Ziggy for one final performance at London's Marquee Club which was filmed especially for American television and helped record Bowie's 'Pin-ups' album with him in France. Unfortunately, Mick's solo career failed to fully take off and he replaced Mick Ralphs in Mott the Hoople, but only appeared on one single with the group, which was entitled 'Saturday Night Gigs'. He left Mott the Hoople together with ex-Hoople frontman, Ian Hunter and formed the Hunter/Ronson band, touring and recording with Hunter albums such as 'Once Bitten, Twice Shy'. Mick also called up for the tour and the album, ex Rat and friend Geoff Appleby. The collaboration with Hunter lasted on and off for the rest of his career.

Later in the 1970s Mick formed a friendship with Robbie

Robertson of the Band and appeared with them on Bob Dylan's 'Rolling Thunder 'Tour which also included backing guest stars such as Leonard Cohen. In 1976 he also produced former 'Byrd' Roger McQuinn's acclaimed solo album ' Cardiff Rose'. From 1976 until his death in 1993 Mick continued to play live including tours with Ian Hunter, and T Bone Burnett, gigging in the small New York clubs and also playing occasional concerts back in London. Mick also produced many other albums including to name but a few, those of the 'Rich Kids' who featured two ex-'Sex Pistols' and Midge Ure, Hull 70's group 'Dead Fingers Talk' 'Storm The Reality Studios' album and an album for Morrisey.

In 1992 Mick joined David Bowie on stage for the song 'All the Young Dudes' at the Freddie Mercury Tribute Concert. He also that year appeared on Bowie's 'Black Tie, White Noise' album track, 'I Feel Free' a song he had last performed with Bowie 20 years before. Bowie appeared on Mick's posthumous album 'Heaven and Hull' on the track 'Like A Rolling Stone' but he didn't appear at either of the two memorial concerts.

The recently released 'Rats' CD is a fitting tribute to Mick Ronson and captures the sound of his guitar playing as you would have heard it in the late Sixties if you'd turned up for say, a gig at Hull's Portobello Youth Club or the Anlaby Common Scout Hut.

Mick Ronson (Hull - 1966)

417

Discography:

Singles:

Under the name **'RONNO'**

'Fourth Hour Of My Sleep' c/w 'Powers of Darkness'
1970   Vertigo 6059 029

Under the name **'MICK RONSON'**

'Slaughter On 10th Avenue' c/w 'Leave My Heart Alone'
1974   RSC LPBO5022
'Love Me Tender' c/w 'Only After Dark'
1974   RSC APBO212

MICK RONSON WITH THE RATS

'The Rats'   ANGEL AIR RECORDS   1998

MICK RONSON SOLO ALBUMS:

'Slaughter On 10th Avenue' 1974 RSC APW0353
'Play, Don't Worry'   1974 RSC APLI0681
'Heaven and Hull'   1994
'Powers of Darkness'   1995
'Just Like This'   1999 BURNING AIRLINE
                                  RECORDS

MICK RONSON with DAVID BOWIE

ALBUMS

Bowie at the Beeb
The Man Who Fell To Earth
Hunky Dory
Ziggy Stardust and the Spiders From Mars
Aladdin Sane
Pin-Ups
Live in Monaco

MICK RONSON with LOU REED

ALBUMS   Transformer

MICK RONSON with IAN HUNTER

ALBUMS - Once Bitten, Twice Shy, Shades Off

MICK RONSON with MICHAEL CHAPMAN

ALBUMS -   Fully Qualified Survivor, Millstone Grit

MICK RONSON ON VIDEO

The Rise and Fall of Ziggy Stardust - The Movie
The Freddie Mercury Tribute Concert
The History of Rock - The 70s

RUMBLE	1967 - 1971	GRIMSBY

Drums   Keith Line

Bass   Steve Curry

Lead   Noel Skelton (The Aztecs)

Sax   Phil Wyatt

Guitar/Vocals   Dave Ranshaw

Other Members: Geoff Mackrill (Lead Guitar)

Potted History: 'THE RUMBLE'

The Rumble band had various line-ups during its existence and in its latter days was simply called 'Rumble'. The band was formed after local youths were encouraged by jazz musicians at Grimsby's South Bank Jazz Club. The original group included organ, sax and brass and it is possible that in the early days the Rumble line-ups incorporated both a 5 piece rock group as well as a 10 piece Jazz Band. The Rumble were the resident group at the South Bank Club where many Hull groups also played. Several stories exist as to how the Rumble got their name. One is that a group member noticed that when they were rehearsing the group made a low rumbling sound! Another story concerns a Grimsby Jazz musician who originally formed the Southbank Jazz Club in the late 1930s. The name of the guy was Harry 'Rumbelow', who according to legend, died in the old Southbank Jazz Club at the Riverhead and consequently haunted the premises. Dave Larder ran the SBJ Club in 1968-1970, and despite several attempts to lure the legendary ghost out, he never appeared. The readjusted 1969 line-up of the group signed a recording contract with Warner Bros. and released the single 'Rich Man, Poor Man'. Steve Curry then joined Marc Bolan in T Rex and sadly, like Marc, was later killed in a road accident. In 1974 Noel Skelton featured on John Gladwin's (late of The Amazing Blondel) solo album, but unfortunately, this was never released. Keith Line later toured with Eddie and the Hot Rods, also worked with Marc Bolan and toured America with Bram Tchaikovsky. He also recorded with them and appears on the album 'Pressure'.

The good news is that in 1985 the Rumble Band reformed for a one-off 'Live Aid' gig and they went down so well that they have continued playing ever since. You can hear their rumble again at gigs anywhere between Grimsby and London.

Discography:

Singles:

'RICH MAN, POOR MAN'
1970   WARNER BROS.   WB8011

SATALITES   circa 1962   **BEVERLEY**

Drums   Colin Cooper

Bass   Dave Hutchinson

Guitar   Barry Donald

Vocals   Barry Hastings

Potted History: 'THE SATALITES'

Another of Beverley's early beat groups, the Satalites were obviously influenced by tracks like Telstar by the Tornadoes. Barry Hastings went on to manage top Beverley group the Strollers. The Satalites, with various line-up changes, developed into the Foot-Tappers.

SCARLET FARMYARD	1967 - 1968	HULL
Drums	John Burgess	
Bass	Tom Roantree	
Rhythm	Tony Soames	
Lead	Rod Turner (Penjants)	
Sax	Colin Moore	
Sax	Geoff Pamplin	
Vocals	Jerry O'Connell (Penjants), Kevin Corbett (Variations)	

Potted History: 'SCARLET FARMYARD'

Psychedelia going at full throttle. Both the arrival of Pink Floyd and Jimi Hendrix on the scene had a big effect not only on the local groups music but on their names as well. Several, just like the Floyd, linked two totally unconnected words together, hence Scarlet Farmyard. The night the Scarlet Farmyard were launched they were appearing at the Brid Spa. The group played the first set using their former name the 'Penjants' then changed their clothes and played their second set as the Scarlet Farmyard. The group had learnt a full set of extra songs and really socked it to the audience. They played R & B, soul and chart covers, anything that kept the audience entertained. The Farmyard rehearsed anywhere they could, including bedrooms and ex-railway goods wagons. They played regularly at the Regal Ballroom in Beverley and the Brid Spa where they supported the likes of the Moody Blues and the Move.

However, even though gigging 3 to 4 nights a week they got relatively little money for their efforts. The group were together for two years. When they split, John Burgess went on to form the rock band 'Wine' with Laurie Burnett while Rod Turner and Colin Moore joined Terra Nova.

SCARLET RAINBOW	circa 1968	HULL

Drums	Alan Carey
Bass	Steve Wright replaced by Geoff Appleby
Lead	Steve Smith
Potted History:	'SCARLET RAINBOW'

Formerly known as the Un-Named, ex-Rat Geoff Appleby took over the bass position with the group after leaving 'Treacle'. Scarlet Rainbow tended towards playing the Top Ten and Beatle songs such as 'Come Together' and 'Something'.

SCENE	circa 1968	HULL

Drums	Barry Jeffrey
Bass	George Garton
Lead	Brian Betham
Organ	Roy Neave
Vocals	Philip Barraclough
Potted History:	'THE SCENE'

A real 'mod' sounding name but the Scene didn't last very long. Local gigs included the Beverley Regal and the Enterprise Club in York. The Scene supported PP Arnold at the Brid Spa. Roy Neave went on to join the excellent 'Chest Fever'.

SCORPIONS	1963 - 1965	HULL

Drums   Pete McLeod

Bass   Mike Wright

Lead   Ian Kirkman

Sax   Chris Fairbanks (Swingin Dukes)

Vocals/Harmonica   Val Buffrey replaced by Eric Silver

Potted History: 'THE SCORPIONS'

Based in Kirkella, the Scorpions played mostly Top 20 material and had a local fan following. The group featured Pete McLeod on drums who would later establish his own Entertainments Agency. Busy on the local scene, out-of-town gigs included Filey Pavilion. Chris Fairbanks would go on to join the Rats and Roger Bloom's Hammer.

SCORPIONS   **1993 -1964**   **YORK**

Drums   Phil Calvert

Bass   Ray Morris

Rhythm   Tim Rothwell replaced by Mick Colley

Lead   John Makin

Vocals   Stuart Harrison

Other Members   Linda Cook

Potted History: 'THE SCORPIONS'

This group were originally called Gary Yorke and the Scorpions. When Phil Calvert auditioned for the band along with several other drummers, he didn't think that he would get the job because he had a very big old fashioned bass drum latterly used in dance bands. But the group liked the look of it and signed him up. Phil then discovered that the Scorpions themselves were pretty much equipped with home-made gear with amplifiers that looked mysteriously like old valve radio sets which plugged into home-made speaker cabinets. The Scorpions gigged wherever they could, playing any church hall that would have them including gigs at the Acombe Hotel where a lot of York groups first started out. The group soon became popular and updated to Vox and Selmer 30 watt combo amplifiers. Towards the end of their time together the group took on female vocalist Linda Cook who was particularly good at Diana Ross and Supreme numbers. The group eventually evolved into the 'Four Shades Of Black' and a couple of its members (John Makin and Ray Morris) later went on to join recording band 'Middle of The Road'. They also provided the backing group for Paul and Barry Ryan.

SCREEN	circa 1967	YORK

Drums — Bobby Grice

Bass — Ian Hall

Lead — Eric Wragg

Sax — Keith Kidding

Trumpet — John Jagger

Vocals — Michael Miller

Potted History: — 'THE SCREEN'

Towards the end of the mid Sixties', in an effort to create an exciting on-stage sound, several local groups began adding brass to their line-up. The Screen did this and became one of the top York groups of that period. They toured Britain and played such prestigious venues as the Tiles Club down Oxford Street whose DJ was Kenny Everett. Nevertheless, by the end of 1968 the group had split with several members forming new local supergroup 'Matchbox'.

SEDATION 1968 - 1969 **HULL**

Drums Jim White (Strange Experience)

Bass Tony Soames (Rip Van Winkle)

Lead Rod Turner (Scarlet Farmyard)

Potted History: 'SEDATION'

A rock band influenced by the sounds of Hendrix, Cream and Beck. They supported several top stars including Geno Washington. Both Tony Soames and Rod Turner had begun their musical career with the Penjants. Jim White had been playing the drums since he was 12 and later joined Nothineverappens.

SEMI-TONES   **1964 - 1969**   **HULL**

Drums   Brian Chapman

Bass   Gordon Suddaby replaced by
                         Mike Millington

Rhythm   Dave Oriss

Lead   Peter Loft, Keith Carver

Vocals   Margaret Boutelle

Potted History: 'THE SEMI-TONES'

One of many bands to be managed by the mother of a group
member. The Semi-Tones name was suggested to them when
they were first starting out and were appearing at a local youth
club. The group played mostly Top Ten material and gigged at
pubs, clubs and talent competitions. They got their gigs via Pete
McLeod and on recommendation. The Semi-Tones supported
many top bands including the Fortunes, the Nashville Teens,
Tom Jones and the Squires, the Kinks, the Searchers and
Manfred Mann. The group recorded at Keith Herd's studio and
sent demo tapes to various London record companies. They also
made their own record entitled 'Intuition' which they sold
several copies of in the area. The Semi's also auditioned for
Television's 'Opportunity Knocks'. One of the longest surviving
local groups of the 1960s, the Semi-Tones did eventually
disband as the various members got married. Road Manager
Dave Bell remembers early gig fees ranging from £5 in town to
£10 for out. He also recalls The Semi-Tones having some of their
best nights at the Beverley Regal where they played alongside
the Zircons, the Crestas, Mandy and the Moonrakers, the Rats,
Barry Graham and the Mustangs and the Strollers. This also

occasionally included joining forces with top Beverley group, the Strollers, for a joint number. Ten musicians, their Goodman speaker cones being truly tested as they blasted out the Coasters 'I'm A Hog For You, Baby'.

The Shapes (Hull - 1967)

SET	circa 1967	HULL
Drums	Dave Bradfield (Statesmen)	
Bass	Brian Hairsine (King Bees)	
Lead	Dave Webster	
Vocals	Gary Landis	
Potted History	'GARY LANDIS AND THE SET'	

Formed by experienced musicians on the local scene the band was managed by Pete Bocking. Singer Gary Landis came from Bristol. This group was typical of the many musicians who crossed-over from being main stream 'pop' groups into playing the clubs and cabaret circuit once they got beyond the dangerous age of 21!

The Semi-Tones (Hull - 1965)

SHADES   circa 1968   **GOOLE**

Drums   John Harrison

Bass   Mike Gawtry

Lead   Alan Knight

Potted History: 'THE SHADES'

The Shades were Goole's best-known pop group of the Swingin' Sixties'. They were on the road for many years. During this time they had several changes in line-up and at one point even turned professional. In the 1970s they were resident at Goole's Capricorn Night Club and produced an album 'Reflections' which comprised of many of the songs they had played on stage during the Sixties'.

Alan Knight has fond memories of the group scene during the swingin' 60s, most of which revolve around being packed like sardines in the back of 'poorly ventilated' Bedford vans and playing with unreliable equipment. He puts the Shades popularity down to playing what the audiences wanted to hear. He say's, 'I'm not sure whether Mick Ronson or Robert Palmer ever played Swinefleet WMC, but in 1968, when we took to the stage, we were The Beatles .... '

SHANTELLS	circa 1963	SCUNTHORPE

Drums	Pete Johnson
Bass	Pete Hornsby
Guitar	Mal Turner
Lead/vocals	Jimmy Ryder
Potted History:	'THE SHANTELLS'

The Shantels were formed out of Scunthorpe's earliest rock 'n' roll group, Jimmy Ryder and the Nightriders. Soon after the Nightriders had become the Shantells they took their first trip to France. For over a month they played at a US army hospital base in Toule. On returning to the UK they played a gig in Sheffield and after it were asked if they would be interested in teaming up with late Fifties recording star Jimmy Crawford. Crawford had released several records including his biggest hit, 'I Love How You Love Me'. Despite deciding to join the star, the group still had to rough it, sleeping in the back of their Commer van where every member had their own special place to sleep. Life on the road also meant eating at 'greasy spoon' cafes. But the group did now support many top stars including the Kinks, Dusty Springfield, Freddie and the Dreamers, Herman's Hermits, the Honeycombs, Dave Berry, the Nashville Teens and the Pretty Things. They also stood in for Julie Rodgers (The Wedding) when her backing group failed to turn-up for a gig. While there were several changes in line-up, Jimmy Ryder eventually appeared several times with the group on Television's weekly talent show 'Opportunity Knocks'. This also included a special Christmas performance. All of which were filmed at the ABC studios at Manchester

The Moody Brothers get some decent gear!

The Shapes (Hull - 1967)

The Shapes (Hull - 1967)

Ray Moody (with his greatest fan)

SHAPES	1966 - 1968	HULL

Drums   Michael Moody

Rhythm   Dennis 'John' Moody

Lead   Ray Moody

Potted History: 'THE SHAPES'

The Shapes began life as the 'Raydens' playing 'Shadows' instrumental's and most of the tunes from the Chuck Berry Songbook. They later changed their name to the Raydenmics and finally the Shapes after the Yardbirds hit. The Shapes played the Top Ten including numbers like the 'Move's 'I Can Hear the Grass Grow'. Donovan's 'Mellow Yellow', Jeff Beck's 'Hi Ho Silver Lining', Lulu's 'The Boat That I Row' and the obligatory 'Midnight Hour' and 'Johnny B Goode'. There seemed to be no urgency to write your own material at this time.

I remember sitting for hours, with the record player speed slowed down to 33 and a third, trying to pick up the bass lines off a single. I also remember always being short of decent equipment, using cheap guitars, cheap second-hand amps, cheap second-hand mikes, etc.

With the age of pyschedelia on us we were originally going to be called 'Anim-Yard' after our two favourite groups the Animals and the Yardbirds, but decided to give it a miss after finding out that roughly translated into Latin it meant 'Windy Passage'!

Musically, the Shapes really came of age in the 1970s, with all members going their separate ways and being involved in some good bands, recording, etc.

Personally, in 1977 I got a recording deal with the Independent Cambridge label 'Raw Records'. The Raw stable of groups at that time included the Troggs, Downliners Sect, Kevin Rowland, then of the Killjoys, later singer with Dexy's Midnight Runners, the Softboys (most of whom became 'Walking On Sunshine' and Eurovision band Katrina and the Waves), the Hammersmith Gorillas, the Users, Lockjaw and the Unwanted who later provided members for the Cure, and the Psychedelic Furs.

Our single was RAW 22 and we recorded it in Manfred Mann's 'Workhouse' studio on the Old Kent Road in London the day after Ian Dury and the Blockheads had finished recording their 'New Boots and Panties' album. We had been quite excited when the record company had told us that they were providing us with a real live Record Producer. A member of a pop duo who had recently had a number one summertime hit. But when we saw the guy arrive at the studio on a moped we began to have doubts. Apart from continually trying to give our vocalist elocution lessons he also unfortunately, tried to give the same treatment to our rock single as he had to his pop tune and totally ruined it. Thankfully, the record company agreed and we then re-recorded the record in the Kinks Studio, 'Konk' in Hornsey. The production this time was much better. Unfortunately, just before the date for its release, Raw Records went under (after heavy spending on an album by the Hammersmith Gorillas). Our master tape to this day still remains in the Konk Studio vaults. On recently making enquiries at Ray Davies' Studio we were informed that the tape will be made available to us on the payment of the sum of £1,600!

SHERBURN PANTHERS	1960 –1963	SCARBOROUGH

Drums · Dave Pinkney

Bass/Vocals · Sidney Beal

Lead · Geoff Harrison

Keyboard · Derek Boyes

Vocals · John Dennison

Potted History: · 'THE SHERBURN PANTHERS'

The Panthers originated from the North Yorkshire village of Sherburn. On the scene for quite a while they won the semi-pro section of Scarborough's Gaiety Theatre Band Contest. Derek Boyes was the first person in the area to use a Clavinet electric organ. The Sherburn Panthers were also the first local group to play at Butlins Holiday Camp, Filey. In 1963 the Panthers along with Jonty and the Strangers, Rikki and the Blue Stars, the Moonshots and the Coasters, dominated the Scarborough scene. The group later shortened their name to the Panthers. When Derek Boyes and Danny Darley left the group they joined the Dave Kirby Five who would eventually evolve into the Tennesseans.

SHOTS   1966 - 1967   SCARBOROUGH/YORK

Drums   Geoff Gill (The Viceroys)

Bass   John Lund (The Viceroys)

Rhythm   Phil Peacock (The Moonshots)

Lead   Malcolm Luker (The Viceroys)

Vocals   Mick Rowley (The Moonshots)

Potted History: 'THE SHOTS'

A unique combination of Scarborough and York musicians. The Shots were created out of a mixture of some of the former members of Scarborough's 'Moonshots' and York's 'Viceroys'. The various members believed that in their original outfits they had gone as far as they could on the local scene and that to make it in the music business they really needed to be based in London. After moving to London and finding day jobs, the group had their management taken over by millionaire Alan Brush. He got them a contract with Columbia Records who released the single 'Keep A Hold On What You've Got Now Baby'. The Shots appeared on 'Ready Steady Go' to promote the record and also made appearances at the Scarborough Spa and York Assembly Rooms. Unfortunately, the record failed to chart and after Phil Peacock left, the band changed its name to the Smoke. (See entry for Smoke)

Discography:

'Keep A Hold of What You've Got' c/w 'She's A Liar'
1965   Columbia DB7713

SILKIE   1963 - 1967   HULL UNIVERSITY

Bass   Kevyn Cunningham

Guitar   Mike Ramsden

Guitar   Ivor Aylesbury

Vocals   Silvie Tatler

Potted History: 'THE SILKIE'

A folk group formed by four Hull University Students, they named themselves after the 'Silkie' a legendary Hebridean sea. After several months on the road the Silkie sent a demo tape of themselves to Beatles manager Brian Epstein. He then visited a Northern Club to see them play. Liking what he saw, he signed the group into his famous 'stable' of pop artists. The group then recorded their first single "Blood Red River' which they wrote themselves. This failed to chart and so next they recorded Lennon/McCartneys 'You've Got To Hide Your Love Away' which was a minor hit for them in the States. John Lennon and Paul McCartney produced the record and McCartney can be heard on backing vocals. A clip of the Silkie live in the studios with the Beatles adding their support is still available on film and was recently broadcast on Television as part of a documentary on 'Brian Epstein. The group, like the Hullaballoos toured America and formed part of the 1965 'British Invasion'. In 1966 the Silkie released their third single 'Keys To My Soul' and soon afterwards the further single 'Born To Be With You', both of which failed to chart. Apart from this they also recorded two albums, one entitled 'The Silkie Play the Songs of Bob Dylan'. The group made several television appearances including appearing on 'Thank Your Lucky Stars'. Despite all of this the band split in 1967, apparently due to 'lack of success!'

Discography:

Singles:

'Blood Red River' c/w 'Close The Door Gently'
1965   Fontana TF556

'You've Got To Hide Your Love Away' c/w 'City Winds'
1965   Fontana TF603

'Keys To My Soul' c/w 'Leave Me To Cry'
1966   Fontana TF659

'Born To Be With You' c/w 'So Sorry Now'
1966   Fontana TF709

Albums:

'You've Got To Hide Your Love Away'
1965   Fontana MGF27548

'The Silkie Sing The Songs of Bob Dylan'
1965   Fontana

SKYSOUNDS	1965 - 1969	HULL
Drums	Cal Winestroube replaced by Glen Petty	
Bass	Frank Murphy replaced by William Bolton	
Lead	Albert Barley	
Vocals	Lynda Harrison replaced by Carol Peak	
Organ	Anthony Brown	
Potted History:	'THE SKYSOUNDS'	

'Sensible, smart and well worth hearing' summed up one reporter's description of this band. Born out of the 'Panthers', the group took its name from the 'Skyline Ballroom' where they were resident. The band had numerous line-ups during its existence and these are only a few of them! The Skysounds released several of their own records and also auditioned for Televison's 'Opportunity Knocks' but were unsuccessful. Sadly, bass player Bill Bolton was killed in a car crash. Other Skysound members included Charlie Nicholson, Tim Myers, Derek Flower, Philip Parkman, Alan Glave, Eric Caldow, Jean Playfoot, Dave Fowler, Johnny Lever, Janet Hassan, Mike Smith, Brian Levitt, etc, etc, etc.

SLICE   **1969 - 1970**   **HULL**

Drums   Jimmy Dad

Bass   Duggie Scott

Organ/Vocals   Rex

Potted History: 'SLICE'

Remembered for their 'psychedelically' painted van, their version of Arthur Brown's 'Fire', for having a drummer who looked like Frank Zappa and for not featuring a guitar player! Slice played often at the free concerts held in Hull's Parks during the late Sixties'.

SMALL FOUR   1965 - 1967   **HULL**

Drums   Dave Morris (Blue Berries)

Bass   Johnny Patterson (Aces)

Lead   Tony Gosling (Blue Berries) replaced by
                    Steve Trice (Tycoons)

Vocals/Keyboard   John Small (Fabians)

Potted History: 'THE SMALL FOUR'

The Small Four were a group of musicians who had been
around since the days of Skiffle. They were formed by Tony
Gosling, Dave Morris and Johnny Patterson. They had
originally called themselves the 'Small Four' because there were
only three of them. Then strangely enough they took on a new
member named John 'Small'. John played one of the early
electronic keyboards. The Small Four supported several top
groups during their existence including the Kinks, the Pretty
Things and the Hollies. Tony Gosling left the group in 1966 but
the Small Four continued with new member Steve Trice. The
new line-up successfully auditioned for and appeared on
Television's 'Opportunity Knocks'. Their appearance created
interest amongst the record companies and they released the
single 'One Up on Me' in October 1966. The song was written
for them by John Small. The Small Four were also one of the
lucky local groups who supported Jimi Hendrix when he
appeared at Hull's Skyline Ballroom on March 9, 1967.

Discography:

'One Up On Me' c/w 'I Find Him' 1966 Pye Records IN7191

SMALL SOUNDS   **circa 1966**   **YORK**

Drums   Keith Jackson

Bass   Don Gargott (Cheavours)

Lead   John Loughram

Vocals   Chris Queminet

Potted History: 'SMALL SOUNDS'

Local gigs for the Small Sounds included the Enterprise Club and the Beverley Regal. Chris and Don had been members of very popular York group the Cheavours.

SMOKE   1967 - 1969   SCARBOROUGH/YORK

Drums   Geoff Gill (The Viceroys)

Bass   John Lund (The Viceroys)

Lead   Malcolm Luker (The Viceroys)

Vocals   Mick Rowley (The Moonshots)

Potted History: 'THE SMOKE'

The Smoke were formed out of the Shots who had been an amalgamation of York's Viceroys and Scarboro's 'Moonshots'. When Phil Peacock left the Shots, the remaining members presented some newer more psychedelic demos to Producer Monty Babson and under their new name the Smoke released the great single 'My Friend Jack' which reached no 45 in the British Singles Chart. Unfortunately, the National Radio Stations banned the record because of the line 'My friend Jack eats sugar lumps' which they felt was a reference to the taking of LSD! Nevertheless, the underground press and radio picked up on the song and it was a massive hit throughout Europe. It reached No. 2 in Germany and stayed in the charts for 16 weeks. The Smoke became most successful in mainland Europe and their one official LP 'It's Smoke Time' was released there.

The Smoke's follow-up single 'If the Weathers Sunny' wasn't a hit and the band left Columbia in 1967. They then signed to Island Records and released singles both under their own name and under the name 'Chords Five'. The Smoke's first release on Island was 'It Could Be Wonderful' followed by 'Utterly Simple' which was written by Dave Mason of 'Traffic'. Both singles failed to chart. The singles released under their other name, 'Chords Five' also failed to chart.

Around this time Geoff Gill also produced several of the records released by some of the groups from the area including those of Distant Jim and Cliff Wade.

Eventually Lund, Luker and Gill took up an offer to became resident musicians at Morgan Studios in London and they were soon joined by former Roll Movement frontman 'Cliff Wade'.

With guest musicians Lund, Luker, Gill and Wade continued releasing singles throughout the early 70s, but non charted in the UK, although they did have some success in Holland. Geoff Gill became a producer/songwriter for successful 70s group 'Boney M' and they also recorded a version of the Smokes 'My Friend Jack' which reached 57th position in the UK Charts, in April 1980.

Discography:

THE SMOKE

'My Friend Jack' c/w 'We Can Take It'
1967   Columbia DB8115
'If the Weathers Sunny' c/w 'I Would If I Could'
1967   Columbia DB8252
'It could be wonderful' c/w 'Have Some more Tea'
1967   Island WIP6023
'Utterly Simple' c/w 'Sydney Girl'
1968   Island WIP 603
'ITS SMOKE TIME' LP
1967   GULL INT 128301

SMOKEY'S BALLOON	**1968 - 1969**	**YORK**

Drums   Al Reeve

Bass   Roger Goodrick

Guitar   Dave Britton

Lead   Phil Quin

Vocals   Dave Parkinson

Potted History: 'SMOKEY'S BALLOON'

A very popular and busy York group, local gigs included the Beverley Regal. Smokey's Balloon supported the Love Affair when they appeared at the Bridlington Spa.

SNAKE EYE	1970 - 1972	HULL

Drums	Steve Jackson
Bass	Ken Giles
Lead	Ron Hales
Vocals	Dave Richardson

Potted History: 'SNAKE EYE'

Formed out of 'Red Dirt', a pro band managed by the Hull Brick Company. 'Snake Eye' played throughout the country and supported many top bands. Most of the members had waist-length hair!

Ron Hales had started his rock career in 1965 with the Aeriels whose teenage members included Gavin, Steve Wilson, John Coldwell and Susan Bratley. Ron would develop into one of the finest rock guitarists ever to come out of Hull.

SOCIETY   **1965 - 1966**   **MARKET WEIGHTON**

Drums   Philip Gray

Bass   Paul Thomas

Rhythm   John Illingworth

Lead   Chris Ford

Vocals   Dave Peacock

Potted History: 'THE SOCIETY'

Society were an R & B group who rehearsed 'down on the farm'.
Chris Ford and John Illingworth went on to play with
'Locomotion.

SONS OF WITCH   1966 - 1967   POCKLINGTON

Drums   Tony Fiddler

Bass   Brett Wilson

Rhythm   Adrian Wilson

Lead   Clive Elliot

Vocals   Barry Appleby

Potted History: 'SONS OF WITCH'

Previously known as the 'Rockin Helliots', the Sons of Witch rehearsed in a hut on Pocklington's old Wartime airfield. The group were managed by Brian Sellers. They played support to many top bands including the Searchers, the Mojos, the Who, the Herd, Manfred Mann, Paul and Barry Ryan and Long John Baldry. They also auditioned for weekly TV show 'Opportunity Knocks'. During a gig at the Hull City Hall, the Sons of Witch did a 'Who' and began smashing their guitars, drums, and amplifiers up, which was much to the delight of the audience, J P Cornell, Gough and Davy and other local musical instrument suppliers.

SOUL IMAGE   circa 1967   **HORNSEA**

Drums   Gary Burroughs

Bass   John Crooks

Guitar   Graham Southwell

Potted History: 'SOUL IMAGE'

This was the group future drummer, singer, recording engineer and producer Gary Burroughs started out with. Soul Image played 'Cream' and 'Quo' numbers including 'Pictures of Matchstickmen'. Gary Burroughs went on to join the Pink. Apart from Soul Image Hornsea had several good groups around this time including Blue Circle and Tall Story. Tall Story's members included a really tall lead guitarist. They featured several 'Lovin' Spoonful' numbers in their set and had quite a fan following.

SOUNDS OF SILENCE	circa 1968	HULL

Drums	Martin Jebb
Bass	Bruce Kirton (Harvey Brookes)
Lead	Alfred Hopper
Vocals	Geoffrey Thompson
Potted History:	'SOUNDS OF SILENCE'

While playing dance halls like the Beverley Regal alongside female fronted 'Twiggy's People' the Sounds of Silence were mainly geared towards playing the club scene.

SPANISH LEATHER circa 1967   BRIDLINGTON

Drums   Paul Jenkinson

Bass   Ken Giles

Guitar   Allan Black

Guitar   John Lewis

Vocals   Steve 'Snips' Parsons

Potted History: 'SPANISH LEATHER'

The name of this group came from the Bob Dylan song 'Boots of Spanish Leather'. Allan Black and 'Snips' both attended Bridlington Grammar School and were musical soul mates - they both wore black arm-bands the day Otis Redding died! Allan Black remembers Snips as a young 15 year old teenager being one of the most extrovert characters he had ever met. He recalls him at a Youth Club dance, the crowd around him just stood gawking as Snips danced wildly and shouted 'Sock It To Me'! Spanish Leather, like many young groups just starting out, rehearsed more often than they gigged. But they did play locally including the Seabirds Pub, the Ace of Clubs and various youth club gigs. Their music was that of the Byrds, Jefferson Airplane, the Doors and Bob Dylan. The group evolved into the Mutiny.

SPICE   **circa 1969**   **HULL**

Drums   Graham Keenan

Bass   John Parker

Lead   Geoff Purschion

Vocals   Phil Wingfield

Potted History: 'SPICE'

Busy gigging around Hull, the group had to change their name slightly as 'Spice' kept getting confused with another local band called 'Slice'. One was never too sure just whose gig one was going to see. Spice changed their name to the 'Apple Spice Band.

460

SPREADEAGLE   1969 - 1970   HULL

Drums   Russ Aisthorpe

Bass   Stan Saye

Organ   Rod Temperton

Vocals   John Parker

Potted History: 'SPREADEAGLE'

This group were formerly known as the 'Hammer'. Spreadeagle had a very professional sound and released an album on Page One Records. The group also doubled-up as Camelot 'earning bread' from playing more commercial gigs. I will never forget the sight of the ex-Peighton Checks' singer, standing on the top of Rod Temperton's keyboard. Dressed like an Ancient Greek in a off-white bedsheet he belted out a rock version of the song 'Who Will Buy' from the musical 'Oliver'. Rod Temperton went on to greater things in America, writing and recording with Michael Jackson some of his finest albums. He is reputed to be one of the highest earning songwriters of all time.

John David Parker also did OK. After Spreadeagle split he joined the Boston Showband and worked six hours a night at the Star Club and Top Ten Club in Hamburg. When John left, the band joined forces with Gary Glitter and became the Glitter Band. John stayed on in Hamburg and eventually went on to become a top International songwriter and producer with two worldwide number one hits and over 40 gold, platignum and silver discs to his name. John met up again with Rod temperton in Hollywood in 1984 where he enjoyed dinner with him which was paid for by Quincy Jones.

STATESMEN   **1964 - 1965**   **HULL**

Drums   Dave Bradfield (Batmen)

Bass   John Griffiths (Mariners)

Lead   Rick Kemp

Vocals   Harry Shortland

Potted History: 'THE STATESMEN'

Originally called Vince Ford's 'Statesmen', the group was made up of experienced musicians. Dave Bradfield later joined Mick Ronson in the Crestas. The group is unusual in that it features future Steeleye Span member, Rick Kemp on lead rather than in his later more familiar role on bass.

STEREOTONES   circa 1962   **HULL**

Drums   David Barron replaced by Jim Simpson

Bass   Brian Buttle

Rhythm   Joe Donnelly

Lead   Frank Ince

Vocals   Rocky Stone replaced byBenny Marshall

Potted History: 'ROCKY STONE AND THE
                 STEREOTONES'

This group's name was based on 'Shane Fenton and the Fentones'. It is claimed that singer Rocky Stone spoke with an American accent both on and off the stage despite coming from the depths of Hull! Rocky was replaced by Benny Marshall and the band after various comings and going's was renamed 'Peter King and the Majestics'.

STRANGE EXPERIENCE	circa 1967	HULL

Drums	Jim White
Bass	Frank Murphy (5 Objeks)
Lead	Ken Barrett
Rhythm/Vocals	Ken Allbourne
Potted History:	'STRANGE EXPERIENCE'

The Strange Experience were named after two of the most influential rock bands around in 1967, the 'Jimi Hendrix Experience' from whom they took the last part of their name and 'Cream's single 'Strange Brew' from which they took the front part of their name. The Strange Experience played gigs at the Hull City Hall and the Beverley Regal. Other members include Richard Foster. Drummer Jim White was later a member of pro band 'Nothineverappens'.

The Stereotones (Hull - 1963)

STRANGERS	1961 - 1964	SCARBOROUGH

Drums   Dave Brown, Simon (Sam) Rotherham

Bass   Roy Piper

Lead   Mick Hill

Guitar/Vocals Jonathan Hartley

Potted History: 'JONTY AND THE STRANGERS'

Jonty and the Strangers were the first Scarborough group to hit the local beat scene and they broke down many barriers for other groups. They were for instance the first local group to play both the Scarborough Olympia and Spa, both venues had previous to this only booked traditional dance bands. The group were also for many years resident at the Scarborough YMCA. When 'Jonty and the Strangers' appeared on the same bill as fellow Scarborough group the Panthers they would often join forces on stage for a joint number. The group eventually split when Roy Piper joined the Tennesseans. Jonathan Hartey, better known as 'Jonty' then actually joined the Panthers and Sam Rotherham teamed up with Filey group the Urge, playing keyboards.

STRAWBOA FANTASY	circa 1968	SCARBOROUGH

Drums   Norman Davies

Bass   Derek Gill (Drogo's Trolls)

Lead   Pete Hudson (New Religion)

Vocals   Eric Brooks

Potted History: 'STRAWBOA FANTASY'

Arguably, the most psychedelically named of all the local Sixties' bands. Strawboa Fantasy was a band formed by musicians who would only play the music they liked and not give in to pressure to play popular music just for the money. Their tastes at that time were Cream, Jimi Hendrix and American West Coast Music (The Doors, Buffalo Springfield, etc,) which was not to the liking of the general local gig-goers at that time and consequently their career was short-lived. The high spot of their career was playing at an all-night concert near Hull where their music was really appreciated. The band played their farewell gig at a 21st birthday party in Scarborough before the members went their separate ways. Derek Gill joined the Mandrakes, Pete Hudson joined Brave New World, Norman Davies joined the Urge and Eric Brooks became a disc jockey.

STROLLERS	1962 - 1968	BEVERLEY

Drums   Peter Cuthbert

Bass   Philip (Ali) Barber

Rhythm   Dave Cuthbert

Lead   Gavin Dixon replaced by Laurie Burnett (Penjants)

Organ   Norman Cowey (Foot-Tappers)

Vocals   Dave Park

Potted History: 'THE STROLLERS'

One of the longest surviving and talented local groups of the Swingin' Sixties. For nearly six years they featured their original line-up. The group was formed by a set of school friends who each had an interest in music. They began with acoustic guitars and a snare drum borrowed from the local Church Lads Brigade and would play to anyone who was willing to listen. But their first 'major' gig was at a Women's Institute gathering which included tea and cakes, it was in the building which now houses Radio Humberside on Lord Roberts Road. The Strollers were all in their final year at Longcroft School and invited some of their school friends along to support them. The group had just learned to play the Beatles 1963 hit 'She Loves You' and a reporter from the Beverley Guardian, present at the gig, wrote an article which appeared in that newspaper the following week. In it he dubbed the Strollers sound the 'Beverley Beat'.

The Strollers were raw but they were keen and that appearance gave them the 'bug'. They began to go for it in a big way convincing their parents to sign hire purchase agreements enabling them to obtain electric guitars and amplification. They had also settled on a name, while ideas such as the Becksiders, the Minstermen and the Bev Beats had been put forward, they wanted a name which reflected the musical trend at that time. The Beatles had (beat) – Gerry and the Pacemakers had (pace) – the Swingin' Blue Jeans had (swinging) so they came up with 'Strollers' (roll) and the Strollers were born.

Although well under age, but keen for experience, the Strollers soon after this played in a couple of Beverley pubs including the Grovehill Hotel on Holme Church Lane and the Lady le Gross on Norwood. They were the entertainment on a Friday or Saturday evening. At these early 'bookings' the Strollers wore suits and 'dickie bows' and thought that they looked oh, so classy! They also one evening played at the old British Legion Club on Grovehill Road. But they soon found that It was difficult to play such places as they were so small and there was little room for the equipment. In later years they ended up turning down bookings for this reason.

But they were now in business and while initially playing Cliff Richard and the Shadows numbers 'note perfect' (including copying the Shadow's 'walk'), with the advent of the 'Mersey Sound' the Strollers repertoire started to develop. They began to play more Beatle songs. The group had already begun to learn harmonies and a lot of the Beatle songs were good practice for them. As the Strollers name began to spread their bookings started to increase. They began to play dances at local Youth Clubs, in Cherry Burton, Walkington and Wawne, they also played at RAF Leconfield. Gavin lived in Wawne and that's how they got to play there. They were then asked to play at a dance at Hodgsons Ballroom in Beverley. Dave remembers that the Dave Clark Five hit 'Glad all Over' was Number One in the charts. 'We were basically a pop group at that time and played

The Strollers (Beverley - 1965)

Top Twenty stuff. When we played 'Glad all Over' at Hodgsons ballroom that night, the kids stamped their feet on the floor to the beat of the song. The floor bounced quite heavily and the organisers of the dance told us never to play it again as apparently the stamping of feet was so loud that that the downstairs doors of the ballroom had flown open!

The Strollers would practice anywhere they could. They originally rehearsed in their own homes, usually number 2 or number 11 Crathorne Road. Garth lived at number 11 and Pete and Dave lived at number 2. The neighbours of that time were quite reasonable. But later they managed to practice on a Sunday afternoon at Hodgsons Ballroom. This really helped because they could try out different kinds of songs for long periods of time and not have to worry about the neighbours. This was especially true when they later bought more powerful equipment. When the group took on Barry Hastings as their manager, he allowed them to practice in an old barn he owned down by Beverley Beck and they could then rehearse for as long as they liked.

In 1965 the Strollers entered a 'Beat Contest' in Leeds for which the top prize was an appearance on Television's premier rock show 'Ready Steady Go'. But the group soon realised that they were really not quite ready for it. Around this time the Strollers were asked to play at the Beverley Youth Centre on Coltman Avenue. They were the first group to play there and would go on to play many nights at the Youth Centre, meeting many other groups there over the years. It was at the Youth Centre that they first played on the same bill as Scarborough's top group the Mandrakes and it was the first of many times they would meet.

By now the Strollers had quite a local fan following and on his way to work each morning vocalist Dave Park would often have to run the gauntlet of adoring schoolgirls. As well as dances the Strollers were being asked to do other functions including weddings, birthdays and anniversary do's. These bookings took them into Hull and district and they were soon playing regular dances there. They also began to make regular Friday and Saturday night appearances at the Beverley Regal and Saturday evening dances at the Hull City Hall. To cope with the increase in size of venue their equipment was totally upgraded.

The Strollers had initially been unable to get booked in at the Beverley Regal. This was because many of the first wave groups, such as the Aces, the Tycoons, the Small Four and the Keith Herd group, were still very popular there, playing their early rock 'n' roll, Elvis, Chuck Berry, Everly Brothers and that kind of stuff. But it was the new 'beat' that was beginning to attract the younger crowds and a lot of the older customers were moving on, so the Strollers were booked for their first appearance at the Regal.

At the Regal on a Friday and Saturday night, usually two groups played two sessions each. Because the Strollers were new at the venue they had to go on first and Dave remembers that there weren't many people there at the first session. By this time they had wanted to get away from their suit and tie outfits and were experimenting with stage dress. Anything was acceptable but it was very uncoordinated. Dave wore a pyjama jacket top over a tee shirt that night. Because they looked so very different from the suit and tie groups they drew immediate attention. From that night on the Strollers became regulars at the Regal and most of the time were topping the bill. Some nights they would also join forces on stage with other groups, such as the Semi-Tones, the Crestas and the Zircons, three drummers and up to nine guitarists playing a number together.

The Strollers (Beverley - 1967)

The Strollers (Hodgson's Ballroom)

The most difficult gig the Strollers played at the Regal was as a favour at a Saturday morning children's matinee in front of a load of kids! Dave remembers that they had to set up their equipment between the curtains and the screen and were to go on before the movies started. When they were announced and the curtains opened, they were immediately pelted with sweets, popcorn and other unidentifiable objects. They didn't mind though as the crowd really enjoyed them. The kids cheered after every song, but it was hard work dodging sweets and singing at the same time. Dave made the mistake of throwing one back and got bombarded in the process. He considers that to have been one of the Strollers toughest audiences.

By the end of 1965, the Strollers were playing many Beatle songs, especially those off the very influential album 'Rubber Soul'. They were also playing tracks by the Who, including 'Substitute' and Can't Explain and a particularly good version of James Brown's 'I'd Go Crazy' featuring some excellent keyboard playing. The Strollers would launch into their set with a blistering version of the Hollies 'Come On Back'.

By 1966 the Strollers had developed a truly professional sound featuring strong harmonies. They were introducing more Beach Boy numbers into their set and played absolutely brilliant versions of 'California Girls' and 'Wouldn't It Be Nice'. The band were now also wearing loud green, blue, yellow and white striped jackets like the Troggs. They wore white 'turtle' necked jumpers underneath and grey slacks. They had their jackets especially made for them out of 'deckchair' material! Always smiling, tambourine slapping and strutting, vocalist Dave Park, then known affectionately as 'Garth' had great stage personality, very reminiscent of Davy Jones of the Monkees and he used it effectively to win his audiences (and many girls in the audiences) over!

The Strollers were now playing further afield, with bookings at Brandseburton village hall, Scarborough, Bridlington and Hornsea. Hornsea Floral Hall was a place they played at quite regularly. It was there that they supported hit recording groups like the Mojos, the Pretty Things and Paul and Barry Ryan.

The Bridlington Spa was a great favourite of Dave's. The Strollers backed the Alan Price Set there one evening and they allowed the Strollers to use their professional PA System which was quite a blast!

Other chart topping groups the Strollers supported included the Small Faces, the Searchers, Dave Dee, Dozy, Beaky, Mick and Tich, and the Fortunes. They also, along with the Mandrakes and the Small Four supported Jimi Hendrix when he appeared in Hull in 1967 at the Skyline Ballroom.

The night the Strollers supported Hendrix, Dave remembers it as being a really special event as Hendrix's music was changing the whole scene and subsequently would even change the Strollers sound. Talking, along with others, to Hendrix backstage, Dave remembers him as being quiet and unassuming and wearing some pretty 'way-out' clothes.

In 1967 the Strollers career took a surprising turn when one night they were invited to play at the Young Conservatives Club in Cottingham. It proved a interesting break for them. Dave guesses that, that night they must have been seen by some of the 'Upper classes' and that their sound and style proved acceptable to that crowd. Dave believes that their now infamous striped outfits might just have swung it for them! He also reflects that it was funny how they had gone from suits to wearing anything and back to suits. He thinks that they felt that they needed more stage presentation as they were now playing a lot of these classy do's and it seemed the obvious thing to do.

As a direct result of the Cottingham gig the Strollers were booked to play Wednesday evenings at the Trees Country Club in Ferriby. They were then asked to play at the South Cave Castle and became a favourite turn at birthdays, weddings and anniversaries with this crowd. But the real highlight of this period came when they were booked in 1968 to play at Hoveringham Hall for the 21st birthday party of Angela Worsley (the Duchess of Kent's sister). Dave recalls that this was really classy and he remembers driving down the long driveway to get to the 'House'! The Strollers really enjoyed that evening and got to see how the rich folk lived. The parking lot didn't have anything cheaper than a Jaguar in it!

Another highlight of the Strollers career was winning the final of one of the yearly Talent Competitions held by Hull City Leisure Services most years throughout the 1960s. The various heats being held in the local parks with the final at the Hull City Hall. Winning the competition gave the group some useful publicity, but directly afterwards they were a little bit deflated because after winning the final in front of an audience of 1500 people and having their photograph taken, it was never featured in the Hull Daily Mail. Instead the Mail used a photograph of the winners of the Junior section, a dance troupe!

The Strollers were also one of the first groups to record in Keith Herd's Studio in Willerby. While recording several numbers from their stage set, which they had put onto disc, they also recorded a song called 'Felicity' which was written by Keith Herd and Rick Kemp. Keith had contacts with Columbia Records and sent this recording off to their Studios. Unfortunately, it failed to rouse interest, but the group weren't surprised, as they didn't like the song either!

One of the group's worst moments around this time was at a

Youth Club dance in Hedon where some of the local youths took a dislike to two of the group's members because of the attention the local girls were giving them. They caused trouble to such an extent that the gig had to be abandoned with the Strollers having to make a hasty retreat.

In 1968 lead guitarist Gavin, emigrated to Canada and Laurie Burnett of the Penjants replaced him. Pete Cuthbert left the group sometime later followed by Norman. Pete was replaced by John Burgess (Bodge) also of the Penjants. With the new look to the group and changes generally happening musically there were brief flirtations with the idea of changing the Strollers name. Laurie Burnett came up with the 'happening' name 'Funky's Idol'. But thankfully the group decided to stick to their original name. However, with the exceptional guitar skills of Mick Ronson contemporary Laurie Burnett, they now began to take on more of the new sounds by groups such as the Move, Moby Grape, Cream, Hendrix and the Moody Blues, and the Strollers original image began to change.

That year the Strollers signed a management deal with the Pete McLeod Agency and gigs continued to pour in. They quite often appeared with the Mandrakes around this time and Dave recalls that whenever they played the same gig together, Robert or Allen Palmer as he was then known, would often ask the Strollers to play some Beatle numbers, of whom he was a great fan. At a dance at Burton Constable Hall, Robert Palmer actually joined Dave on stage to duet on the Strollers version of the Beatles 'Hey Jude'. Another person who also joined Dave up on stage one evening, at the Brandesburton village hall, was Rats drummer John Cambridge. In-between sets the two of them, stood side by side, whistling 'I Was Kaiser Bill's Batman' to a stunned and mesmerised audience!

The pressure of holding down a day job and gigging at night for such a long period of time eventually took its toll and after a tour of Northern towns in January 1969, Dave Park decided to leave the band and the Strollers disbanded altogether. In 1973 Dave emigrated to Canada.

One of Dave's favourite memories of his time with the Strollers is of when they supported the Searchers at the Brigg Cinema in Filey. The year was 1968 and the Brigg had booked a few acts for the summer in an attempt to draw in more people to the resort. The Strollers were to play a matinee and an evening session. They were big fans of the Searchers and of all the Liverpool groups, so this really was a special gig. When they met the Searchers at the Brigg, they turned out to be a really great bunch of guys. The group at the time consisted of Mike Pinder, John McNally, Frank Allen and John Blunt. Their last big hit in 1966, was 'Take Me For What I'm Worth' so by the time they came to Filey they had disappeared from the Top Twenty charts and were not as popular. The Strollers played the matinee performance in front of 14 people and couldn't believe it. A group who had, had so many hits over the years and yet so few people had showed up. They decided to join the audience when the Searchers went on and after each song, tried to make as much positive noise as they could. The Searchers were very appreciative and after the matinee session both groups went down to the beach and played football. The Searchers versus the Strollers (Liverpool v Beverley)! The evening session also wasn't much better with only about 2 dozen people showing up and one couple actually complaining because they thought they had come to see 'The Seekers'! But Dave really enjoyed that day and couldn't believe that he had actually played music and football with the Searchers and it lives long in his memory.

As a Canadian, Dave's lifestyle has now changed, but he will never forget those halcyon days of the Swingin Sixties'.

THE STROLLERS

SUGAR 'N SPICE   1968 - 1969   **HULL**

Drums   Glen Petty (Dimes)

Bass   Barry Donald (Fabians)

Lead   Tony Auld (Fabians)

Organ   Norman Cowie (Strollers)

Vocals   Margaret Wedgner (Girlfriends)

Potted History: 'SUGAR 'N SPICE'

Sugar 'n' Spice signed a record deal with Columbia Records and recorded at the legendary Abbey Road Studios where the Beatles produced so many hits. EMI Recording Manager Bob Barrett actually travelled to Hull to see the group in action before bringing them down to London. Sugar and Spice featured the excellent keyboard skills of former 'Strollers' member Norman Cowie, but his new group tended more towards cabaret.

SUNSETS	1961 - 1964	HULL

Drums   Les Lamb replaced by Doug Thurlow, Brian Sleight

Bass   Pete Edward Green

Lead   Pete Green

Vocals   Irvin Gordon replaced by Rod Ellis

Potted History: 'TONY MARTIN AND THE SUNSETS'

I saw this great sounding group playing on the bill of one of the 'Beat Nights' held in Hull's West Park during the summer of 1964. Rod Ellis had taken over the vocals spot after being invited on to the stage to sing a couple of Cliff Richard numbers when the original Sunsets were playing at a Bridlington Youth Club. So impressed were they by Rod's vocals that the band (minus their original singer) went round to his house the next day and signed him up! Original vocalist Irvin Gordon then left the group and formed the rival 'Dean Curtis and the Phantoms', later emigrating to Australia. Between 1963-65 the Sunsets were the resident group at Hull's Gondola Club, supporting and backing many of the top bands who played there. While getting their own bookings locally, they had Cleethorpes agent Martin Yale for their out-of-town work and they travelled quite extensively. In 1964 Martin Yale, decided that it was time that the group had a new image and he came up with new name the 'Mods'. To go with their name the group had a new set of stage gear created, the like of which at that time had only been seen being worn by the Rolling Stones.

| SWEET SUGAR | 1967 - 1969 | HULL |
| SOUL SET | | |

Drums   Dave Spenceley

Bass   Colin Bell

Rhythm   Rob Fleet

Lead   Al Wright

Vocals/Harmonica   Dave Topham

Potted History: 'THE SWEET SUGAR SOUL SET'

The Sweet Sugar Soul Set was started by Dave Spenceley. The group originally concentrated on playing soul music, like several East Riding groups around this period. Busy in the local area, gigs included the Beverley Regal. But the group played all over Lincolnshire and the Ridings including the Whitby Spa, Brid Spa and gigs in Scarborough. The Soul Set supported several top groups including 'Cupid's Inspiration', the Hurt, P P Arnold, Love Affair, the Paper Dolls, Amen Corner and the Move. They also shared the bill with many local groups including Mick Ronson and the Rats. The Soul Set were yet another band to suffer at the hands of jealous youths. At a gig in York a gang of them climbed on to the stage and carrying knifes, cut their way through the group's guitar leads. Alan Wright eventually left the band due to travelling distances and the group's van being involved in a road accident whilst returning from a gig at Gainsborough Drill Hall. When Ron Hales joined the group to replace him, they shortened their name to 'Sweet Sugars'.

SWEET SUGARS   circa 1969   **HULL**

Drums   Dave Spenceley

Bass   Colin Bell

Lead   Ron Hales

Vocals   Dave Topham

Potted History: 'SWEET SUGARS'

Formed out of the 'Sweet Sugar Soul Set', Sweet Sugar played Cream, Hendrix and Tamla Motown numbers. The first 'real' sighting of ace guitarist Ron Hales on the local scene was with this group. He had apparently spent the previous year in London. When Ron joined the group, their sound became much heavier and they began playing bigger venues. Sweet Sugar were managed by Pete McLeod and they supported many top groups. Local DJ Ricky Dobbs took the Sweet Sugar into Keith Herd's Willerby studio which was then based in the front room of Keith's home. Here with the technical refinement of egg boxes stuck on the walls they recorded the Isley Brothers track 'Behind A Painted Smile'. Ricky had a disc cut of it and took it to London. The London Record companies were apparently impressed by the recording but rumours about the possibility of the Isley Brothers re-releasing the record meant nothing became of it. 'Sweet Sugar' eventually evolved into a showgroup called 'Autum', adding two girl singers (Lynn Andreason and Lynn Clark). Ron Hales later joined recording group 'Red Dirt'.

Sweet Sugars (Hull - 1969)

Barry Adams and The Swingalongs (York - 1961)

SWINGALONGS   **1961 - 1965**   **YORK**

Drums	Ron Cooper replaced by Steve 'Sticks' Bennet
Bass	Ian McClaren
Sax	Norman Hughes
Lead	Geoff Oakland
Vocals	Barry Adams
Potted History:	'BARRY ADAMS AND THE SWINGALONGS'

Originally, called Danny Adams and the Challengers the Swingalongs were formed for a residency at York's White Horse Hotel, down Coppergate. The group soon built up a reputation for themselves, both on the local scene and further afield. They didn't just play Top Ten numbers but quite a wide range of music and were very versatile. In 1963 they made their first broadcast on BBC Radio and attracted a lot of publicity in the national and local press. The group also won their way through to the North's Top Group Finals in Leeds where they fought it out for the title of 'North Top Group' along with five other groups. The Swingalongs where also one of the first groups to put together a charity concert for a world 'Freedom From Hunger' campaign. This was held at York's Carr Lane Junior School and was long before Bob Geldolf got a similar idea!

SWINGING DUKES 1964 - 1965   HULL

Drums   John Marshall

Bass   Brian Harrison

Rhythm   Peter McLeod

Lead   Terry Barrett

Vocals   Clive Dunn

Potted History: 'THE SWINGING DUKES'

The Swingin Dukes were one of the first Hull groups to have a fan club. Sax player Chris Fairbank was also at one time a member of the band. The Swingin' Dukes made a demo tape which included the self-penned track 'Love Can Last'. Local gigs included the Hessle Town Hall and they also gigged out of town. The Dukes were particularly popular on the club scene.

SYNDICATE 5	1963 - 1965	DRIFFIELD
Drums	Tony Knaggs	
Bass	Tony Simms	
Rhythm	Mike Rogerson	
Lead	John Beyley	
Vocals	Tal Taylor	

Potted History: 'THE SYNDICATE 5'

The Syndicate 5 were a top Driffield group who played all over the East Riding. They were particularly popular in York at such venues as the Tramways and the Enterprise Clubs and could often be seen in Hull at dances at the City Hall. The Syndicate 5 also appeared regularly at the Brid Spa where they played support to many top outfits including Tom Jones, the Hollies, the Swinging Blue Jeans, Cliff Bennet and the Rebel Rousers, the Fenmen, Manfred Mann, Spencer Davis, the Moody Blues and the Bow Street Runners. So popular was the group that they were also able to attract large audiences on a Wednesday evening when they topped the bill at the Spa themselves. Sixties' girl's magazine 'Jackie' tipped the 'Syndicate 5' for stardom. One moment captured of them in time is in the summer of 1965 when the Syndicate 5 appeared at the Brid Spa supporting the Moody Blues. That night the group performed on stage. wearing their famous blue and white hooped long-sleeved Tee-shirts. The Byrds number one hit 'Mr Tambourine Man' topped the charts and whilst performing this up on stage the lead guitarist climbed onto the singer's shoulders to play the guitar solo. Halcyon Days!

TELSTARS   circa 1963   **GOOLE**

Drums   John Gardiner

Rhythm   Pete Robinson

Lead   Mike Trickett

Potted History: 'THE TELSTARS'

The early 1960s was the era of 'Space flight'. Uri Gagarin had been flown into space and circled the earth, Russians dogs had also circled the earth. Not to get left behind the USA had sent monkeys up into space to circle the earth and the first satellite had also been launched. Many groups began to name themselves after things connected with space. While nationally we had the 'Spotnicks' and the Tornadoes (who released the brilliant record 'Telstar'), locally we had the Martians (Hull), the Blue Streaks, the Moonshots (Scarborough), the Astronauts (Hull and Scarborough), the Satalites (Beverley), the Flyaways (Hull), UFOs (Hull), the Vulcans (Hull) and both the Satalites and the Telstars from Goole. The Telstars were one of many groups influenced by the Shadows and they featured several instrumentals in their repertoire. Mike Trickett went on to become a member of top Goole group Us 'n' Im.

TENNESSEANS	1964 - 1966	SCARBOROUGH
Drums	Dave Pinkney	
Bass	Danny Darley replaced by Roy Piper	
Lead/vocals	John Hutchinson replaced by Paul Downing (Tycoons)	
Keyboards	Chow Boyes	
Potted History:	'THE TENNESSEANS'	

I remember seeing this great group several times at the Hull Parks Beat Nights in the summer of 1964. I also saw them again later in 1966 when they regularly appeared at the Hull City Hall. Other regular gigs included the Candlelight Club in Scarborough and Filey's Belle Vue Club. Even in 1964 the Tennesseans had a very modern rock sound to the guitar playing and seemed a couple of years ahead of their time. The group had named themselves after the Gretsch 'Tennessean' guitar and had Nashville influences. They used no echo units and evolved into the three piece style of playing. The Tennesseans supported many of the early rockers including Little Richard, Johnny Kidd and the Pirates, and Gene Vincent. On stage the group wore red shirts and black ties and had a great front man in 'Hutch'. When he left the group in 1965 to go to Sweden, former Tycoon, Paul Downing took over his spot. The Tennesseans were then still very busy and popular on the local scene and also followed John in touring Sweden. But on their return Paul Downing moved to Los Angeles and John Hutchinson then replaced him in the Tennesseans, until the group finally split. An afternote is that Paul Downing actually came over on holiday from the USA to Scarborough in September 1996 and joined Hutch live on stage.

491

TERRA NOVA	1969 - 1970	HULL

Drums   John Wilson

Bass   Keith Russell

Lead   Rob Kuch

Vocals   Rick Wilson replaced by
                 Rod Turner (Sedation)

Sax   Terry Dunn and Colin Moore (Penjants)
                 replaced by 'JJ'

Potted History: 'TERRA NOVA'

Managed by McLeod Holden Enterprises, Terra Nova began life as a four-piece and then added two horns and began to produce exciting Soul and Tamla sounds. Turning pro they were a very busy band including playing the prestigious Top Ten Club in Hamburg made famous by the Beatles. They supported such top groups as Status Quo and Johnny Johnson and the Bandwagon. Terra Nova also played at the huge Boston Glidadrome. A famous venue in those days, where more often than not, the 'phantom conductor' would appear. This eccentric would be dressed in starched white shirt and tails, his shiny hair slicked back, as though performing at the 'last night at the proms'. And with as much sensitivity, he would stand at the front of the stage and conduct the group through their set.

The Tennesseans (Scarborough - 1964)

TEXANS　　　　　1963 - 1968　　　　　HULL

Drums　　　　　Peter Robinson replaced by
　　　　　　　　　Dave Bradfield

Bass　　　　　　Roger Kendall replaced by Tim Myers

Rhythm　　　　　James Buttery replaced by Alan Morris

Lead　　　　　　Ron Wilkinson replaced by Danny Wood
　　　　　　　　　replaced by John Whitewood

Vocals　　　　　Doreen Towle replaced by Jenny
　　　　　　　　　replaced by Dane Roberts
　　　　　　　　　replaced by Malcolm Hunt
　　　　　　　　　replaced by Bob Rivet

Potted History:　　'THE TEXANS'

The Texans were formed in 1963, for quite a while they were
known as Jenny and the Texans and originally dressed up in
cowboy outfits. They played Top Ten material and while being
popular as a club group they did play at dances including the
Skyline Ballroom, Locarno Ballroom, the Hull City Hall and the
Regal Ballroom, Beverley.

The Texans also played out of town on the Sheffield, Doncaster,
Scunthorpe and Grimsby Clubs. Much longer journeys in those
days because it was before the building of the M62 and the
Humber Bridge, which meant that they spent weekends away,
staying at bed and breakfast establishments and eating fry-ups
at 'greasy spoon' transport cafes.

One of the Texans' highlight gigs was appearing on Reckitt's
private Riverboat Shuffle, playing on one of the Hull - New

494

Holland ferries along with 'Johnny Kidd and the Pirates. Unfortunately, that evening they couldn't get their PA to work and like so many groups had to do, plugged their mikes into their Vox AC30's and sang along with their guitars.

The Texans also supported Brian Poole and the Tremolos at Leeds Locarno and 10 days later appeared with them again at the Brid Spa.

When Dane Roberts took over on vocals the Texans style changed with them tending to cater more for the clubs.

The highlight of the Texans career was passing the audition for Television's weekly talent show 'Opportunity Knocks'. This was to be filmed at the Granada Studios in Manchester. For months the Texans eagerly waited for their television date but were eventually told that because so many acts had successfully passed the auditions, they had, had to slim down the number of available spots and so their TV appearance never came off, disillusioned the band eventually split.

THAK J S   circa 1969   **HULL**

Drums   Mike Heap

Bass   Rick Kemp

Lead   Steve Trice

Vocals   John Small

Potted History: 'J S THAK'

Born out of 'Johnny Small and the Little People' J S THAK was a name made up from the abbreviations of the group's collective surnames, e.g. J S (John Small), T (Trice), H (Heap) And K (Kemp). Rick Kemp went on to greater things, first with Michael Chapman including featuring as the bass player on the classic 'Fully Qualified Survivor' album and then as a member of 'Steeleye Span'. John Small went to live in the USA.

THAT FEELING   circa 1967   HULL

Drums	Kevin Corbett
Bass	Dick Heaton
Rhythm	Dave Jefferson
Lead	Dave Carmichael
Organ	Phil Mullet
Vocals	Graham 'Gaz' Taylor
Vocals	Tony Brown
Potted History:	'THAT FEELING'

Formed out of Plague 66, That Feeling came into being during the second half of their New Year's Eve gig at the Hull City Hall in 1966. They had played the first half of the gig as Plague 66 and played their second set as the newly born 'That Feeling.' While in existence for only eight and a half months, just like their previous band they were one of the most exciting local groups of the mid-Sixties'. They had many original ideas for their stage act including using Go Go Dancers, smoke bombs, and a singer who wore Wellington Boots! Drummer, Kevin Corbett, also took to reciting poetry during long lead breaks (Later copied by Jim Morrison of the Doors). That Feeling supported several top groups including the Small Faces and the Soft Machine. Several other local bands attempted to emulate them but most failed to capture the unique excitement that this band could generate. On splitting, Kevin Corbett and Dave Carmichael formed the Variations, while Graham Taylor went off to the 'Third World.

That Feeling (Hull - 1967)

THIRD WORLD   **circa 1968**   **HULL**

Drums   Glenn Petty

Bass   Graham Wilkinson replaced by
                 Nigel Dalton

Lead   Martin Glover

Vocals   Graham Taylor (That Feeling) replaced by
                 Dave Marshall (Locomotion)

Potted History: 'THIRD WORLD'

The Third World came into being on the wave of the 'Wah Wah' Pedal and the 'Fuzz Box'. The group were formed by former 'That Feeling' vocalist Gaz Taylor. A 'Way out' group they intended to shock audiences both with their music and their style of dress. Tending towards the West Coast sounds of The Mothers of Invention and Jefferson Aeroplane they had to lower their horizons a little. Dave Marshall went on to front the Variations and took Nigel Dalton with him.

THIS GENERATION 1969 -1970   GRIMSBY

Drums   Geoff Byman

Bass   Dave Taylor

Lead   Robert Hinchliffe

Potted History: 'THIS GENERATION'

This Generation were influenced by 'Cream' and 'Jon Hiseman's Colossean'. They turned pro and played all over the UK. One of the highlights of their career was when they were booked to play live on Radio One's Lunchtime pop show. Unfortunately, the group's van broke down on the way and they arrived too late to go on the air. 'This Generation' split in 1969 but reformed the following year with 'longer hair'. Changing their name to 'Black Jasper' they played loud progressive rock music and supported such top groups as 'Gypsy'. Black Jasper always finished their set with the classic Cream number 'I'm So Glad'.

THREE PLUS ONE   *circa 1965*   **HUTTON CRANSWICK**

Drums   Derek Atkin

Bass   Graham Price

Rhythm   John Guy

Lead/Vocals   Brian Nicholson

Potted History: 'THREE PLUS ONE'

Three Plus One were previously known as the 'Chevrolets'. They were the eventual winners of the 1965 Broadgates Talent Competition despite strong opposition from local groups the Strollers and the Raydenmics! Managed by David Thorley, Three plus One supported many top groups including the Animals, the Mersey Beats and the Four Pennies. They had regular work in Hull, Hornsea, Bridlington and York with local gigs including the Beverley Regal.

**TOMORROW'S
TOPIC**   circa 1968   **HULL**

Drums   Brian Levitt (Riverbeats) replaced by
                       Keith Stutt

Bass   Paul Ashurst (Magpies)

Lead   Ron Wilkinson (Mods)

Vocals   Malcolm Hunt (Crestas)

Potted History: 'TOMORROW'S TOPIC'

Tomorrow's Topic played dances, clubs and cabaret. Local gigs
included the Beverley Regal. At one time the group featured
two dancing girls in their stage act, just like several other Hull
groups had done including 'That Feeling' and 'Disturbance'.
On occasion they also used 'psychedelic' lighting and smoke
effects in their act. The group found their name while one of the
band members was browsing through a Motor Car magazine, in
it one of the features was 'Tomorrow's Topic'.

TORNADOES circa 1961 **HULL**

Drums Rod Nicholson

Bass Rod Stubbs replaced by Mike Lilley

Guitar Malcolm Bradley

Lead John Robinson

Vocals Eric Lee

Potted History: 'ERIC LEE AND THE TORNADOES'

The Tornadoes had evolved out of skiffle group the 'Cotton Pickers.' They were resident several nights a week at the Halfway House, Spring Bank, Hull. The group whipped up such a storm at this venue that people flocked in from miles around to seem them whenever they played. The group folded when Eric Lee and John Robinson went on to join the Four Aces and later Eric Lee was vocalist with Hull's first recording group of the 1960s the 'Aces'.

TREACLE	circa 1968	HULL

Drums	John Cambridge
Bass	Geoff Appleby replaced by Keith Cheesman (Jellyroll)
Lead	Mick Ronson
Vocals	Pete 'Benny' Marshall
Potted History:	'TREACLE'

A temporary name change for the 'Rats'. This was the period when Don Lill, late of the Majority took over their management for a while. Keith 'Ched' Cheesman was formerly lead guitarist with the Jellyroll Blues Band and turned to the bass to be in a band with guitar hero, Mick Ronson. Very busy gigging in the area, one notable gig was when the group stood in for Julie Driscol at Hull University when she failed to turn up. 'Sticking to it' they went down well in her absence. While using the name 'Treacle' the group recorded a three-track acetate at the Fairview Studios in Hull. The songs from the session were released on the 1994 limited edition vinyl album 'Bernie Gribblestone and the Rats From Hull' and also on the more recently released CD version of the same album. Despite much marketing as 'Yorkshire's Top group' and using the slogan 'Stick To It Treacle', the group eventually reverted back to its original name, the 'Rats'.

Treacle (Hull 1968)

TRENDS **1965 - 1966** **HULL**

Drums   Trevor Wilson replaced by Noel Cundall

Bass   George Clarke

Lead   Geoff Prest

Vocals   Colin Biggs

Potted History: 'THE TRENDS'

Another great name for a group, the Trends rehearsed in St. Saviours Church bell-tower. Local gigs included the Sombrero Club later known as Prohibition 66. The group supported the New Vaudeville Band when they appeared at the Brid Spa.

TROLLS	1964 - 1966	HUNMANBY

Drums	Tony Mainprize replaced by Dave Hann
Bass	Bob Fox
Rhythm	Stuart Black replaced by Derek Gill
Lead	John Harris replaced by Colin Bardsley
Vocals	Maurice 'Jock' Scullion replaced by Mick Bowen

Potted History: 'THE TROLLS'

The Trolls were formed late in 1964. They specialised in R & B and rehearsed at Grisethorpe Village Hall. A later replacement member was John More on Lead guitar. In 1965 the Trolls played for the season at 'Drogo's Den' which was based in the Linzi Coffee Bar, Skipsea. The Trolls liked the name of the venue so much that they later changed their name to 'Drogo's Trolls'. (All previous resident outfits at the 'Den' had signed recording contracts!) In January 1966 the Trolls supported the 'Mindbenders' at the Scarboro' Olympia. Shortly afterwards the band folded with Mick Bowen and Dave Hann joining 'Big Change' who later became 'Brave New World'. Derek Gill joined the Mandrakes.

| TURNABOUTS | circa 1965 | SCUNTHORPE |

TURNABOUTS   *circa* **1965**   **SCUNTHORPE**

Drums   Toyne Tomlinson

Bass   Paddy O'Connor

Guitar   Ernie Boynton

Potted History: 'THE TURNABOUTS'

The Turnabouts were a very popular Scunthorpe band. For such a small town Scunthorpe had a thriving group scene at this time which included recording band the Dimples, the Imps, the Chechakos and the Nightriders.

Maureen and the Freeways were another popular local group and included brother and sister John and Maureen Stevenson, also Rex Garton. They featured in Scunthorpe's first Battle of The Bands contest in 1964. That night the bill also included the Kingpins, the Kraakans, the Dimples, the Ensigns, Blues Anonymous, the Tropics, the Colarados and the Imps.

TYCOONS 1961 - 1965 **HULL**

Drums Dave Kristian

Bass Malcolm Duke

Lead Peter Nutbrown replaced by
Paul Downing

Organ Phil Naylor

Vocals Billy Kent replaced by Harry Shortland

Potted History: 'THE TYCOONS'

The Tycoons were professional for two years, during which time they toured the country, gigged in London and undertook a holiday camp residence at the 'Rock Ballroom', Butlins Holiday Camp, Ayr. While playing at the camp, the Tycoons were given a taste of fan worship when about 50 screaming girls chased them back to their chalet. The Tycoons also made a record which was entitled 'Quo Vardis'. But they eventually returned to Hull and went semi-pro. The bus which they had used to travel the country in was taken over by recording group the 'Hullaballoos'. Playing R & B they had regular gigs at the Hull City Hall and Memorial Hall, Beverley. Other members of the group included Steve Trice. The Tycoons lead guitarist, Paul Downing, was a left-handed player and instead of restringing his guitar he taught himself to play it 'upside-down' whereby he was able to produce some unique sounds. After the Tycoons split, Paul joined the Tennesseans later emigrating to the USA where he provided guitar support for Mama Cass. Today he lives in Los Angeles.

The Tycoons (Hull - 1964)

TYCOONS	1964 - 1966	YORK

Drums   Phil Calvert

Bass   Ron Alpress

Rhythm   John Olive

Lead   Dave Nettleship

Vocals   Mal Addison

Potted History: 'MAL DYMAN AND THE TYCOONS'

The York Tycoons gigged mainly in the West Riding and South Yorkshire, including Universities. They were resident group at the Buckles Inn on the Tadcaster Road.

The Tycoons played Hollies, Manfred Mann and Beatles numbers, drummer Phil Calvert also wrote songs and the group played a few of them. The group became so 'tight' when playing together that instead of just dancing, they noticed that their audiences were beginning to stand in front of the stage and listen. Often at their gigs, when the stage curtains opened the group were faced by a 'wall of people'.

A highlight of the Tycoons career was when they auditioned for agent Stanley Jospeth at the Leeds City Varieties. He sat in the stalls while up on stage the group played him three songs, the last being Phil Calvert's song 'Stop My Greaving'. So impressed was Jospeth by the song that he suggested to the Tycoons that if they produced a demo tape of it, he would take it to London as he felt sure that he could get them a contract with Columbia Records. The group quickly arranged to record the song and spent a day in session at the Morton Sound Studios in

Newcastle (where the Animals had first recorded). Flushed with success, drummer Phil Calvert also wrote off to Television Producer 'Johnny Hamp' requesting an audition for a slot on the popular nightly TV show, 'Scene At Six-Thirty'.

Phil remembers the group celebrating their success at a gig at Morley Town Hall. But the success was short-lived because it slowly began to dawn on the various group members that in order to be able to reap their success they would have to turn pro. Two of the band members were studying for their careers and didn't want to give them up. The doubts had set in and shortly afterwards the band split. A few weeks later, Phil Calvert received a letter from Johnny Hamp inviting the group to audition for his television show!

UFOs   **circa 1964**   **HULL**

Drums   Glen Petty

Bass   Geoff Appleby

Guitar   Steve Smith

Potted History: 'THE UFOs'

This group never really 'took-off' as the UFO's and soon evolved into the 'Yorkies'. Geoff Appleby developed into one of the finest bass players around. He took his style from Jack Bruce of Cream and later used it effectively in the Rats. In the 1970s Geoff toured and recorded with the Hunter/Ronson Band.

UNIT IV   **circa 1964**   **FILEY**

Drums   Alan Whitehead

Bass   Dave Hammerton

Guitar   Pete Rickard (Vikings)

Guitar/Vocals   Mike Hepworth

Potted History: 'UNIT IV'

Formed by ex-members of Filey's 'Vikings', Unit IV were influenced by Johnny Kidd and the Pirates and Jerry Lee Lewis. Mike Hepworth played a Burns 'Jazz Guitar'. The group gigged locally at such venues as Flamborough Village Hall and Hunmanby Youth Club. They also had bookings in Scarborough at such venues as the Condor Club. Dave Hammerton went on to play with top Bridlington group, Mark Antony and the Avengers and was also later a member of the Exodus.

UNKNOWNS   circa 1967   **BRIDLINGTON**

Drums   Roger Scales

Bass   John Lawn

Rhythm   Dave Berriman

Piano   Len Foster

Potted History: 'THE UNKNOWNS'

Popular in the area, the Unknowns supported the 'Searchers', 'Tom Jones' and the 'Hollies' at the Brid Spa. They later had a surge of energy and changed their name to 'High Voltage'. Bridlington had several good groups around this time including Mark Anthony and the Avengers, the Zircons, the Electrons and the Corvettes who later changed their name to the 21st Century.

UNNAMED	1966 - 1968	HULL

Drums   Alan Carey

Bass   Godfrey Dack replaced by
Richard Whittles (Dimes)

Lead   Ken Barrett replaced by
Steve Smith (Yorkies)

Keyboard   Mike Smith replaced by
John Bartlett (Cock-a-Hoops)

Rhythm/Vocals   Steve Wright

Potted History: 'THE UNNAMED'

Around the mid-Sixties' it was becoming increasingly difficult to come-up with a new name for a beat group beginning with the prefix 'The' and it became gimmicky to become 'Un' something. Such as 'Unknown', 'Unnamed', 'Unheard-of', etc. The Unnamed played Top Ten material at local dances and clubs and could often be seen playing at the Hull City Hall. The group were managed by Mrs Carey. A highlight of their career was recording a demo tape at Hull's Fairview Studios. The group eventually changed their name to 'Scarlet Rainbow'.

URGE	1966 - 1970	FILEY

Drums   Martin Haxby

Bass   Phil Blowman replaced by Mick Mason

Lead   Rich Hodgson replaced by Dave Brown

Keyboards   Sam Rotherham replaced by
                 Barry Gossland

Vocals   Alec Cammish

Other replacement members John Dunwell (Lead), John Harris (Lead)

Potted History: 'THE URGE'

The 'Urge' were formed out of Filey groups the Mosaics and the Voodoos. The band had got their name from the title of a Jerry Lee Lewis recording. Their repertoire included lots of Tamla Motown. Lead guitarist, Rich Hodgson played a Gibson Les Paul 'Junior' which he saved up for and bought for the sum of £37.10.0d. When he bought it (in 1966) he was offered a Fender 'Strat' for the same price but declined because it was very old and rusty! Rich had started out with Filey group the Voodoos. He had learnt to play guitar by copying Hank Marvin note for note and then bought a chord book. He progressed by listening to Eric Clapton, Jeff Beck and Jimi Hendrix tracks. Rich also used to exchange guitar tricks with Mick Ronson backstage at gigs.

Whilst the Urge became very popular, Rich Hodgson left the group after future 'Blue Eyed Soul' singer Robert Palmer turned up to see him play during an Urge gig at St Peters Youth Club in Scarborough. Liking what he saw, Palmer invited Rich to join the Mandrakes. Rich had been lucky to still be around, because shortly before this, while playing at the Tramways Club in York he had badly electrocuted himself after 'earthing' a mike stand. Such a shock did Rich receive that he fused all of the club's electric's and had the burn marks of six guitar strings branded into his hand for several weeks!

Despite Rich leaving, the group continued and by 1968 were wearing bright yellow trousers on stage - as part of a drive to create an exciting stage act. That same year they won the first round of a local Pop Group Knockout Contest held at the Capital Cinema in Scarborough. The Richard King Set from York were the Judges. At the deciding contest held the following week the Urge lost to future York recording band 'Angel Pavement'. During their career the Urge supported many top bands including the Herd, Dantallions Chariot. the Tremeloes and Black Sabbath.

One story about the Urge is that during their early days their Road Manager, Frank Cammish, drove them to their gigs in his dad's wet fish van. It is claimed by some group members that when the band's old valve amps heated up at a gig there was some awful strange smells wafting across the stage to the audience!

The Urge (Filey - 1967)

US N' IM'	1964 - 1966	GOOLE

Drums   John Gardener

Bass   Malcolm Tune replaced by Jimmy Carroll

Rhythm   Stu Jarvis replaced by Mike Trickett

Lead   Mike Trickett replaced by Geoff LeVogue

Vocals   Phil LeVogue

Potted History: 'US 'N' IM'

Formed out of the 'Telstars', 'Us 'n' Im' played pop music and rock 'n' roll. The group got its unusual name from a liking for Van Morrison's R & B group 'Them'. 'Us 'n' Im' apparently being a Yorkshire way of saying 'Them'! The group played all over Yorkshire including such gigs as the Scala Club in Doncaster, the Brid Spa and a regular gig at the 'Winning Post', Thorn-Moorends. One of the group's finest moments was winning the 1965 'Best Band' contest held in Goole's West Park. One of the worse moments for the band was when their lead guitarist had his treasured Vox 'Phantom' guitar stolen from the van after thieves had hacked the door to pieces to get it.

Us 'n' im (Goole - 1965)

VARIATIONS   1968 - 1969   **HULL**

Drums   Frank Preston

Bass   Ray Hussey

Lead   Dave Carmichael (That Feeling)
                    replaced by Paul Sutton (Disturbance)

Keyboards   Nigel Dalton

Vocals   Dave Walkerley
                    Janet Hassan, Dave Marshall, replaced
                    by Noel Caroll
                    Kev Corbett (That Feeling)

Potted History: 'THE VARIATIONS'

The original Variations had their roots in the defunct 'That
Feeling' and featured ex-Feeling members Kevin Corbett and
Dave Carmichael together with their former Roadie, Dave
Walkerley. The new band featured three singers up front, Kevin
Corbett, Janet Hassan and Dave Walkerley. Their repertoire was
Tamla Motown, especially numbers by the 'Impressions' and
hits such as 'Put Yourself In My Place', 'Going To A Go Go', and
'Get Ready'. The group didn't intend to feature the flamboyance
and gimmicks of their previous groups 'Plague 66' and 'That
Feeling'. The new band intended to play it straight with the
emphasis being on good four-part harmonies.

The Variations rehearsed in a house next door to the Trafalgar
Street Church on Beverley Road in Hull. They were very busy
on the local scene and were particularly popular in York at
venues such as the Cliffe Ballroom. But by the winter of 1967
vocals Janet Hassan had left the band and during 1968 there

were several more changes in line-up with Kevin Corbett and Dave Carmichael also leaving. The arrival of Paul Sutton and Dave Marshall as replacements meant that the band began to take a totally different direction. The established line-up became a professional band and did what every dedicated musician would have wanted to do back in the Swingin' Sixties', lived together in a house so that the emphasis was very much all day on music. When Dave Marshall left the band he was replaced by out of town vocalist Noel Caroll.

I saw the Variations play at Hull's Arblemarle Youth Centre during 1969. They had a great sound with an excellent front man in Noel Caroll. That year the group had gigged all over the UK, including colleges, army bases, clubs, and a tour of Scandinavia. They had also supported several top groups including the 'Gods', 'Love Affair', the Move and 'Dave Berry'. The Variations looked like pop stars and certainly 'appeared' on their way to 'making it', when sadly, a car crash on the Leven Road killed singer Noel Caroll and seriously injured Nigel Dalton. Late in 1969 a memorial concert was held at the Skyline Ballroom in memory of Noel and an impressive line-up of Hull groups performed to show their respect. These included the Rats, Roger Bloom's Axe, Hammer, Flesh, Chest Fever, Childhood and Terra Nova. The remaining members of the Variations topped the bill and at the end of the evening, after singing 'Auld Lang Syne', they changed their name to 'Karaelious' and for a while carried on as a four-piece.

Tony Adams and the Viceroys

The Variations (Hull - 1969)

524

The Variations (Hull - 1968)

The Variations (Hull - 1968)

VICEROYS   circa 1961 - 1965   **YORK**

Drums   Derek Waugh replaced by Geoff Gill

Bass   John Lund

Rhythm   Keith Hunt

Lead   Malcolm Luker

Vocals   Tony Adams

Potted History: 'TONY ADAMS AND THE VICEROYS'

The Viceroys were voted York's Top group in a poll held in the Ouse Beat magazine. The Ouse Beat magazine was from 1964 until 1967 York's own pop paper. The Viceroys were resident at the Burns Hotel in Market Street, playing there every Thursday, Friday and Saturday night during 1964. They also played gigs at the Boulevarde Night-club on the Tadcaster Road and won a Beat Contest at the Rialto Cinema. One of the early songs they included in their repertoire was Screaming Lord Sutch's 'Jack The Ripper' but they generally played mostly Top Ten hits including many Beatle and Stones numbers. They did also give their own arrangements to songs such as 'Summertime'. The Viceroys supported several big stars including Jerry Lee Lewis, Gene Vincent, the Animals and Lulu. On stage the group had great charisma and looked like pop stars. They had long hair before many of their contemporaries. When the Viceroys split, Tony Adams went on to form the Dawnbeats. The remaining three members of the group teamed up with two members of top Scarborough group the 'Moonshots'. Basing themselves in London the new group gave themselves the new name 'The Shots.'

VODS	circa 1964	BRIDLINGTON
Drums	Jeannie Neil	
Bass	Linda Bozley	
Lead	Wendy Key	
Vocals	Monica Ross	

Potted History: 'THE VODS'

Everyone wanted to be in a beat group in 1964. The Vods were Bridlington's attempt   at an all-girl group, but unlike Hull's Mandy and the Girlfriends they didn't last long. Their name was probably a pun on 'Mods'.

VOODOOS   circa 1964   **FILEY**

Drums   Alec Cammis

Bass   Phil Blowman

Lead   Rich Hodgson

Vocals   Ted Cammish replaced by
                Dave McFegan

Potted History: 'THE VOODOOS'

Liverpool had its black magic charm group the Mojos, London had its Black Cat Bones, York had its Boneshakers and Filey had the Voodoos. The Voodoos played R & B and Top Ten music, including the Animals hit 'House of The Rising Sun'. Local gigs included Filey Pavilion (now the Navy Cadets hall), Filey YHA (now private flats) and the Print Union's Convalescent Hall (Northcliffe). Lead guitarist, Rich Hodgson, originally played a Vox 'Pacific' single pick-up guitar through an 8 watt Shaftsbury Amplifier. To make the amp look bigger Rich added four coffee-table legs. Taking pity on the group, one of the sisters of a band member bought them a 17 watt Watkins 'Dominator' amplifier (two speaker, triangular model) a technology which all of the guitarists immediately plugged into and shared. Most of the group members went on to form the Urge.

WATERSONS   1963 - 1968   HULL

Guitar   John Harrison

Vocals   Elaine Waterson

Vocals   Norma Christine Waterson

Vocals   Mike Waterson

Potted History: 'THE WATERSONS'

Even if one had never seen them, one had heard of the Watersons and their connections with the City of Hull. The 1960s was a time of revolution and in the early Sixties, with the arrival of 'Ban The Bomb' marches and protest, we got 'Beatniks'. Many of the Beatniks carried acoustic guitars and sang folk songs and many of the beatnik girls always seemed to have long black hair. In early photographs, the Waterson girls fit this stereotype image. With two males and two females the group concentrated on vocal harmonies and created a unique sound. They appeared regularly at the Blue Bell Inn down Lowgate, where the Freedom Folk Club (later Phase Two) were based. Such was the talent of the Watersons that they recorded several albums. Their first, 'New Voices' achieved almost cult status and it has been suggested that the track 'John Barleycorn' from their 'Fire and Frost' album was the inspiration behind Traffic's later album 'John Barleycorn Must Die'.

Discography

'NEW VOICES'	TOPIC 12T125 1965
'FROST AND FIRE'	TOPIC 12T136 1965
'WATERSONS'	TOPIC 12T142 1966
'A YORKSHIRE GARLAND'	TOPIC 12T167 1967

WAYFARERS 1963 - 1965 YORK

Drums Billy Bearpark

Bass Dave Ploughs

Guitar Brian Perry

Potted History: 'DAVE AND THE WAYFARERS'

Local gigs for the Wayfarers included York pubs such as the Burns Hotel, the Coach and Horses, the Lonsborough Arms, the Rialto Cinema and the Boulevard Nightclub. York had a thriving group scene at this time which included the Viceroys, the Dominoes, the Pentagons, the Ousebeats, the Rockafellas, the Escorts, the Embers, the Blackjacks, the Vampires, the Tycoons, the 'N' Chants, the Misfits and the Cheavours.

WAYS 'N' MEANS 1967 – 1968   HULL

Drums	Trevor
Bass	Stan Saye
Rhythm	Mike
Lead	Geoff replaced by Chris Ramsdale
Vocals	Stuart
Potted History:	'WAYS 'N' MEANS'

'Ways 'n' Means' were managed by John Ranby and their Sole Agency was with Pete McLeod. The Means sported original suits designed by themselves. They tended more towards the cabaret and club type of audience. Two of the 'Means', Chris Ramsdale and Stan Saye later joined the Hammer.

WEE 3   **1965 - 1966**   **HULL**

Drums   John Costello

Bass   Paul Brannon

Lead   Martin Glover

Potted History: 'WEE 3'

Formed out of the 'Neutrons'. Local gigs included the Hull City hall. The first tentative sighting on the local group scene of ace rock guitarist, Ron Hales. was with this outfit.

WEST 28 STREET   1968 - 1969   HULL

Drums   John Costello (Napoleon's Trust)

Bass   Jed Vivian (Napoleon's Trust)

Lead   John Green (Night Starvation)

Organ   Steve Mayor (Impact)

Vocals   Kevin Mulligan (Night Starvation)

Potted History: 'WEST 28 STREET'

West 28 Street named themselves after Hammonds city centre Department Store boutique. Their repertoire was Tamla Motown, soul and rock music. The band also later featured brass with trumpeters Mike and Bernie. West 28 Street supported several top groups including Ike and Tina Turner. They gigged all over the East and North Ridings and were particularly popular at the Enterprise Club in York.

WHITE MAGIC   circa 1969   HULL

Drums   Ron Newlove (Circuit One)

Bass/Vocals   Dave George (Guys and Gals)

Lead   Richard Foster (Strange Experience)

Potted History: 'WHITE MAGIC'

Formerly called the 'Combine', while this band disappeared without a trace its members went on to form top local group 'Bare Sole' who had quite a bit of success.

WILLIAM	1967 - 1968	HULL
COTTON BLUES		
BAND		

Drums   Keith Stutt

Bass   Steve Powell

Lead   Les Nichol

Vocals   Dave Ritchie

Potted History: 'THE WILLIAM COTTON BLUES BAND'

Formed to provide Hull with a 'real' blues band. Several of its members played with Michael Chapman's Electric Army of Friends. In 1968 Les Nichol obtained the lead guitarist slot with Scunthorpe recording group 'Gospel Garden' and the band folded.

The Winsors (Hull - 1965)

537

WINSORS **1962 - 1968** **HULL**

Drums Chris Bennet

Bass Alf Simpson

Rhythm Arthur Platten

Lead Norman Moore

Vocals Allen Melling

Potted History: 'THE WINSORS'

The Winsors were named after the Windsor Hall, Argyle Street, Hull, where they rehearsed. In the late 1950s the Hall ran a weekly Jazz club, featuring such stars as Kenny Ball, Chas McDermott and Nancy Whiskey. The Winsors guitarist Alf Simpson, had begun his musical career with a local group which featured future 'Aces' Brian and Adrian Gatie and also Dave Tenny. Vocals Allen Melling had spent several years singing and playing piano around the City's pubs.

The Winsors were resident during their career at several venues, including the Halfway House Hull, the Tiger Inn in Cottingham, and the Griffin Inn in Market Weighton. They were also at one time offered the residency at Hull's Locarno Ballroom but because of existing commitments were unable to take it.

While tending towards the clubs, the Winsors also played at dances and had a wide repertoire. The group played the latest hits and if something was in the 'Pick Of The Pops' chart on a Sunday evening it would be in their repertoire by the following Friday.
The Winsors made a four-track EP which was recorded by Hull's

Malconi Studios. In 1967 the group auditioned for televisions weekly talent show 'Opportunity Knocks'. The auditions were held at the Farmery Hall in Hull and the group remember an impatient Hughie Green shouting, 'Where's the Winsors, where's the Winsors?'

The Winsors certainly knew how to 'bring the house down'. At a local rugby club gig they played in a large tent, with one of Hull's top contemporary groups playing in a neighbouring tent. Perhaps due to the fickleness of the crowd preferring straight pop music, the Winsors tent gradually grew fuller and fuller as the evening drew on and they had most of the rugby club audience dancing in it. But as the Winsors played away to this capacity crowd they suddenly found the tent falling down around their's and the audience's ears, and a general turmoil ensued. Once the tent had been stabilised, it was found that the rival group had mysteriously disappeared!

Another story about the band is that one evening they arrived to play at the Majestic Ballroom in Hull and on entering the dressing room were shocked to find a 'coffin' lying there in wait for them! Was it a sleeping vampire they wondered? No, it later turned out to be the property of 'Screaming Lord Sutch' who had been playing there the previous week. He used to be carried on stage in it!

The Winsors must be one of the few bands who never really wanted to become famous and saw their six years on the road together as one of fun and friendship, a friendship which still remains with the group today. They came back together for a reunion gig a few years ago and future reunions are not ruled out!

WORRYING KIND **1967 - 1969**   **SCUNTHORPE**

Drums   Alan Beasty

Bass   Martin Street

Lead   Alan Boyd

Keyboards   Ray Johnson

Vocals   Dave Waterland

Potted History: 'THE WORRYING KIND'

The Worrying Kind could often be seen playing at the Beverley Regal. They eventually turned pro and changed their name to the 'Monday Morning Glory Band' and went on to gain a recording contract.

YE BARONS	1963 - 1965	HULL

Drums   Charles Nicholson replaced by
Mike Kelly

Bass   Graham Tiplady

Rhythm   Rod Yeomans

Lead   Chris Keech replaced by
Ian Kirkman (Scorpions)

Vocals   Keith Howland

Potted History: 'YE BARONS'

Originally called 'Dave Tulsa and the Barons' other members included Wally Scarra. 'Ye Barons' played R & B and ballads and Ian Kirkman was considered to be one of the best beat instrumentalist in the city at this time. Managed by Gerry Gribben and later Brian Hudson the Barons had regular gigs at the Halfway House in Hull and the Ferryboat Inn in Hessle. Rod Yeomans and Graham Tiplady later joined 'Cain's Kultur'.

YORKIES	1964 - 1966	HULL

Drums   Glen Petty (Martians) replaced by Clive Taylor

Bass/Vocals   Geoff Appleby

Rhythm/Vocals   Pete Spencer

Lead/Vocals   Steve Smith (Martians)

Potted History: 'THE YORKIES'

Formed by two former members of the Martians, the Yorkies began life with local DJ, Ricky Dobbs on vocals. The group had regular gigs at the Hull City Hall. They also auditioned for television's weekly talent show 'Opportunity Knocks' but were unsuccessful. Both Geoff Appleby and Clive Taylor went on to become members of the Rats.

YOUNG ONES   circa 1964   **DRIFFIELD**

Drums   Les Watson

Bass/Vocals   Frank Gillanders

Rhythm   Alan Wilmott (Fabulous 006 and the
                   Agents)

Lead   Billy Mack

Vocals   Dennis Petch

Potted History: 'SMALL PAUL AND THE YOUNG
                   ONES'

Probably named after the Cliff Richard movie of the same name, Small Paul and the Young Ones were very popular at both Brid and Scarborough Spa's. They supported several top stars including Gene Vincent and the Applejacks. Driffield produced several good groups during the 1960s including the Fabulous 006 and the Agents', the Road Runners, and the Syndicate 5. It also sired several successful musicians notably Mick 'Woody' Woodmansey. Driffield's Town Hall and Club Bohemia were also regular venues for 'beat groups' and the excellent Beatcomber magazine, which reported on the East Riding music scene was published there.

ZEBEDEE'S PEOPLE	circa 1967	YORK

Drums	Sydney Locker
Bass	Derek Scale
Lead	Phil Quin
Potted History:	'ZEBEDEE'S PEOPLE'

Zebedee's People were originally known as the 'N' Chants and they later merged with York's Crawdaddies including members Mick Unas and Graham Robson. Like Zebedees People there were several local groups around at this time who included the word 'People' in their name. While recording groups included 'Rupert's People', locally, Hull had its Twiggy's People, Goole had 'Gullivers People' and Scunthorpe simply had the 'People'.

ZEROES   1962 - 1965   **POCKLINGTON**

Drums   Trevor Buttle

Bass   Tony Walker replaced by Steve Rolley

Rhythm   Derek Dennington replaced by
Kenneth Hurley

Lead   Brian Barrett replaced by Graham Burnett

Vocals   Roy Frear

Potted History: 'ROY AND THE ZEROES'

The Zeroes rehearsed on Pocklington's old wartime airfield, in an old hangar. Originally an R & B group, they later played Top Ten material. The Zeroes won the 1964 Hornsea 'Beat Contest' and were also that year Northern Beat Contest Finalists representing Yorkshire along with Huddersfield's 'Embers'. They supported several top groups including the Who, the Four Pennies and Jimmy Saville. The Zeros gigged at most resorts on the East Coast and had quite a large fan following. They became the most popular group in Pocklington.

ZIRCONS   1963 - 1965   BRIDLINGTON

Drums	Calvin Winetroube replaced by John Baker
Bass	Nev Moore replaced by Paul Marsh, John Lesingtone
Rhythm	Ray Stannard
Lead	Ian Casson

Potted History: 'THE ZIRCONS'

The Zircons played R & B, rock 'n' roll, instrumentals and Top Ten, especially numbers by the Hollies. They originally tended to concentrate on instrumentals like the 'Shadows' and the 'Spotnicks'. The group drove to their gigs in a hand-painted blue, red and yellow striped van! One of the highlights of a 'Zircon' gig was to see them thrilling their audiences by playing the Can-Can and kicking their legs high up in the air in time with the music. The Zircons represented the Hull area in the regional final of a national beat contest after beating 8 other local groups at the 'Locarno' Ballroom. They also won another Beat Contest in Hornsea in 1967, with top Beverley group, the Strollers coming second. One of the highlights of the Zircons career was supporting Gerry and the Pacemakers at the Brid Spa. The Pacemakers were number One in the charts with their single 'How Do You Do It'. While setting their gear up on stage at the Spa Gerry Marsden arrived and offered to let the Zircons use the Pacemakers gear. He then suggested that they all had a jam session, which they did and he turned out to be a really nice guy. The Zircons eventually disbanded when Ian developed a back problem (possibly due those early days when they did the 'Can-Can'). One of the best versions of the Who's 'My

Generation' ever heard was reputedly played one Friday evening in 1965 at the Beverley Regal. A combined session with the Zircons, the Strollers and the Crestas (who at that time featured Mick Ronson). The three groups playing live together on stage. It must have nearly taken the roof off!

ZOFFANY	1970 - 1971	SCARBOROUGH
Drums	John Cambridge	
Bass	Derek Gill	
Lead	Rich Hodgson	
Lead/vocals	Allan Black	
Vocals	Maggie	
Potted History:	'ZOFFANY'	

Originally tentatively called 'Myzophony', Zoffany were formed out of the remnants of the Mandrakes after the departure of Robert Palmer. Working for Peter Pitts they were very busy in the area and now fronted by a female vocalist called Maggie played regular gigs at Scarborough's 'Scene One' and the 'Ocean Room'. On finally splitting Allan Black went on to form 'Milk Train' and then Rinky Dink and the Crystal Set gaining a recording contract and cutting an album.

THE GROUPS OF HULL AND THE EAST RIDING, SCARBOROUGH, YORK, SCUNTHORPE AND GRIMSBY 1960 - 1970

ABC	circa 1966	HULL
ABSOLUTE DIRGE	circa 1968	YORK
ACES	circa 1963	HULL
ACES, JOHNNY HAWK AND THE	circa 1959	HULL
AERIALS	circa 1965	HULL
AFFLUENT SOCIETY	circa 1966	YORK
AGENTS	circa 1965	DRIFFIELD
ALPHA-BEATS	circa 1964	HULL
ALPHABETICAL ALARM CLOCK	circa 1968	SCUNTHORPE
ALPINES, TONY AND THE	circa 1964	SCARBOROUGH
ALICE'S RESTAURANT	circa 1969	HULL
AMAZING BLONDEL	circa 1969	SCUNTHORPE
AMAZONS	circa 1965	HULL
ANGEL PAVEMENT	circa 1969	YORK
ANSERMET SWING	circa 1966	YORK
APPLE SPICE BAND	circa 1969	HULL
ARIELS	circa 1965	HULL
ASTRONAUTS	circa 1963	HULL
ASTRONAUGHTS	circa 1963	SCARBOROUGH
ATMOSPHERE	circa 1969	HULL
ATTACK	circa 1966	HULL
AVENGERS	circa 1963	PICKERING
AVENGERS, MARK ANTONY AND THE	circa 1963	BRIDLINGTON
AXE, ROGER BLOOM'S	circa 1969	HULL
AZTECS	circa 1967	GRIMSBY
BADGE	circa 1969	YORK
BADD LADS	circa 1966	SCUNTHORPE
BARE SOLE	circa 1969	HULL
BARONS, DAVE TULSA AND THE	circa 1962	HULL
BARRONS	circa 1965	HULL
BASKERVILLE MOOD	circa 1966	YORK
BATMEN	circa 1964	HULL

BATMEN, VINCE FORD'S	circa 1962	HULL
BEATBOYS, RAY CHARLES AND THE	circa 1964	YORK
BEAT CULT	circa 1966	SCARBOROUGH
BEAT SECT	circa 1965	YORK
BEAUTIFUL DELILAHS	circa 1963	YORK
BIG CHANGE	circa 1967	SCARBOROUGH
BINNS THURSTON	circa 1969	NORTH FERRIBY
BIRDS GROOVE	circa 1967	HULL
BLACK CAT	circa 1969	POCKLINGTON
BLACK HAWKS	circa 1965	SCUNTHORPE
BLACKJACKS	circa 1965	YORK
BLEU KATS KLAN	circa 1968	
BLIND LEMMON	circa 1969	GRIMSBY
BLITZKRIEG	circa 1970	HULL
BLUEBERRIES	circa 1964	HULL
BLUE CIRCLE	circa 1968	HORNSEA
BLUE MAX	circa 1969	SCARBOROUGH
BLUE STARS	circa 1964	SCARBOROUGH
BLUE STREAKS	circa 1963	HULL
BLUES ANONYMOUS	circa 1964	SCUNTHORPE
BLUES SYNDICATE	circa 1965	SCUNTHORPE
BLYND COMPREHENSION	circa 1969	SCARBOROUGH
BOLTONES	circa 1964	HULL
BONAPARTE'S RETREAT	circa 1967	HULL
BONE	circa 1969	GILBERDYKE
BONESHAKERS	circa 1964	YORK
BOYFRIENDS, SANDRA AND	circa 1961	SCUNTHORPE
BOYS, JONNY AND THE	circa 1964	SCUNTHORPE
BRAVE NEW WORLD	circa 1968	SCARBOROUGH
BUCCANEERS, DAVY JONES AND THE	circa 1963	HULL
BURNS BEAT COMBO	circa 1963	HULL
CADILLACS, TONY AND THE	circa 1964	SCUNTHORPE
CAINS KULTUR	circa 1967	HULL
CHALLENGERS, BARRY ADAMS AND THE	circa 1964	YORK

CALMEN WATERS	circa 1968	GRIMSBY
CAMELOT	circa 1970	HULL
CAROL'S KNIGHTS	circa 1965	HULL
CASTAWAYS	circa 1969	YORK
C-BEATS	circa 1964	WITHERNSEA
CHALLENGERS, DANNY ADAMS AND THE	circa 1963	YORK
CHAPMAN, MICHAEL	circa 1967	HULL
CHAPTER SIX	circa 1964	SCUNTHORPE
CHEAVOURS	circa 1964	YORK
CHECHAKOS	circa 1965	SCUNTHORPE
CHERRY TREE FARM	circa 1968	
CHERRY BLOSSOM CLINIC	circa 1968	
CHEST FEVER	circa 1969	HULL
CHEVOLETS	circa1964	HUTTONCRANSWICK
CHEVRONS	circa 1965	YORK
CHICAGO LINE	circa 1966	GRIMSBY
CHICAGO STYLE BLUES BAND	circa 1967	HULL
CHILD	circa 1970	HULL
CHILDHOOD	circa 1969	HULL
CHILLS	circa 1966	SCUNTHORPE
CHORDELLS	circa 1963	BEVERLEY
CHOW'S MEN	circa 1965	SCARBOROUGH
CIRCUIT FOUR	circa 1966	YORK
CIRCUIT ONE	circa 1967	HULL
CITADELS	circa 1964	SHEFFIELD
CLASSICS	circa 1964	BARTON ON HUMBER
CLASSICS, IAN KING AND THE	circa 1964	SCUNTHORPE
CLUBMEN	circa 1964	YORK
COASTAL EROSION	circa 1968	WITHERNSEA
COASTERS	circa 1966	SCARBOROUGH
COCK-A-HOOPS	circa 1964	BROUGH
COLARADOS	circa 1964	SCUNTHORPE
COLOURS PURPLE	circa 1967	
COMBINE	circa 1968	HULL
COMACHES	circa 1964	SCARBOROUGH
CORTINA'S	circa 1963	MARKET WEIGHTON

CORVETTES	circa 1964	YORK
CORVETTES	circa 1964	BRIDLINGTON
COSSACKS	circa 1964	HULL
COUM TRANSMISSIONS	circa 1969	HULL
COUNTERPOINTS	circa 1964	YORK
CRAZE	circa 1965	SCUNTHORPE
CRAWDADDIES	circa 1964	YORK
CREATIVE INNOCENCE	circa 1968	SCARBOROUGH
CREEKY BEDD	circa 1970	SCARBOROUGH
CRESTAS	circa 1961	HULL
CRESTAS, JOHNNY HAWK		
AND THE	circa 1961	HULL
CRESTERS	circa 1964	YORK
CROWD, KEITH KELLY AND THE	circa 1963	HULL
CRUSADERS, RICKY KNIGHT		
AND THE	circa 1963	HULL
CRY HAVOC	circa 1970	
CUCUMBER	circa 1968	YORK
CULT	circa 1965	YORK
CURRENTS	circa 1968	
CYCLONES	circa 1966	HUNMANBY
CZECHERS	circa 1966	YORK
DAWNBEATS, TONY ADAMS		
AND THE	circa 1965	YORK
DAY RETURN	circa 1969	SCARBOROUGH
DECCANAIRS	circa 1965	SCARBOROUGH
DECOYS	circa 1965	SCUNTHORPE
DELLMEN	circa 1964	HULL
DELTONES	circa 1964	SCARBOROUGH
DEMOLITION	circa 1966	YORK
DEMONS, TONY DIAMOND AND	circa 1960	SCUNTHORPE
DETROIT SOUL SOUND	circa 1967	
DIAGONALS	circa 1965	HULL
DIAMONDS, IAN AND THE	circa 1964	YORK
DIARY	circa 1969	HULL
DIMES	circa 1967	HULL
DIMPLES	circa 1965	SCUNTHORPE

DINGOS	circa 1960	BRADFORD
DIZZY WHEELA	circa 1969	SCARBOROUGH
DISTURBANCE	circa 1967	HULL
DOMINANT FIVE	circa 1966	SCARBOROUGH
DOMINOES	circa 1965	YORK
DROGOS	circa 1965	HUNMANBY
DUSTY BLUES	circa 1969	HULL
DYNAMITES	circa 1964	SCARBOROUGH
EASYBEATS, BRIAN AND THE	circa 1965	YORK
ECHOES	circa 1961	IMMINGHAM
ELECTRAZ	circa 1965	SCARBOROUGH
ELECTRONS	circa 1965	BRIDLINGTON
ELITE	circa 1967	HULL
EMBERS	circa 1964	HUDDERSFIELD
EMBERS	circa 1965	YORK
ELMA FUDD	circa 1968	WHITBY
ENSIGNS	circa 1964	SCUNTHORPE
ESCORTS, STEVE CASSIDY AND THE	circa 1964	YORK
ESCORTS, SYLVIA AND THE	circa 1966	YORK
E TYPES	circa 1963	DRIFFIELD
EXCURSIONS	circa 1968	
EXCUTIVES	circa 1962	GOOLE
EXILES	circa 1964	YORK
EXODUS	circa 1965	BRIDLINGTON
FABIANS	circa 1964	HULL
FABULOUS 006 AND THE AGENTS	circa 1964	DRIFFIELD
FAINTLY BLOWING	circa 1969	YORK
FALCONS, JOHNNY HAWK AND THE	circa 1964	DRIFFIELD
FALCONS, WALLY AND THE	circa 1963	HULL
FIVE TRAX	circa 1964	HULL
FIX	circa 1966	YORK
FLINTONES	circa 1962	SCARBOROUGH
FLYAWAYS	circa 1963	HULL
FLESH	circa 1969	HULL

FOOT-TAPPERS	circa 1964	BEVERLEY
FOUR JUST MEN	circa 1964	SCARBOROUGH
FORGERS	circa 1964	BRADFORD
FOSSILS	circa 1964	POCKLINGTON
FOUR ACES, ERIC LEE AND THE	circa 1962	HULL
FOUR CENTS, NICK JAMES	circa 1963	SCUNTHORPE
FOUR Js, BILLY AND THE	circa 1964	YORK
FOUR OF A KIND	circa 1966	YORK
FOUR SHADES OF BLACK	circa 1964	YORK
FREEWAYS, MAUREEN AND THE	circa 1965	SCUNTHORPE
FRIENDS	circa 1969	SCARBOROUGH
FUZ	circa 1969	SCARBOROUGH
GARDEN GATE	circa 1970	
GARY LANDIS AND THE SET	circa 1967	HULL
GAZELLES	circa 1962	HORNSEA
GEMINIS, GEOFF DRAKE AND THE	circa 1963	HULL
GEMINIS	circa 1964	HULL
GENGHIS KHAN	circa 1965	PICKERING
GENIE'S LAMP	circa 1968	HULL
GENTRY	circa 1966	HULL
GIDEON'S FEW	circa 1965	YORK
GIRLFRIENDS, MANDY AND THE	circa 1965	HULL
G MEN	circa 1964	SCARBOROUGH
GOLDEN VALLEY	circa 1967	BEVERLEY
GONDOLIER	circa 1964	HULL
GONX	circa 1965	HULL
GOSPEL GARDEN	circa 1968	SCUNTHORPE
GOVERNMENT	circa 1970	SCARBOROUGH
GREEN GINGER	circa 1968	BRIDLINGTON
GRID	circa 1967	YORK
GRIT	circa 1966	YORK
GROUP	circa 1965	YORK
GROUP 29	circa 1964	SCARBOROUGH
GULLIVER'S DREAM	circa 1967	GOOLE
HAMMER	circa 1968	HULL
HARVEY BROOKES, SACK OF WOE	circa 1966	LEVEN

HARVEY BROOKES SKUTTLE	circa 1967	LEVEN
HEDZ	circa 1969	YORK
HENRY STREET JAILERS	circa 1967	COTTINGHAM
HERBIE'S iii's	circa 1967	SCARBOROUGH
HI-FI's	circa 1963	YORK
HIGH NUMBERS	circa 1966	HULL
HIGH VOLTAGE	circa 1966	BRIDLINGTON
HONEYS	circa 1967	HULL
HORNETS, GERRY B AND THE	circa 1963	YORK
HOUSE	circa 1969	YORK
HUTCH	circa 1968	SCARBOROUGH
HYBRIDS	circa 1964	HULL
IDES OF MARCH	circa 1965	HULL
IGUANAS	circa 1965	SCARBOROUGH
ILLUSIONS	circa 1969	GRIMSBY
IMAGE	circa 1967	HULL
IMPS	circa 1965	LINCOLN
IMPS	circa 1965	SCUNTHORPE
IMPACT	circa 1967	HULL
IMPACTS, ADRIAN KAYE	circa 1964	YORK
INCAS	circa 1964	SCARBOROUGH
INNER MIND	circa 1968	
INNER MOVEMENT	circa 1968	SCUNTHORPE
INNOCENTS	circa 1964	SCARBOROUGH
INNOMINATES	circa 1965	YORK
INSECTS	circa 1963	HULL
INSEX	circa 1964	HULL
INSPIRATION	circa 1970	HULL
INVADERS	circa 1964	HULL
IOTAS	circa 1969	GRIMSBY
JAGUARS	circa 1964	HULL
JELLY ROLL BLUES BAND	circa 1968	HULL
JESTERS	circa 1964	SCUNTHORPE
JETS, JOHNNY AND THE	circa 1962	HULL
JETSONS, JOHNNY STARR AND THE	circa 1964	YORK

JIMMY PARKER SOUL SUPPLY	circa 1967	HUDDERSFIELD
JOHNNY BALLAD GROUP	circa 1964	SCUNTHORPE
JOHN'S FOLLOWERS	circa 1967	GOOLE
KALEIDOSCOPE	circa 1969	GRIMSBY
KARAELIUS	circa 1970	HULL
KAREMA 4	circa 1968	HULL
KEITH HERD RHYTHM GROUP	circa 1964	HULL
KERBSIDERS	circa 1964	HUNMANBY
KINGDOM BRUNEL	circa 1970	HULL
KING BEES	circa 1964	HULL
KING BEES	circa 1964	SCARBOROUGH
KING BEES	circa 1967	GRIMSBY
KINGPINS	circa 1965	SCUNTHORPE
KLAN	circa 1968	
KODIAKS	circa 1967	ROTHERHAM
KOKOMOS	circa 1966	HARROGATE
KRAAKANS	circa 1965	SCUNTHORPE
KUDOS	circa 1965	HULL
LATE STARTERS	circa 1970	HULL
LAWMEN	circa 1964	SCUNTHORPE
LAZY POKER	circa 1969	SCARBOROUGH
LIMITED COMPANY	circa 1967	BEVERLEY
LISTEN	circa 1970	HULL
LITTLE DEDICATION	circa 1967	YORK
LITTLE PEOPLE	circa 1968	HULL
LIVEWIRES	circa 1965	SCARBOROUGH
LOCOMOTION	circa 1968	EAST RIDING
LOLLIPOPS	circa 1967	YORK
LOVING WAY	circa 1967	LINCOLN
LUCIFER	circa 1969	HULL
LUKE	circa 1969	HULL
McCOYS	circa 1964	SELBY
MACHINE	circa 1967	YORK
MAGNETS	circa 1964	HULL
MAGPIES	circa 1965	HUTTONCRANSWICK

MAGPIES	circa 1965	HOLDERNESS
MAGYARS	circa 1964	
MAIDEN PRAYER	circa 1968S	CARBOROUGH
MAJESTICS, PETER KING		
AND THE	circa 1963	HULL
MAJORITY	circa 1965	HULL
MAKIN' TIME	circa 1966	YORK
MALE SET	circa 1968	SHEFFIELD
MALIBU	circa 1967	
MAMA'S LITTLE CHILDREN	circa 1967	LEEDS
MANDRAKES	circa 1965	SCARBOROUGH
MANICK DEPRESSION	circa 1967	HULL
MARINERS	circa 1964	HULL
MARTIANS	circa 1963	HULL
MANX UNION	circa 1970	HULL
MATCHBOX	circa 1968	YORK
MERLIN	circa 1970	HULL
METAPHORS	circa 1965	HULL
METHODS	circa 1964S	CARBOROUGH
METHUSELAH	circa 1968	SCUNTHORPE
MICHAEL CHAPMAN	circa 1967	HULL
MIDNIGHT EXPRESS	circa 1969	SHEFFIELD
MINORITY SOUL SET	circa 1968	SHEFFIELD
MISFITS	circa 1964	YORK
MODERATION	circa 1966	SCUNTHORPE
MODS	circa 1966	HULL
MODS, TONY MARTIN AND THE	circa 1964	HULL
MOLES	circa 1965S	CUNTHORPE
MONDAY MORNING GLORY BAND	circa 1969	SOUTH LINDSEY
MOOD	circa 1965	YORK
MOODS	circa 1968	SCARBOROUGH
MOONRAKERS, MANDY AND THE	circa 1964	HULL
MORVANS, JOHNNY MORRELL		
AND THE	circa 1962	YORK
MOSAICS	circa 1964	FILEY
MOONSHOTS	circa 1963	SCARBOROUGH
MOTIVES	circa 1965	YORK
MOUSETRAP	circa 1968	YORK

MUSTANGS, BARRY GRAHAM		
AND THE	circa 1963	HULL
MUTINY	circa 1968	BRIDLINGTON
MYZOPHONY	circa 1970	SCARBOROUGH
NAPOLEON TRUST	circa 1967	HULL
'N' CHANTS	circa 1966	YORK
NEUTRONS	circa 1964	HULL
NEWCOMERS, JOHNNY AND THE	circa 1961	YORK
NEW MIDNIGHT TRAIN	circa 1967	
NEW RELIGION	circa 1967	SCARBOROUGH
NIGHT PEOPLE	circa 1964	HULL
NIGHT RIDERS, JIMMY RYDER		
AND THE	circa 1960	SCUNTHORPE
NIGHT STARVATION	circa 1967	HULL
NOTHINEVERAPPENS	circa 1970	HULL
NSU	circa 1968	
OBJEKS 5	circa 1965	HULL
ODD ONES, ODEIN AND THE	circa 1964	GOOLE
ORBIT	circa 1969	HULL
OUSEBEATS, BRIAN AND THE	circa 1965	YORK
OUTCASTS	circa 1964	SCARBOROUGH
OUTERLIMITS	circa 1967	LEEDS
OX	circa 1966	SCARBOROUGH
PAGE THREE	circa 1966	HULL
PAKT	circa 1967	YORK
PANTHERS	circa 1963	HULL
PANTHERS	circa 1965	SCARBOROUGH
PATHFINDER 5	circa 1966	HULL
PATTERN	circa 1967	HULL
PEACEBREAKERS	circa 1968	HULL
PEIGHTON CHECKS	circa 1966	SCUNTHORPE
PENJANTS	circa 1965	BEVERLEY
PENTAGONS	circa 1965	YORK
PENTODE	circa 1967	
PEOPLE	circa 1969	SCUNTHORPE

PERFUMED GARDEN	circa 1967	
PHANTOMS, DEAN CURTIS AND THE	circa 1964	HULL
PHARMACY	circa 1969	YORK
PINK	circa 1969	HOLDERNESS
PINK EFFLUENCE	circa 1967	GRIMSBY
PITIFUL	circa 1967	SHEFFIELD
PITIFUL SOULS	circa 1968	SOUTH LINDSEY
PLAGUE 66	circa 1966	HULL
POACHERS	circa1965	MARKET WEIGHTON
POLITICIAN	circa 1969	SCARBOROUGH
PRIVILEGED	circa 1967	YORK
PURPLE HAZE	circa 1967	HULL
PURPLE MIST	circa 1967	SCARBOROUGH
Q JUMPERS	circa 1965	BEVERLEY
QUADRANT	circa 1968	HULL
RANDOM DESTINY	circa 1968	YORK
RANGERS, SCOTT MADISON AND THE	circa 1962	HULL
RASCALS	circa 1965	HULL
RASCALS, JOHNNY LEVER AND THE	circa 1966	HULL
RATS	circa 1964	HULL
RAYDENMICS	circa 1965	HULL
REASONS WHY	circa 1967	CLEETHORPES
REBELS	circa 1964	BARTON ON HUMBER
REBELS	circa 1963	GOOLE/ SCUNTHORPE
RED DIRT	circa 1969	HULL
RED MILL	circa 1969	SCARBOROUGH
REFLECTIONS	circa 1969	HULL
REFORMATION	circa 1969	HULL
RELATIONS	circa 1963	HULL
RENEGADES	circa 1965	WHITBY

RETALIATION	circa 1970	HULL
RELAYS	circa 1965	HULL
REVELATIONS	circa 1970	HULL
REVOLUTION KIND	circa 1967	
R G SIMPSON BAND	circa 1968	YORK
RIP VAN WINKLE	circa 1966	HULL
RIVALS	circa 1964	HULL
RIVERBEATS, JON AND THE	circa 1963	HULL
RIVERBEATS	circa 1965	HULL
ROAD RUNNERS	circa 1964	DRIFFIELD
ROCKAFELLAS, GERRY HARRISON AND	circa 1965	YORK
ROCKING HELLIOTS	circa 1964	POCKLINGTON
ROCK MACHINE	circa 1970	SCARBOROUGH
ROCKY ROAD FOUR	circa 1960	HULL
ROGER BLOOMS HAMMER	circa 1967	HULL
ROLL MOVEMENT	circa 1966	YORK
RONSON, MICK	circa 1963	HULL
ROGUES	circa 1963	BEVERLEY
RUMBLE	circa 1969	GRIMSBY
SATALITES	circa 1962	BEVERLEY
SATELLITES	circa 1963	GOOLE
SAXONS	circa 1965	HULL
SCARLET RAINBOW	circa 1968	HULL
SCARLET FARMYARD	circa 1967	BEVERLEY
SCENE	circa 1968	HULL
SCORPIONS, GARRY YORK AND THE	circa 1966	YORK
SCORPIONS	circa 1963	HULL
SCREEN	circa 1967	YORK
SECRETS	circa 1965	SCARBOROUGH
SECT	circa 1967	
SEDATION	circa 1968	HULL
SEMI-TONES	circa 1964	HULL
SENATORS	circa 1965	HULL
SENSATIONS	circa 1965	
SESSION MEN	circa 1969	SCARBOROUGH

SHAPES	circa 1967	HULL
SHADES	circa 1969	GOOLE
SHADES OF BLUE	circa 1963	HULL
SHARKS	circa 1964	SHEFFIELD
SHERBURN PANTHERS	circa 1964	SCARBOROUGH
SHE TRINITY	circa 1966	HULL
SHIFTERS, IAN AND THE	circa 1963	YORK
SHOTGUN PACKAGE	circa 1967	YORK
SILKIE	circa 1965	HULL
SIX SHADES OF BLUE	circa 1967	ROTHERHAM
SKYSOUNDS	circa 1965	HULL
SLICE	circa 1969	HULL
SMALL FOUR	circa 1964	HULL
SMALL SOUNDS	circa 1968	YORK
SMOKEY'S BALLOON	circa 1969	YORK
SNAKE EYE	circa 1970	HULL
SNOWIE WOODS MAGICAL CIRCUS	circa 1968	YORK
SOCIAL ATMOSPHERE	circa 1969	HULL
SOCIETY	circa 1965	SHIPTONTHORPE
SOLIDS	circa 1960	HULL
SOME PEOPLE	circa 1967	HULL
SONICS	circa 1965	SCARBOROUGH
SONS OF WITCH	circa 1966	POCKLINGTON
SOUL IMAGE	circa 1967	HORNSEA
SOUNDS 4	circa 1964	HULL
SOUNDS 6	circa 1965	SCARBOROUGH
SOUNDS OF SILENCE	circa 1968	HULL
SOUTHLANDERS	circa 1965	SCUNTHORPE
SPANISH LEATHER	circa 1968	BRIDLINGTON
SPARTANS	circa 1963	YORK
SPECTRE INC.	circa 1966	MALTON
SPELL	circa 1967	SCARBOROUGH
SPICE	circa 1969	HULL
SPREADEAGLE	circa 1969	HULL
SQUELCH	circa 1968	SCARBOROUGH
STARLINERS	circa 1964	YORK
STATESMEN	circa 1963	HULL

STATESMEN, VINCE FORD'S	circa 1963	HULL
STEREOTONES, ROCKY STONE AND THE	circa 1963	HULL
STORMERS, TONI GALE AND THE	circa 1963	SHEFFIELD
STRANGE EXPERIENCE	circa 1967	HULL
STRANGERS, VIC AND THE	circa 1965	HULL
STRANGERS, JONTY AND THE	circa 1964	SCARBOROUGH
STRANGERS	circa 1961	SCUNTHORPE
STRAWBOA FANTASY	circa 1968	SCARBOROUGH
STRAY	circa 1966	YORK
STREETS OF SADNESS	circa 1968	
STROLLERS	circa 1962	BEVERLEY
STROLLERS	circa 1965	BRADFORD
STYLISTS	circa 1963	HULL
SUGAR AND SPICE	circa 1968	HULL
SUNSETS, TONY MARTIN AND THE	circa 1961	HULL
SUNSETS	circa 1964	GOOLE
SUNSETS	circa 1964	YORK
SUN SPOTS	circa 1960	SCUNTHORPE
SWEET IMAGE	circa 1966	YORK
SWEET SUGAR SOUL SET	circa 1967	HULL
SWEET SUGAR	circa 1969	HULL
SWINGALONGS, BARRY ADAMS AND THE	circa 1963	YORK
SWINGIN DUKES	circa 1964	HULL
SYNDICATE 5	circa 1964	DRIFFIELD
SYRACUSE	circa 1969	YORK
TALL STORY	circa 1967	HORNSEA
TEAM BEATS	circa 1965	SCARBOROUGH
TEETH	circa 1970	SCARBOROUGH
TENNESSEANS	circa 1964	SCARBOROUGH
TERRA NOVA	circa 1969	HULL
TEXANS, JENNY AND THE	circa 1963	HULL
TEXANS	circa 1963	HULL
THAT FEELING	circa 1967	HULL
THAK J S	circa 1969	HULL

THIRD WORLD	circa 1967	HULL
THIS GENERATION	circa 1967	GRIMSBY
THREE PLUS ONE	circa 1965	HUTTONCRANSWICK
THUNDERBOLTS	circa 1965	YORK
TOBY JUG	circa 1969	HULL
TOMORROWS TOPIC	circa 1968	HULL
TONICKS, JOEY YOUNG AND THE	circa 1968	YORK
TORNADOES,		
WALLY STEWART AND	circa 1960	SCUNTHORPE
TORNADOES	circa 1961	HULL
TRACK	circa 1970	SCARBOROUGH
TRAP	circa 1967	
TRAVELLERS EXPRESS	circa 1968	SHEFFIELD
TRAX	circa 1965	SHEFFIELD
TREACLE	circa 1968	HULL
TREMULOS, EDDIE FALCON		
AND THE	circa 1961	SCUNTHORPE
TRENDS	circa 1965	HULL
TRIFFYDS	circa 1964	SCARBOROUGH
TROLLS	circa 1964	SCARBOROUGH
TROPICS	circa 1964	SCUNTHORPE
TRUETONES	circa 1964	YORK
TURNABOUTS	circa 1965	SCUNTHORPE
TWENTY-FIRST CENTURY	circa 1966	BRIDLINGTON
TWIGGY'S PEOPLE	circa 1966	HULL
TYCOONS	circa 1960	HULL
TYCOONS, MAL DYMAN		
AND THE	circa 1964	YORK
TYKES	circa 1967	YORK
UFOs	circa 1965	HULL
URGE	circa 1966	FILEY
UNION BLUES SOLE BAND	circa 1967	HULL
UNIT IV	circa 1964	FILEY
UNITY	circa 1967	HULL
UNKNOWNS	circa 1966	BRIDLINGTON
UNNAMED	circa 1966	HULL
US 'N' IM	circa 1964	GOOLE

VAMPIRES	circa 1964	YORK
VARIATIONS	circa 1967	HULL
VELVET OPERA	circa 1963	COTTINGHAM
VERTEBRAE, LEN BONE AND THE	circa 1964	HULL
VICEROYS, TONY ADAMS		
AND THE	circa 1964	YORK
VIKINGS	circa 1964	FILEY /
		SCUNTHORPE
VODS	circa 1964	BRIDLINGTON
VOODOOS	circa 1964	FILEY
VULCANS	circa 1962	HULL
WANDERERS	circa 1964	SCARBOROUGH
WAYFARERS, DAVE AND THE	circa 1965	YORK
WAYS N MEANS	circa 1967	HULL
WEST 28 STREET	circa 1967	HULL
WEE THREE	circa 1966	HULL
WELLINGTON BOOT	circa 1968	YORK
WHITE MAGIC	circa 1968	HULL
WILLIAM COTTON BLUES BAND	circa 1967	HULL
WINSORS	circa 1962	HULL
WINDY	circa 1970	HULL
WINE	circa 1970	BEVERLEY
WORRYING KIND	circa 1967	SCUNTHORPE
XENONS	circa 1964	YORK
YE BARONS	circa 1964	HULL
YOUNG ONES, SMALL PAUL		
AND THE	circa 1964	BRIDLINGTON
YORKIES	circa 1964	HULL
ZEBEDEE'S PEOPLE	circa 1966	YORK
ZEROES, ROY AND THE	circa 1964	POCKLINGTON
ZIRCONS	circa 1964	BRIDLINGTON
ZODIACS	circa 1964	HULL
ZOFFANY	circa 1970	SCARBOROUGH

LET ME TAKE YOU DOWN

1963

'THE ROAD TO ROCK'

An A.B.C. Theatre

REGAL - HULL

Manager: J. B. FISHER

Telephone: 15530

ON THE STAGE FOR ONE DAY ONLY

WED. 19TH MARCH 6.15 TWO SHOWS 8.30

Prices CIRCLE 10/6, 8/6, 6/6, 4/6
STALLS 10/6, 8/6, 6/6, 4/6, 2/6

BOX OFFICE NOW OPEN—BOOK NOW

LEW & LESLIE GRADE Ltd. Presents

THE GREAT AMERICAN RECORDING STARS

BUDDY HOLLY

HIT RECORDER OF "PEGGY SUE"

AND THE

CRICKETS

FAMOUS FOR THEIR GREAT DISCS "THAT'LL BE THE DAY", 'OH BOY', etc.

THE PYE-NIXA RECORDING STAR

GARY MILLER

Featuring his Hit Record
'THE STORY OF MY LIFE'

OF STAGE, RADIO & RECORDING FAME

THE TANNER SISTERS

COMEDIAN WITH THE MODERN STYLE

DES O'CONNOR

BRITAIN'S NEW MUSICAL SENSATION

RONNIE KEENE AND HIS ORCHESTRA

567

1963

CITY HALL
Tuesday, October 15
at 6.30 and 8.40 pm

✳ JOHNNY KIDD
and The Pirates
(I'll Never Get Over You')

✳ HEINZ
('Just Like Eddie')

✳ THE ROLLING STONES
('Come On')

✳ SAINTS
('Wipe Out')

✳ SAMMY KING AND VOLTAIRS

✳ GARTH CAWOOD
("Mr Shake")

✳ ERIC LEE and FOUR ACES
(Hull's Top Group)

BOOK NOW at

PARAGON MUSIC STORES
PARAGON STREET
3/6 4/6 5/6 6/- 7/0

THE ACES

WITH THEIR FIRST RECORDING
ON THE PARLOPHONE LABEL

PARLOPHONE R5094

"WAIT TILL TOMORROW"

and

"THE LAST ONE"

IN THE RECORD SHOPS NOW

THE ACES APPEARING AS USUAL

ELLOUGTON - Friday, Dec 6th

BEVERLEY ROAD BATHS - Saturday, Dec 7th

COME AND GET YOUR RECORD AUTOGRAPHED

BEVERLEY ROAD BATHS
SATURDAY BEAT CLUB - SATURDAY NOV 23rd
7.30 pm to 11.30 pm

The Fabulous Group

THE ACES

supported by

'THE MAJESTICS' and ALAN EDWARDS DJ

Admission 4/-   Late Transport

FERRYBOAT INN
HESSLE

TONIGHT

THE JAGUARS

THURSDAY

WALLY and the
FALCONS

FRIDAY

THE JAGUARS

568

The Aces, The Mods, The Rangers, The Mustangs (Four of Hull's earliest Beat groups)

1963

1963

HALFWAY HOUSE
Spring Bank

RHYTHM AND BLUES
With
THE KING BEES
Hull's Most Exciting Group

THURSDAYS AND SATURDAYS

ALL NIGHT RAVE
THE DOLPHIN CLUB, BRIDLINGTON
Saturday, January 23rd

BARRY GRAHAM AND THE MUSTANGS

10 pm - 6 am Tickets 7/6 obtainable from the
Dophin Club, Queen Street, Bridlington

Beverley Road Baths

SATURDAY

THE 5 TRAX

4/-   4/-
ALAN EDWARDS DJ

7.30 pm to 11.30 pm

SKYLINE
BALLROOM
2-38 Jameson Street

DANCING

TONIGHT - QUARTER FINAL

ROCK 'N' ROLL
BAND CONTEST

2/6.   7 - 11

Bands Competing

**THE MUSTANGS
RICKY KNIGHT AND
THE CRUSADERS
JOHN.T.HUNTER
AND THE PANTHERS
THE BARONS
THE MARTIANS**

THURS - QUARTER FINAL
ROCK 'N' ROLL
BAND CONTEST
2/6   7 - 11
Bands Competing

**SCOTT MADISON AND
THE RANGERS
JOHNNY LEVER AND
THE RASCALS
THE REBELS**

**TOMORROW
NIGHT**
ELLOUGHTON

THE FABULOUS

**F O U R
A C E S**

FEATURING

**ERIC LEE
THE ACES OF BEAT**

**Owing to commercial
Reasons this group will in
Future be known as
THE ACES**

MAJESTIC Ballroom
HULL
Phone 29094

THE BEATLES

7..30 pm - 11 pm Admission 3/6

With **ERIC LEE** and
THE FOUR ACES

571

OUSE
BEAT

february

1964

1s 6d

wn pop music magazine. york's own pop music magazine. york's

1964

The Humber Sound

You've heard about the Merseybeat,
Which in the past has made much
ground,
But wait, just wait, until you've heard
That thumping, twitchin Humber Sound,

It swings and rocks you to an fro,
this sound just makes you go, go, go,
So if you're low and wear a frown
Listen to this Humber Sound,

Oh! we've not hit the charts just yet,
But in the future you can bet
This sound will hit the top one day
And we'll hear less of yeah! yeah! yeah's!

So watch yourself you Liverpool groups,
As we from Hull just start to troop,
To top the charts, the world around
With our own type, the Humber Sound.

Roland Pexton (1964)

573

1964

SATURDAY
BIG BEAT NIGHT
at the
C ITY HALL
with

3 GROUPS 3

**THE BLUEBERRIES
THE DELLMEN
DEAN CURTIS AND THE
PHANTOMS**

7.30 - 11.30 pm   Late Transport
ADMISSION ONLY 4/-

**JIMMY SAVILLE
"CRAWLS"**
Holme-on-Spalding Moor
Village Hall

FRIDAY. JULY 13TH
Dancing 9 pm to 3 am.
to **THE CORVETTES and
THE ZEROES**

Buffet   Admission 7/6

THE CRICKETERS
NORTH MARINE ROAD

FRIDAY
* ## JONTY AND THE STRANGERS

SATURDAY
* ## GROUP 29

SUNDAY
* **The Fabulous**
TENNESSEANS

**DRIFFIELD TOWN HALL
FRIDAY, AUGUST 28**

THE FABULOUS McCOYS
with Glamour Girls Liz and Joan
plus the **ROAD RUNNERS**

Dancing 9.30 pm - 2 am

Admission 5/-   Bar
Refreshments

THE PAVILION - FILEY
F A B   D A N C E
8.30 pm till 1 a.m - Tickets
Wed Aug. 19   **7/6**

* **STAR GROUPS**

3

**SCREAMING LORD
S U T C H
and THE SAVAGES**

THE McCOYS

ROAD RUNNERS

TICKETS
BOOKING
OFFICE

BERNARD DEAN MUSIC CENTRE

BERNARD HADDOCK PROMOTIONS

576

577

HISTORY - AND HULLABALLOO - AT THE BARONIAL HALL

As 20th-Century Mistrels Make Their Disc Debut

SOME ten miles from Hull, in Yorkshire's East Riding, there
stands the great, centuries-old baronial hall, Burton Constable, with
its 100 rooms and its history. On its 6,000-acre estate are 32 farms.
Fish abound in its 17 acres of lakes, and from the woods dotted about
its 230 acres of lush parkland they once cut down giant oak trees to
build ships for Nelson's fleet at the Battle of Trafalgar.

Inside Burton Constable - a King of France was once a
house guest there - the vast state rooms display fine porcelain and
valuable pieces of furniture. On the high walls hang 400 paintings
by such world-renowned artists as Lely, Kneller and Paninni. On the
library shelves there are rare first editions among the 7,000 books.

Not far from the house, in the shadow of the imposing,
turreted tower with its flagpole and royal blue and gold standard
flying at its head, is one of the few indoor riding schools in this
country. It is the second largest indoor riding school in Europe.

And in the riding school is a beat group.

SO WHAT?

"So what?" asks Burton Constable's owner, 37-year-old former
Rifle Brigade officer and Old Etonian, John Chichester-Constable, who
inherited with the estate the feudal title of Lord Paramoun of the
Seigniory of Holderness. "My forbears lived here for 900 years, and
they had their minstrels. The boys in our beat group are our
20th-century minstrels."

Mr. Chichester-Constable's minstrels are The Hullaballoos -
four blond-haired, long-haired young men from Hull named Andy Woonton,
Ricky Knight, Harry Dunn and Geoff Mortimer. John Chichester-Constable
and his wife Gay first heard them playing at a dance in a nearby village
hall. It was later, when they invited them to play at a barbecue at
Burton Constable, that they realised The Hullaballooes were 'pop'
potential.

YORKSHIRE

is THE LARGEST COUNTY

IN ENGLAND

Kingston-upon-Hull

is THE LARGEST FISHING PORT

IN ENGLAND

IN LANCASHIRE, NOTTINGHAMSHIRE, LINCOLNSHIRE AND

YORKSHIRE, WITH A TOTAL POPULATION OF OVER

11½ MILLION PEOPLE

THE LARGEST CROWDS

ARE DRAWN BY THE

"RATS"

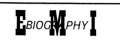

THE RATS

One of Hull's claims to fame is that it has the only independent telephone service in Great Britain - in fact, there is only one other in the whole world - and that this service has a special system whereby callers who dial 21411 can hear the Hull Record of the Week..

In February, 1965, subscribers dialling the above number were able to hear a new record called "Spoonful", sung by a group calling themselves The Rats! This record marked their entry into showbiz.

For eighteen months they had been whipping up riot-like enthusiasm among the teenagers of the North, resulting in a large fan club and many gifts of large felt rats - not to mention tee-shirts emblazoned with that animal.

Bunny Lewis took an interest in the group, and was sufficiently impressed with their talent to bring them down to London and record them. "Spoonful" is an old Howlin' Wolf number that the Rats have been doing on stage for many months, and the audience reaction convinced them that the number was commercial enough enough to merit single release.

THE RATS ARE:

BENJAMIN MARSHALL, the group's vocalist and harmonica-player, is 21 years old and a native of Hull. Since leaving school at 15, he has been a bricklayer's labourer and a pork butcher. His interests are jazz and blues, aside from girls, although he dislikes work and salad cream. He also lists the East Riding Police Force as something to be avoided! He eats either steak or fish and chips and likes a vodka and lime. With grey eyes and dark brown hair, he stands six feet tall, and he's one of the reasons that the Rats are so popular with Northern girls.

JAMES SIMPSON, the drummer. He's seventeen and left school two years ago to become a apprentice refrigerator engineer. His only other job, he claims, was "Milk monitor"! His only claim to any musical background is the fact that his father played the Jaws Harp - although this would hardly account for his other interests, which are "buttons and combs". He likes kissing girls and dislikes not kissing them; he has dark brown hair, hazel eyes, weighs 11st. 4lbs, and eats spaghetti bolognaise.

BRIAN BUTTLE, the bass guitarists, is now 22 years old, and stands six feet tall. He's powerfully built, and since leaving school at 15, he has been a signwriter, a labourer and anTV engineer. His principal interests are cars and electronics, and he has a passion for R & B. He dislikes buses, getting up and going to bed, but raves over salads and vodka. He describes both his hair and eyes as "mousey", and spends most of his spare time chasing girls.

FRANK INCE, guitarist, is a 22-year-old native of Wigan who has had various jobs in the last four years, graduating from a shoe salesman to a clerk. His musical interest was aroused by some friends in a folk group, and he learned the guitar in order to join such a group. Eventually R & B took over and he joined the Rats. He likes music of all kinds and enjoys travelling with the group, while his dislikes are toll bridges, ferries, the group's van, and echoed guitars. On the culinary side he digs cheese, steak, spaghetti, chicken and fired rice, and he will not touch alcohol, for he prefers either tea or coke. His hair is blond, and eyes are blue-grey; and his powerful guitar-playing is one of the main features of the Rats' sound.

FLORAL HALL
HORNSEA

TUESDAY, SEPTEMBER 8th

POP-IN

FINAL OF BEAT GROUP
COMPETITION

featuring

THE ZEROS	THE CHEVELETS
(POCKLINGTON)	(ROTHERHAM)
THE DELLMEN	THE STATESMEN
(HULL)	(HULL)
THE BLUE STARS	THE FABIANS
(SCARBOROUGH)	(HULL)
THE ZIRCONS	THE SCORPIONS)
(BRIDLINGTON)	(HORNSEA)

DANCING 8 p.m. to 1 a.m.

Admission 4/- Car-park.

Hull Parks Department

OPEN AIR

BEAT NIGHTS

with the Top Groups

Commencing 7.30 p.m.
Admission :
Adults 1/-. Children 6d.

TUESDAY
West Park
JENNY
and THE TEXANS

THURSDAY
East Park
THE FABIANS
and
THE COSSACKS

Introducing . . .

THE NORTH'S TOP GROUP

BARRY GRAHAM

AND HIS FABULOUS

MUSTANGS

(MEMBERS OF M.U.)

NATIONAL FINALISTS AT BRIGHTON
MARCH 1964

Rock :: Rhythm :: Blues

Enquiries to:-

J.J.W.WIGLEY	Telephones
20 DENT ROAD	846368
BRICKNELL AVENUE	506809
HULL	505369

J ENTERPRISES promote the biggest

BIG
BEAT **Bar-B-Que !**

at REIGHTON HALL COUNTRY HOTEL
(TWIXT BRID. AND SCARBOROUGH)

THURS., 6th AUG.

DUSK, 9 p.m. till
DAWN, 3 a.m.
Full T.V. Film Coverage
Licensed Bar

LINZI ENTERPRISES

* * * * PRESENT GRAND GALAXY OF STARS
BERN ELLIOTT'S ORIGINAL

FALEX WINSTONE and the ORIGINAL FLINTSTONES	FENMEN	THE TENNESSEANS
BARRY MILLS and THE LIMELIGHTERS	The McCoys	BARRY GRAHAM and the MUSTANGS
THE Blue Stars	METHODS	Group 29

Non-Stop Music :: Late Transport :: TICKETS (Strictly limited) 15/6

SORRY, NO
BIG SATURDAY
BEAT NIGHT
AT THE CITY HALL
owing to
" TAKE YOUR PICK "
NEXT SATURDAY AS USUAL
with
THE TYCOONS
AND
JENNY AND THE TEXANS

Jay Hoyle Enterprises present
AT THE CITY HALL
BIG SATURDAY
BEAT NIGHT
with
The fabulous
TYCOONS
and
the sensational
JENNY AND THE TEXANS
All the top pops and mime
competition.
7 p.m.-11 p.m.
Admission only 4/-.

KON-TIKI
49, WHITEFRIARGATE

THURSDAY—THE RIVALS. 7.30-11.0. 3/-.
FRIDAY—THE TEXANS. 7.30-12.0. 4/-.
SATURDAY—THE STATESMEN. 7.30-1.0. 4/-.
SUNDAY—THE JAGUARS. 7.30-11.0. 3/-. P

581

582

1965

1965

1965

A.B.C REGAL BALLROOM, BEVERLEY
TOMORROW , FRIDAY, JUNE 18th
Five hours non-stop Rock and Roll, 8 p.m.- 1 a.m., featuring

YE BARONS   THE GONX   THE CRESTAS

Fully licensed bar'   Admission 5/-.

A.B.C REGAL BALLROOM, BEVERLEY
TOMORROW, FRIDAY-- 8.p.m.- 1.a.m.

THE AVENGERS   THE MODS

THE SEMI-TONES

THE BARRACUDA CLUB
1/2, BISHOP LANE, LOWGATE, HULL,
Presents

TONIGHT (THURSDAY)	FRIDAY
The R.B sound of	The sensational
THE NIGHT PEOPLE	TYCOONS
Members 2/6. Guests 3/6	Members 3/- Guests 3/6

Both 7.30 - 11.30.   D.J. Trevor
Refreshments, Snacks. All the Top Pops plus
Atmosphere

THE TOWN HALL HESSLE

FRIDAY, JANUARY 15th   8.00 p.m - 1 a.m

presents

THE KING BEES - THE COCK-A-HOOPS - THE SAXONS

Licensed Bar	Refreshments
Price 5/-	Late Transport to City Centre,

SPA ROYAL HALL   BRIDLINGTON
TEL. 2003

SATURDAY 10th JULY - 8.30 - 11.45 p.m

TOM JONES and the Squires

supported by

THE SYNDICATE 5	THE UNKNOWNS
Admission 7/6	Obtainable at door only

Hull Parks Department

OPEN AIR

BEAT NIGHTS
with the Top Groups

Commencing 7.30 p.m.
Admission
Adults 1/-.   Children 6d.
TONIGHT
West Park
THE SEMI-TONES
and
THE JAGUARS

THURSDAY
East Park
JOHNNY LEVER
and THE RASCALS

Burton Constable
NR.SPROATLEY, HULL

JUNE 26th
THE HULLABALLOOS
plus
THE INN CROWD

Admission 7/6

Hull Parks Department
Open Air

BEAT NIGHTS

TONIGHT
East Park

The Fabulous
RATS
supported by the
METAPHORS

Commencing 7.30 p.m
Adults 1/-
Children and OAPs 6d

586

THE HULLABALLOOS

ENGLAND'S NEWEST SINGING SENSATIONS

587

1965

NEXT WEEK at the **CONTINENTAL**

T H E

MUSTANGS

Farewell engagement prior
to London and Continental
season

BOOK EARLY!

SOULFUL EVENING

Dancing with the
**Alex Harvey Soul Band
The Rats, The Chow Men**

At the SKYLINE BALLROOM

SOMBERO CLUB
Market Place

**JOE COCKER AND HIS
BIG BLUES**

and **THE KING BEES**

Soft Drinks   Refreshments
Price 3/6 Members   4/6 Guests
Late Transport

KON-TIKI
49, WHITEFRIARGATE

THURSDAY - THE NIGHT PEOPLE
    7.30 - 11.00 Members 3/- Guests 3/6
FRIDAY   - JIMMY POWELL AND THE BLUES COUNT
    7.30 - 12.00 Members 4/- Guests 5/-
SAT   - THE POWER HOUSE SIX
    7.30 - 1.00 Members 4/- Guests 5/-
SUN   - THE FABIANS
    7.30 - 11.00 Members 3/- Guests 3/6

FRIDAY, JANUARY 8th, at
REGAL BALLROOM, BEVERLEY
PIC-A-DISC presents
THE KING BEES - THE TEXANS
THE JAGUARS
Late Transport to Hull. Licensed Bar 5/-. 8 p.m. to 1 a.m.

REGAL BALLROOM, BEVERLEY
DANCING - EVERY SAT - 7.30 - 11.45 p.m.

THE SEMI-TONES - THE ZEROS
Admission: Before 8 p.m. 4/-, After 8 p.m. 5/-,
Soft Drinks and Refreshment Lounge.

FERRY BOAT INN
HESSLE
ANNOUNCE FOR YOUR ENTERTAINMENT

TUESDAYS: THE C BEATS
WEDNESDAYS: THE JAGUARS
THURSDAYS: WALLY AND THE FALCONS
FRIDAYS: THE MAGPIES
SATURDAY: THE JAGUARS
A HULL BREWERY HOUSE

THE

C O N D O R
COFFEE CELLER

DROGO'S TROLLS SATURDAY
    SEPTEMBER 11th
Members 2/6, Guests 3/6

SPA BALLROOM

SATURDAY 30th APRIL
✱ 8.30 - till 11.45 pm ✱

DIRECT FROM AMERICAN TOUR

HULLABALLOOS

SUPPORTED BY

KERBSIDERS

Admission .... FIVE SHILLINGS

588

1965

SPA BALLROOM

TOMORROW - SATURDAY

COME AND SAY GOODBYE TO
MICK, PHIL, DAVE, PETE , AND PADDY

THEIR FINAL APPEARANCE

✳ M O O N S H O T S ✳

Admission 5/-: No Jeans: Licensed Bar

TONIGHT AT 8.15

T E N N E S S E A N S

✳ I N C A S ✳

KERBSIDERS
Admission 5/- : Licensed Catering

Saturday Next: THE JOHN BARRY SEVEN

B E L L E   V U E   C L U B

THIS SATUDAY
THE FABULOUS
METHODS

Peter Pitts Management for Filey Swimming Baths Association

TONIGHT in the
PAVILION THEATRE, Southdene, Filey

York's Top Group

T H E   O U S E B E A T S

Dance 8.30 - 12.30   3/-   Cafe

Next Week 15th - The Sensations

PLAGUE 66
(HULL)

Manager:-

HEDLEY M. BILTON,
24 -- 26TH AVENUE,
GREENWOOD AVENUE,
HULL.   854738

TEL. 5 0 5 2 3 0
K. M. CORBETT,
142 BOOTHFERRY ROAD,
HULL.

M J T A

MALCOLM THOMSON
ASSOCIATES LIMITED

IMPERIAL COURT
2 BASIL STREET
LONDON S.W. 3
KENSINGTON 7671

Information

THE MAJORITY

ROBB LONG

Born 20 years ago in Hull, dark, handsome and lithe....plays rhythm guitar, taught himself at the age of 13...interested in body building, wished at one time to be a rugby player...not suprisingly his favourite film is "This Sporting Life"...admires songwriters Carter-Lewis, Lennon-McCartney, Crewe-Caudio... likes spending money on food, the opposite sex, and best bitter....wears five rings on three fingers....enjoys laughing, watching Albert Finney, and listening to youg children talking- he finds their strange logic fascinating....longs to see America and meet Tony Bennett....is an ardent sleeper....rates Sophia Loren as actress and optical delicacy....likes residencies, especially Blaises and The Dolly Club.

ROGER FRANCE

22 year old Roger France, tall, dark and devious, was bound for the Merchant Navy before he turned professional with The Majority....digs the Beach Boys and The Ivy League....is a regular listener to "Teen Scene" on the Light and wishes that more radio programmes had intelligent chat between discs.... dislikes gas meters....appears to be the most sensible member of the group, is soft spoken and amicable....digs suntanned girls, fish and chips, coke and lemon on the rocks.....the falsetto singer of the group, Roger wishes he could hit Streisand's high notes.....though usually conservative in his tastes, he likes brightly coloured, short-sleeved sports shirts - his collection contains vermilion, ultramarine and African violet....thinks sleeping and eating are the greatest time wasters in the world, but admits he enjoys both....collects money.

BARRY GRAHAM

21 years old, born in Hull, electrician turned vocalist.... the shortest of the group, stands 5' 7" in his lettle cotton socks.....stands out as an inventive harmony vocalist.... wanted to become a racing driver but found singing less dangerous.... is rather athletic, loves dancing, especially tap....talks too much, sleeps too much, likes excess in most pleasant things....left school with seven G.C.Es..... befriends strange horses....his favourite pet is his sister Maureen....raves over John Barry, Dudley Moore and Peter Cook.....would love to befriend strange model girls, including 'The Shrimp', Celia Hammond and Playboy Bunnies.... his latest friend is Mike Hurst - they often argue over the interpretation of vintage rock numbers, can't quite agree on "You Aint't Nothing But A Hound Dog"....still wears very tight levis.

DON LILL

Born in Hull, 20 year old Don Lill, The Majority's drummer, is a self-taught musician who enter show business at the tender age of 16....rates Lennon-McCartney and Carter- Lewis as composers....enjoys watching motor racing..... "King Rat" his favourite film to date....clown of the group, hopes to emulate the humour of Sellers and Milligan, and greatly admires the antics of disc jockey Jimmy Saville.... likes Chinese food and James Bond....hates bus queues, dull parties and getting up in the morning....thinks Cathy McGowan is smashing....in anticipation of a number one hit is already recruiting designers of his hoped-for boutique in Hull..... is constantly imitating any strange people he meets..... prefers Bacherach to Bach but Mozart to Mose Allison..... looks forward to the day when he can make a film and live in Scotland.....drinks rum and coke.

KENNY SMITH

Aged 20, born in Hull, plays bass guitar with The Majority.... is blonde and fanciable....was a trainee accountant, now uses his talent to keep an eye on the boys' financial affairs.... likes checked shirts, thin women, and Baroque....yearns to design and paint....The Majority are constantly bombarded with his works of art - their Chelsea flat is plastered with them....rates Rita Tushingham and Harry H. Corbett..... constantly swopping watch straps, lighters, and whatever else is swoppable....has three transistor radios and listens to Radio London on all at the same time....quiet but confident....still rates The Shadows.....often goes to the cinema with rhythm guitarist Robb.....longs to own an Afghan hound called Titian....will probable write a book on the trials and tribulations of a pop group....ambition - to look as good as Cary Grant when he's 60.

1966

FLORAL HALL - HORNSEA
FRIDAY, JUNE 8, 1966

THE

CRYING SHAMES

Supported by the fabulous

Scarborough Group

THE INCAS

8 pm - 1 am

18/6 at the door

Tickets in advance from
The Paragon Music Stores, Hull

SPA ROYAL HALL
SATURDAY, 23rd July

THE WHO

plus

THE MANDRAKES   -   21st CENTURY

SPA ROYAL HALL
SATURDAY, JULY 9th

MANFRED MANN
Supported by

THE SYNDICATE 5   **THE SEMI-TONES**

TOMORROW NIGHT AT THE CITY HALL
BIG SATURDAY BEAT

With THE TYCOONS, PLAGUE 66"

A.B.C making their debut at the City Hall
AND ALL THE TOP POPS

7 p.m - 11 p.m - **ADMISSION ONLY 4/-**
COME EARLY.   "YOU LUCKY PEOPLE"

FLORAL HALL
HORNSEA

Special Attraction July 22

THE TROGGS

THE INCAS

FLORAL HALL
HORNSEA
SPECIAL ATTRACTION
FRIDAY, 9th SEPT
8 p-m.-1 a.m.
Dancing to
THE PRETTY THINGS
supported by
THE STROLLERS
Refreshments and Buffet
Admission 8/6
Tickets in advance from
Paragon Music Stores, Hull
and The Floral Hall, Hornsea.
Tel. Hornsea 2380

PROHIBITION
66 CLUB
MARKET PLACE

FRIDAY
7.30 - 2 p.m.
THE SMALL FOUR
Members 3/- Visitors 4/6

SATURDAY
7.30 till 12
THE TRENDS
Members 3/- Visitors 4/6

SUNDAY
7.30 till 12
THE TRENDS

1966

SENSATION IN SOUL

THAT FEELING

IS COMING

TONIGHT (THURSDAY) ROCK AND ROLL REVUE

ERIC BURDON and THE ANIMALS

plus Philip Goodhart Tait and The Stormville Shakers

BEVERLEY ROAD BATHS

Admission 10/- (at door)

Refreshments   Late Transport

COME - SEE - HEAR

THE EXCITING

LOCOMOTION

ELLOUGHTON
VILLAGE HALL

FRIDAY OCT 7th   8 - 1 am

The Shapes
(Pop Group)

Contact R Moody
15 Brisbane Street
Porter Street
HULL

FACES

HULL COLLEGE OF TECHNOLOGY
STUDENTS UNION

JULY 8, SKYLINE BALLROOM
8.30 pm - 2 am.

THE SMALL FACES

HERBIE GOINS
AND THE NITETIMERS

THE MIKE COTTON SOUND

JIMMY CLIFF

THE MODS

EDDIE GRAY BAND

PRICE 12/6

Tickets from Hammonds
Skyline, Gough & Davy

Late Transport 1 am

FACES

HULL COLLEGE OF TECHNOLOGY STUDENTS UNION
present
the most controversial, sensation group in
Britain today

"THE CREAM"

Hit record "Wrapping Paper"

Supported by Victor Brox BLUES TRAIN
POWERINUS - BIRDS GROOVE - CHAOS

SKYLINE BALLROOM, TONIGHT
12/6   Tickets from Skyline Ballroom

TOMORROW NIGHT AT THE CITY HALL

BIG SATURDAY BEAT

WITH THE TENNESSIANS (SCARBOROUGH)
Las appearance of PAUL DOWNING with this group
prior to his American debut.

THE YORKIES   and   THE 5 TRAX

7 p.m - 11 p.m Admission only 4/- Come early
'YOU LUCKY PEOPLE'

PLAGUE 66'

Before their final booking on Saturday
would like to express their thanks
to all their friends and fans.

PLAGUE 66 - RIP

593

THE TEEN SC[ENE]

The [...] are brothers Dennis, Michael and Raymond Moody.

[...] HAD IT SO GOOD!

They hope to sp[lash] success

A HULL POP GROUP will shortly be launched into the record world with two first-class gimmicks which should focus the beat world's spotlight directly on them.

The first is a musical instrument which, they claim, no other pop group in the world has. It is a phono-harp — a Jew's harp with a horn attachment.

Second — and this should really set the lads' image is an ANTI-DRUG song.

This is quite against the present trend in discs and could give them the originality label.

Centre of attraction is the Sharps, a three-man band of brothers — 7-year-old Raymond Moody, 16-year-old Dennis and 15-year-old Michael, all of Brabane-street, Foster-street.

They are being commanded by their manager and former talent scout, John Reid.

Orinal

Mr Reid [...] the harp in a Hull junk shop and thought it would be an ideal type of instrument for the group to play.

"I knew nobody else had tried to feature one of these in their line-up so I bought

anti-drugs r[...]

it. The Hillbilly groups of America play them but until [...] no pop group has attempted to play one," he said.

The lads should pick up how to play it after a while. When one of them has perfected the method of playing it, then we should get a deep bass sound.

As for the anti-drug song, that was written by a Hull man to show the ugliness and repulsive side of drug taking.

One line in the song—titled "Psychedelic Illusion"— speaks of a person's arm aching where the needle goes in.

It describes the blisters and boils on a junky's arm and how the addict realises that drugs are gradually killing him.

Great chance

"With the Jew's harp and this anti-drug song, I think we have a great chance of getting right to the top at our first go [...] the record business," said [...] a timber worker and the

[...] to the top. It is just [...]

Competition is fierce and the lads will get it on tape quick. A professional outfit are record the number, the [...] turned down [...] a number of times.

Already the boys are competition ... and

No clangers for Hull Misses!

PARIS FASHIONS have gone metallic. But Hull's will stay cloth. This was the unani-

not be the [...] short ones. Hull girls might wear anything too mini[...]

she went as far as to say: "it all boils do[...] to them, not

The Teen Scene

FIND-TH[E]

FIRST PRIZE

50 CO[...] OF

Draw a cross [...] the exact [...]

595

-------- DOUBLE R PRODUCTIONS PRESENT --------

RAVESVILLE NITE

AT THE

Assembly Rooms, York

Friday, May 13th, 1966, 9 p.m ----- 1a.m

-------- PRESENTING -------

TV, RADIO AND PYE RECORDING ARTIST LATEST RELEASE OUT MAY 20,

THE BLUE CHIPS

THE GROUP THE WALKER BROS RAVED ABOUT

THE KOKOMOS

YORK'S BIGGEST SOUND

MAL DYMAN AND THE TYCOONS

BAR – ADMISSION 6/6 – BUFFET

Tickets Available at the Golden Lion Hotel, Gough and Davy Clifford Street, Mackensies Ouse Bridge

---

ASSEMBLY ROOMS YORK
FRIDAY, NOVEMBER 4th 1966
8.30 p.m to 12.30 a.m
Straight from French Television
**RHYTHM AND BLUES
INCORPATED**
And YORK STARS
THE ROLL MOVEMENT
Plus Supporting Group
Bar till 12.30 a.n. – Buffet
TICKETS 7/- Late buses.

SS EMPIRE
SATURDAY DANCE
To THE CRUSADERS
9 p.m. to Midnight
2/6d

Z Z Z ZARF CLUB Z Z Z
Tel 23004   11 Stonegate ,
TONIGHT
THE ROLL MOVEMENT

BURNS WILSON ENTERPRISES present at the
ASSEMBLY ROOMS, YORK
FRIDAY, FEBRUARY 18th,
Dancing 8.30 – 1 a.m.
THOSE SENSATIONAL
S H O T S
- Plus -
MANDRAKES and CHOW'S MEN
PLUS YORK'S OWN FABULOUS
ROLL MOVEMENT

Bar -------------------- admission 6/6

BOULEVARDE

FRIDAY NOVEMBER 4th

Bonfire Night Preview battle of
York's Two Top Groups

THE ROLL MOVEMENT

and

GIDEONS FEW

9 to 1.30 am 6/-

A·GREAT·NEW
RELEASE·TO
START·A·GREAT
NEW·YEAR·FOR~

THE

MAJORITY

"WE·KISS
IN·A·SHADOW"
'RING·THE·BELLS'
JAN·7·DECCA·F12313

1967

FAMILY AFFAIR

Three Hull brothers have formed a new beat group in the city. The Moody brothers of 15 Brisbane Street, Porter Street, have formed a group called the Shapes, which should be out and about on the city's beat scene in the next few weeks. In the group are Raymond Moody (15), Dennis (16) and Michael (13). Raymond is playing lead guitar and Dennis bass. On the drums is Michael who is still at school. The group is being managed by the boys mother. Also taking an interest is Mr John Reid, of Arnold Street Hull. Mr Reid, a former talent scout with a London Agency, hopes that the group will be able to make a demo disc soon after they start working. Already they have been trying out two suitable numbers.

Burns Wilson Enterprises invite you to rave to the sounds of

SOUL '67

At the Civic Hall COTTINGHAM
FRIDAY JUNE 30th
It's all action 9.30 p.m.- 1.30 a.m.

We proudly present the Group that puts allo the big names to
shame, the North-East's No1, its those magnificant

MANDRAKES

PLUS + PLUS

Plus!! Raving records in our "Have Discs will Travel" Show

Doors open 9.15   Buffet   Admission 6/6

PINK FLOYD   PINK FLOYD   PINK FLOYD

WHICH COLLEGE HAS THE

PINK FLOYD

On FRIDAY, JUNE 9th

The ABC   plus The Night Starvation (Formerly the Riverbeats)
Tickets 10/- available from Sydney Scarborough

**For Radio 270 at Burton Constable Riding School,
Sproatley, Near Hull**

Wednesday, 16 AUGUST

All Disc Jockeys there in person including originals

Dance to **THE STROLLERS**

Please book in advance for special Bus leaving Hull
Coach Station 8 p.m. (E.Y.M.S)

599

GROOVY

OCTOBER

2/-

1967

1967

TOP TWENTY CLUB
6.0 - 8.0 - Under 15 years
DANCE CONTEST to find Hull's
BEST MOD, DANCER UNDER 15 years
Plus Best of the Pops. Adm 1/6.

8.0 - 10.30 - Teen Night

THE SHAPES

Saturday, September 24th
Adm 4/-
St. Margaret's Hall, Longhill Estate
TOP TWENTY GROUPS OF TOMORROW

SKYLINE BALLROOM
PRESENTS

THE KINKS
BY POPULAR REQUEST
THE RETURN OF
THE TRAVELLERS EXPRESS
YOUR LOCAL FAVOURITES
THE MANDRAKES
AND THE SENSATIONAL
HERBIE'S iii's

8 - 1 am	LATE TRANSPORT
TICKETS 12/6	BEFORE THE NIGHT
	15/- AT THE DOOR

SPA ROYAL HALL -- BRIDLINGTON
Box Office Tel. 2003
SATURDAY, SEPTEMBER 24th   8.30 - 11.45 p.m.

THE SEARCHERS
PLUS
THE SONS OF WITCH   THE UNKNOWNS
Admission 7/6

A.B.C. REGAL BALLROOM, BEVERLEY
NON-STOP DANCING - EVERY SAT. - 7.30 - 11.45 p.m

THE RIVERBEATS   THE STROLLERS

Admission: Before 8 p.m. 4/-. After 8 p.m. 6/-.
Soft Drinks and Refreshment Lounge.

SKYLINE BALLROOM
THURSDAY JUNE 8

THE SMOKE
(Columbia)
ROGER BLOOMS
HAMMER (CBS)
THE MANDRAKES

RADIO 270 DJs
MIKE HAYES
ROSS RANDELL

THE NEW RELIGION

Tickets 10/- AT THE DOOR
9/- IN ADVANCE FROM SYD SCAR. GOUGH & DAVY

HULL COLLEGE OF
COMMERCE
STUDENTS UNION
presents

from Top London Clubs

THE TRIBE

- with -

THAT FEELING

- and -

THE LOCOMOTION

Saturday, June 17   8 - 11.45
Tickets 7/6

SKYLINE BALLROOM
presents

THE TREMELOES
D/J MIKE HAYES
THE MANDRAKES
THE SACRED MUSHROOMS
THE NIGHT BEATS
THE URGE
THURSDAY, 17th AUGUST
1967
Tickets 10/6 (12/6 at the door) on sale Skyline Box
office
* * * * * * *

- TONIGHT -
CIVIC HALL, COTTINGHAM
BIG BEAT DANCE
6/6
That Feeling
The Disturbance
Refreshments, Late Transport

1967

ASSEMBLY ROOMS, YORK
Saturday April 8th
8 p.m. to 11.45 p.m.

3 GROUP RAVE

TWO STAGES
DISCODELIC LIGHTING

Here's your chance to see the only
British Group to play alongside OTIS
REDDING -SAM and DAVE on their
recent tour. The only group to break
the soul barrier.

THE
NEW
RELIGION

**Featuring Parlophone Recording
Star CHRIS BAGNELL**

Plus

THE SWEET IMAGE

Plus! Plus! York's No.1 Group!

THE LOLLIPOPS

With the GO-GO DANCERS
Tickets 7/6 on the door, 6/6
Advance from ROBERTSON'S
MUSIC SHOP, The Pavement, York

TOMORROW NIGHT
Saturday, June 3

FROM LONDON'S LATEST 'IN' PLACE

'THE SPEAKEASY CLUB'

The Group Jimi Hendrix raves about

THE SOFT MACHINE

With Hull's Top Group **'That Feeling'**

COTTINGHAM CIVIC HALL

TICKETS 7/6 (Students 6/6) Late Transport
From Gough & Davy, Sydney Scarborough

SHERRIF HUTTON Y.F.C
CLIFF BALLROOM, TERRINGTON
DANCING TO
THE PANTHERS
Friday April 7th
8 p.m. to 1.30 a.m.
Bar. Refreshments. Adm 6/-

PINK FLOYD

(Complete with their psychedelic light effects)
Plus **THE DIMPLES, THE RATS, THE DISTURBANCE**

And D.J RIKKI DOBBS

Will appear at

THE "TOP STAR" BEAT DANCE
On THURSDAY, 28TH SEPTEMBER 8 - 1 am

At the SKYLINE BALLROOM, HULL

Usual Refreshment Bars. Late Transport
Tickets 12.6, available at the Ballroom

602

1967

A.B.C REGAL BALLROOM, BEVERLEY
TOMORROW, FRIDAY - 8 p.m - 1 a.m.
THE TALL STORY - THE ROAD RUNNERS
THE STROLLERS

SKYLINE BALLROOM, HULL
THURSDAY, AUGUST 24, 1967, 8 p.m.-1 a m.
THE SMALL FACES
Also Roger Bloom's Hammer, The Mandrakes, The A.B.C
Six Shades of Blue   That Feeling
and Guest Disc Jockey Ray Nortrop
Tickets now on sale 15/- from The Skyline and Gough & Davy
and Sydney Scarborough,
All flower people welcome, Prizes for the most way out
hippy guy and gal

A.B.C REGAL BALLROOM, BEVERLEY
NON-STOP DANCING - EVERY SAT . - 7.30 - 11.45 p.m.
THE PENJANTS - THE STROLLERS
Two top East Riding groups
Admission Before 8 p.m. 4/-. After 8 p.m. 5/-
Soft Drinks and Refreshments Lounge

SPA ROYAL HALL - BRIDLINGTON
Box Office Tel. 2003

SATURDAY, 23rd SEPTEMBER   8 - 11.30 p.m.

THE YARDBIRDS

THE NEW RELIGION   THE URGE

Admission 7/6

Come early, "YOU LUCKY PEOPLE"

" IT'S THE GREATEST "

BIG SATURDAY BEAT

AT THE CITY HALL

THE TENNESSEANS - THAT FEELING
And all the Top Pops
7 p.m to 11 p.m   Admission Only 4/-

THURDAY, MARCH 9th
8 p.m to 1 a.m
Continuous Dancing to the

JIMI HENDRIX EXPERIENCE

SUPPORTING GROUPS

THE FAMILY   THE SMALL FOUR
THE STROLLERS
THE MANDRAKES

Admission   Tickets from the
                       Skyline Box Office
12/6   or the Boutique
                       First Floor Jameson St

Late Transport
SKYLINE BALLROOM
JAMESON STREET

MC.LEOD
ENTERTAINMENT
AGENCY.

ALL NAME & SEMI NAME groups
and artists are available for
engagement through this Agency –
Quotes are always on hand –
Doubles can usally be arranged if
required.

Sole Representation:

ROGER BLOOMS HAMMER –
CBS
THE MANDRAKE –
Scarborough
THE PEIGHTON CHECKS -
Scunthorpe
THE WAYS N MEANS
Hull

THE name in Entertainment
throughout the East Riding

603

That FEELING Feeling

MANDRAKE

CAN BE SEEN
IN OCTOBER

AT

Bradford	Fri. 6th
Hub, Barnsley	Sat. 7th
Hornsea	Sat. 14th
Paradise, Goole	Sat. 21st
Scarborough	Sat. 28th

PETE - plays No. 1 Guitar
and sings.

MICK - plays bass and sings

ALAN - sings lead

MICK - plays drums and sings

ROB - plays No. 2 guitar and
sings.

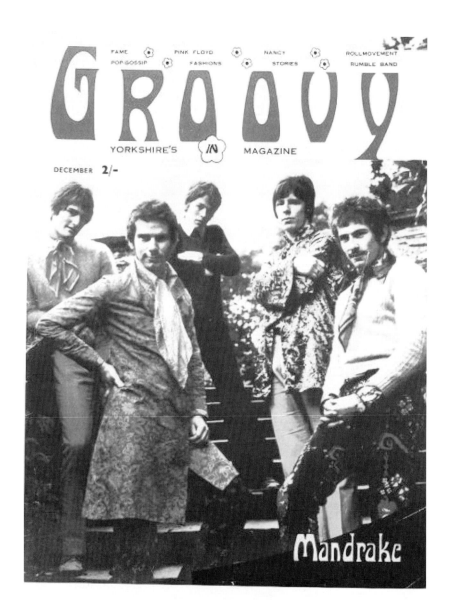

Mandrake

1968

606

1968

607

THE MᶜLEOD ENTERTAINMENT AGENCY

Telephones: HULL 658141 (STD. 0482)
HULL 657311

Direction: P. MᶜLEOD
Licenced annually by E.R.C.C.

24 VALLEY DRIVE,
KIRK-ELLA,
HULL,
E. Yorks.

This contract is subject to the terms and conditions of the Standard Form of Contract of the Variety & Allied Entertainments Council of Great Britain as approved 29th March, 1966.

AN AGREEMENT made the ___13th___ day of ___February___ 196 8

BETWEEN McLeod Entertainments ___ of ___ Hull ___ hereinafter called THE MANAGEMENT of the one part and Sweet Sugar Soul Set ___ hereinafter called THE ARTISTE of the other part.

WHEREBY the Management hereby engages the Artiste and the Artiste accepts an engagement to appear as ___ Known

present ___ their usual act ___ (or in their usual entertainment)

at the Dance Hall/Theatre/Club and from the dates for the periods and at the salaries as stated in the Schedule hereto.

The Artiste agrees to appear at:—

SCHEDULE

Venue	Date	Performances	Salary
Beverley Regal, ABC.Ballroom, Beverley, E.Yorks.	Monday, 15th April, 1968.	1 evening	£12.0.0. Cash

ADDITIONAL CLAUSES

(i) The Artiste shall arrive at the venue by ___7.00.p.m.___ and be ready to commence performance (if required) at ___8.00.p.m.___ and to perform for ___2hrs___ in not less than ___two___ sessions.

(ii) Financial settlement shall be made:✱ By cash on completion of performance.
By cheque on completion of performance.
By cheque within ___ days after performance.

(iii) Commission of ___10___ % is payable on the above engagement(s) and shall be due within 7 days after performance (unless otherwise and separately agreed) — In the case of payment by cheque, commission shall be deducted before forwarding such payment.

(iv) Commission on the above engagement(s) shall be equally divisible between ___mm___ ___mm___ of ___mm___ and McLeod Entertainment Agency.

(v) Any re-engagement made with the above Management shall be subject to a like commission when such is MADE within 12 calendar months of the above performance.

(vi) Should the Artiste fail to keep the engagements as stated in the above Schedule, he shall (without prejudice to any other claim the Management may have against him) be liable to pay the Management, by way of liquidated damages, a like sum to the salary as stated in the Schedule.

I/We, the undersigned, acknowledge that I/We have read the above Additional Clauses and agree that they will be adhered to in detail.

THIS AGENCY IS NOT RESPONSIBLE FOR ANY NON-FULFILMENT OF CONTRACTS BY PROPRIETORS, MANAGERS OR ARTISTES, BUT EVERY REASONABLE SAFEGUARD IS ASSURED.

Signature ___
Address ___

608

JOHN C. SHEARME, M.A., A.I.M.Ent.
Entertainments and Publicity Manager

THE SPA, BRIDL
YORKSHIRE.
(STI

RUNNING ORDER

8.00 to 8.45 p.m.	The Scene
8.45 to 9.45. p.m.	The Sweet Suga Set
9.45 to 10.45 p.m.	P. P. Arnold
10.45 to 11.30 p.m	The Scene

1968

BURTON CONSTABLE
Friday, June 21st

MIDSUMMER NIGHTS DREAM

featuring

LIVE ON STAGE

GENO WASHINTON
and the
RAM JAM BAND

THE MOVE

THE MARMALADE

THE FAMILY

THE
FAIRPORT CONVENTION

SPOOKY TOOTH * TRAMLINE
SAVOY BROWN BLUES BAND

ELMER GANTRY'S VELVET OPERA
BARON RICHTOFEN'S
Rock 'n' Roll Circus

THE ANGEL PAVEMENT

THE MANDRAKES

TICKETS £1

GOUGH & DAVY, SYDNEY
SCARBOROUGH

SPECIAL BUS SERVICES

SKYLINE BALLROOM
HULL. TEL 20364

THURS JUNE 6th 8 - 1

THE AMEN
CORNER

PITYFUL SOULS

STROLLERS

and

THE MANDRAKES

Tickets 13/6 from Gough &
Davy, Syd Scarborough
and The Skyline

Late Transport

SPA ROYAL HALL
BRIDLINGTON

Saturday, 8th June

8 to 11.30 pm

THE

H E R D

Supported by

THE URGE
THE SWEET SUGAR
SOUL SET

Admission 8/6

ABC REGAL BALLROOM - BEVERLEY
NON-STOP DANCING - EVERY SAT - 7.30 - 11.45 pm

SCARLET FARMYARD

THE DISTURBANCE

Admission - Before 8 pm 4/- after 8 pm 5/-
Soft Drinks and Refreshments

ABC REGAL BALLROOM - BEVERLEY
NON-STOP DANCING - EVERY SAT 7.30-11.45 pm

RIP VAN WINKEL

The Sensational Worrying Kind

Admission - Before 8 pm 4/- after 8 pm 5/-
Soft Drinks and Refreshments

611

1968

SPA ROYAL HALL
BRIDLINGTON ·

SATURDAY, 27th July

8 to 11.30 pm

AMERICA'S DYNAMIC
RECORDING STARS

REPARATA
and the DELRONS

with the CLOUDS

PLUS

THE MATCHBOX

THE ·STRAWBOA FANTASY

Admission   8/6

SPA ROYAL HALL
BRIDLINGTON

Saturday, 10th AUGUST

8 to 11.30 pm

SIMON
DUPREE

and the BIG SOUND

plus

THE SONS OF WITCH

THE URGE

Admission   8/6

ABC REGAL BALLROOM - BEVERLEY
NON-STOP DANCING - EVERY SAT - 7.30 - 11.45 pm

THE PURPLE HAZE - THE TREACLE

Admission - Before 8 pm 4/- after 8 pm 5/-
Soft Drinks and Refreshments

SKYLINE BALLROOM   THURSDAY, APRIL 4TH

P.P ARNOLD
CHRIS FARLOWE
THE GOSPEL GARDEN   THE HAMMER
THE QUADRANT

TICKETS 12.6. AT DOOR 15/-
Tickets at Gough and Davy, Sydney Scarborough

TOMORROW NIGHT

DIRECT FROM LONDON'S CROMWELLIAN

'JETHRO TULL'

* M.G.M RECORDING STARS *
Plus!   THE PURPLE MIST
at
COTTINGHAM CIVIC HALL

ADMISSION 7/6   8 - 11.30   REFRESHMENTS

SPA ROYAL HALL
BRIDLINGTON
Tuesday, APRIL 23

FABULOUS, UNIQUE,
SPECIAL ATTRACTION

IKE & TINA
TURNER
with
THE IKETTES

EXODUS SHOWBAND

WEST 28 STREET

DANCING 8.30 pm to 1 am

Tickets in Advance at door 10/-

613

614

Distant Jim

1969

BRIDLINGTON AND
DISTRICT YOUNG
FARMERS CLUB
DANCE
at the
PARISH HALL
BRANDESBURTON
ON
FRIDAY, 15th AUGUST
1969
9 pm,-1 a.m.
DANCING TO
THE MANDRAKES
THE LAZY POKER
Refreshments
Admission 7/6

phase two

HUTCH

Thurs   Sept 18   8 p.m.

BLUEBELL INN   LOWGATE

HULL ARTS CENTRE

FREE
CONCERT

SUNDAY, SEPT 28   12 - 7 pm

EAST PARK,   Wet or Dry

SKYLINE
BALLROOM
FRIDAY, APRIL 10th
8-12 p.m.

BIG
BEAT-NITE

ANGEL PAVEMENT
with
RIKKI DOBBS
RECORD ROAD SHOW

XMAS DANCE
to the
'CHILDHOOD' and
CHESTFEVER
TOMORROW   FRIDAY
DECEMBER 19

TRANSFIGURATION CHURCH HALL
ALBERT AVENUE, HULL
ADMISSION 6/-   REFRESHMENTS

DUKE OF CUMBERLAND
HOTEL
North Ferriby

FRIDAY, APRIL 10
Dance to the
CALMEN WATERS
and
DISCOTHEQUE
Adm 8/-, 10/- after 10.30 p.m
8 to 1 a.m.   Refreshments

IDLE RACE   -   CLOUDS

MANDRAKES
CALMEN WATERS
SKYLINE BALLROOM
8 - 1.30 THURSDAY, 4th September
Late Transport   Refreshments
PAY AT DOOR   12/6

HULL   ARTS   CENTRE
present

THE FREE

BLONDEL   -   CHEST FEVER

FARMERY HALL, BEVIN HOUSE
TUESDAY   28 OCTOBER   8 - 12.30
Late Transport   Tickets 10/-

HULL YOUNG SOCIALISTS

DANCE TO

SWEET SUGARS

FRIDAY   SEPTEMBER 5
8 - 11.30 pm

Blind Institute, Beverley Road, Hull

ALBERMARLE
YOUTH CENTRE
Ferensway
Dance to "**The Variations**'

Tonight, Friday 17   8 - 10.30 pm
Admission 2/-
MEMBERS ONLY

WITHERNSEA
ATTRACTIONS
SATURDAY
BIG BEAT DANCE
Dancing to **The Big Change.**
8.30 p.m. to 11.30 p.m.   Admission 4/-
IN THE
GRAND PAVILION

FREE CONCERT
SUNDAY, SEPT 28 12 - 7 pm East Park, Wet or Dry

THE RATS

HUTCH

CHEST FEVER

MICHAEL CHAPMAN

DAVID BOWIE

MIGHTY BABY

JUNIORS EYES

HULL ARTS CENTRE

617

What Happened?

1970

EASTER IN
HORNSEA

YORKSHIRE'S LAKELAND
BY THE SEA

Floral Hall Dances
Saturday, 28 March
8 pm. - 11.45 pm

KARAELIUS
(Formely Variations) and
COASTAL EROSION

Admission 7/6
Monday, 30th March
8 pm - 1 pm

ANGEL PAVEMENT
(Fontana Records) and
TERRA NOVA

Admission 10/-

THE
PENTHOUSE
25A ST NICHOLAS STREET
SCARBOROUGH TEL 63202

TOMORROW NIGHT

BRAVE NEW WORLD

Admission Only 5/-

9 pm - 2 am   Bar

SPA
ROYAL
HALL
BRIDLINGTON

Saturday, 12 September

BLACK SABBATH
THE APPLE SPICE BAND
THE URGE

---

phase two AND THE ROUND present

david bowie
hype

FEATURING MICK RONSON - LEAD GUITAR
WEST REFECTORY, STUDENTS UNION, UNIVERSITY OF HULL
TICKETS 7/6, 6/6 and at door

HULL BRICK COMPANY

DEEP PURPLE   -   QUINTESSENCE

NOV   CITY
20th   SOLD OUT   HALL

YES   -   **STRAWBS**

in Concert with **RED DIRT**

CITY HALL HULL, WEDNESDAY 9 DECEMBER 7.45

TICKETS 8/-, 10/-, 20/-, STARDISC, SOUTH STREET

S.A.S presents

TONIGHT

RED DIRT

with

CHEST FEVER

BLIND INSTITUTE

8.00 - 12.00
Adm 8/-   at the door

S.A.S presents Tonight

CALMEN WATERS
and
CHEST FEVER

BLIND INSTITUTE
BEVERLEY ROAD
FRIDAY, MARCH 20, 1970
Admission 8/- at door.

619

AGREEMENT NO. 1427

From
PETER PITTS MANAGEMENT
Station Forecourt,
SCARBOROUGH.

Telephone :
SCARBOROUGH 2062 (Robophone)
WEST AYTON 3105 (Residence)

Date : 7th April, 1970

To : ZOFFANY

You have been engaged to appear at SCARBOROUGH SPA OCEAN ROOM, SCARBOROUGH

on SATURDAY, 24TH April, 1970 to arrive : latest and to

perform between : 8 - 12 pm. 2 x 60 min spots

For a fee of £30 payable cash on completion/or cheque via PPM

Other information and instructions: You will be alternating with PILOT from
Morecambe. This is for the National Young Communists and they wanted 2
progressive groups. Mr. Hattersley saw PILOT over at Morecambe and booked
the. He was having LANCASTER (Jack Lancaster - ex Blodwyn Pig) but last Sat
a London group did not arrive until nearly 11pm so they were sent away and he
has cancelled LANCASTER and this will not please CHRYSALIS I'm afraid.

Please complete all parts of the lower half of this agreement, add any special notes and
RETURN SOONEST to PPM.
Go in there and slay 'em. Sincerely
PETER PITTS MANAGEMENT

NOTE: Whilst every care is taken, PPM does not accept liability in the event of non-
fulfilment of agreements by Proprietors, Managers and Artistes.

---

phase two present

MICHAEL CHAPMAN

RICK KEMP (bass)   RITCHIE DHARMA (drums)
Sunday, 19th April 7.30 pm at HULL ARTS CENTRE
SPRING STREET
TICKETS 10/- IN ADVANCE AT DOOR

BRANDESBURTON PARISH HALL
DANCE
to

THE PINK
and
DIZZY WHEELA

Friday, 13th FEBRUARY 1970
Refreshments Adm. 6/-

FRIDAY, MAY 22nd COTTINGHAM CIVIC HALL

American Bluesman
CHAMPION JACK DUPREE
with
THE AMAZING BLONDEL

Tickets 10/- * GUESTS * Late Transport
Gough and Davey Refreshments

CIVIC HALL, COTTINGHAM
SATURDAY, MARCH 21, 1970

The fabulous
DIARY
with
FLESH

Adm. 8/- at the door.
Pass-outs. Late Transport

Barry Nettleton for MHE presents

In concert

Michael Chapman

& Mike Absalom

City Hall, Hull
Friday 23rd March at 8pm

Tickets 60p from Gough & Davy, Savile St., Hull Tel 26525

Festival Information

THE SITE

The Festival Site is near Freshwater in the Isle of Wight, and comprises over 1000 acres of natural grassland. From the site there are extensive views of the Solent and Tennyson Downs.

DATES AND TIMES

The festival will take place over the Bank Holiday weekend from Friday 28th to Sunday 30th August. There will be additional entertainment for the two days leading up to the main programme. The daily concerts will commence at midday and continue until midnight.

TRANSPORT

Special trains will run from the major cities to Portsmouth on the south coast, from where special ferries will operate a constant shuttle service to Ryde, where buses will be waiting to take people direct to the festival site.

For further information write to:

Fiery Creations Limited, P.O. Box No. 1, Freshwater, Isle of Wight. Telephone Freshwater 2162.

Friday £1   Saturday 35/-   Sunday £2   Weekend £3

ISLE OF WIGHT FESTIVAL

FRIDAY 28th AUG
CHICAGO   FAMILY   TASTE
JAMES TAYLOR   ARRIVAL
LIGHTHOUSE   PROCOL HARUM
MELANIE   VOICES OF EAST HARLEM

SATURDAY 29th
DOORS   JONI MITCHELL   WHO
FREE   SLY AND THE FAMILY STONE
CAT MOTHER   JOHN SEBASTIAN
EMERSON, LAKE AND PALMER
MUNGO JERRY   SPIRIT

SUNDAY 30th AUG
JIMI HENDRIX EXPERIENCE
JOAN BAEZ   LEONARD COHEN
DONOVAN   RICHIE HAVENS
MOODY BLUES   RALPH McTELL
PENTANGLE   GOOD NEWS

Latest addition   MILES DAVIS
JETHRO TULL   TEN YEARS AFTER

623

It takes a while, but you eventually get to realise what is important about events in your life like the Isle of Wight Festival. In itself it had nothing of any value, I stood opposite that hill again and did not see one other person where once there had been half a million. I heard no sound where once I could lean against the wall of sound it made. I remembered people I walked with here who are no more. This was nothing to do with it, not the music or the rock stars, or the iron fences or the friends who didn't get this far. In the end it was just the ..... being there.

Free concert in East Park